International Political Economy

D0878874

This book offers a completely new and unique introduction to the economics of international relations. It treats all the traditional major themes of international relations theory while giving each a refreshing new twist with the incorporation of the influence of private power, particularly in the realm of war and peace. It reframes the history of the modern global economy and politics by thoroughly purging the myth of the market, a systematic blindness to private power. It not only draws on, but also illuminates major themes and empirical findings of comparative politics, business history, business strategy, business cycle theory, social evolutionary theory, as well as the practical wisdom of traders and investors.

Part I introduces the major concepts of competing theories of international relations, emphasizing a unique approach: corporatism. Part II introduces the critical importance of dynamic and oppositional analysis of issues. Part III traces the rise of the modern world from the mercantilist period until the rise of modern corporate organizations and the demise of imperialism in the crucible of World War I. Part IV begins with the origins of the contemporary dominance of business internationalism before and during World War II, then analyses three major facets of the postwar era: the unification of much of Europe, the industrialization of the Third World, and the Cold War and its aftermath. The final chapter considers the present and future of a fairly peaceful yet economically unstable world.

This book presents a refreshing and exciting portrayal of the global economy which challenges every major subject from money to markets to the business cycle. This book eschews the economics of dull averages to restore the drama of contending business forces struggling for wealth and, in the process, influencing war and peace.

James H. Nolt is a Senior Fellow at the World Policy Institute in New York and Adjunct Associate Professor at New York University, USA.

International Political Economy

The business of war and peace

James H. Nolt

Routledge
Taylor & Francis Group

LONDON AND NEW YORK

First published 2015
by Routledge
2 Park Square, Milton Park, Abingdon, Oxon OX14 4RN

and by Routledge
711 Third Avenue, New York, NY 10017

Routledge is an imprint of the Taylor & Francis Group, an informa business

British Library Cataloguing in Publication Data
A catalogue record for this book is available from the British Library

Library of Congress Cataloging in Publication Data
Nolt, James H.
International political economy : the business of war and peace /
James H. Nolt. -- First Edition.
pages cm
Includes bibliographical references and index.
1. International economic relations. 2. Economic policy. 3. Business cycles.
I. Title.
HF1359.N6496 2014
337--dc23
2014025515

ISBN: 978-0-415-70076-4 (hbk)
ISBN: 978-0-415-70077-1 (pbk)
ISBN: 978-0-203-79972-7 (ebk)

Typeset in Times New Roman
by Taylor & Francis Books

Contents

PART IV
The rise of business internationalism   **149**

Figures

Preface

> It remains an oddity that although companies are among the most powerful institutions of the modern age, our histories still focus on the actions of states and individuals, on politics and culture, rather than on corporations, their executives and their impacts.
>
> – Nick Robins (2006: 18)

Business crosses borders. It always has. Business is not the only motive for crossing borders. Armies, immigrants, tourists, missionaries, explorers, and others also cross borders, but all of these are also affected by business. Armies may be sent out to fight because of business motivations. No matter what the motive for war, business confidence and finance greatly affect the resources available to fight, and therefore affect who wins wars. Many of the individuals who cross borders are either sponsored by business or participating in business as employees, potential employees, or customers, including tourists. Therefore it is hard to imagine how there could be a reasonable theory of international relations, international politics, or international political economy without addressing the business role. Yet surprisingly many write about international relations today as if business is uninteresting. I aim to change that.

This book is about international relations. However, unlike many authors, I conceive of relations among nations as not merely relations among governments, but among all aspects of a nation, including especially the business organizations that collectively constitute most of a nation's economic life and its day-to-day activity, both in work and leisure. This is a book about international politics too, but politics here is understood as not merely what goes on in government, but the exercise of power both in civil society and government with special attention to business power. As the title says, this is a book about international political economy. Political economy is a term that became popular in the eighteenth and nineteenth centuries to refer to what now includes both economics and politics. Political economy also meant considering together the functions and interaction of government and business. Yet nowadays politics and economics are often seen as separate spheres of life and thus distinct and often mutually isolated branches of social science. This book endeavors to help reunite the study of politics and economies.

Like so many terms in politics and social science, "political economy" is used by different people to mean different things. One common usage of this term today is a label for studying political phenomena with the tool kit of contemporary microeconomic theory. That is certainly not what I am doing. The tool kit of microeconomic theory, designed to examine problems of choosing among alternatives given a budget constraint, can be useful for some problems, but not, broadly speaking, for politics or political economy the way I conceive these. My objections to microeconomic theory become most obvious in the first two parts, but are also evident in my treatment of business behavior in historical and political context in the second half of this book. Some have misunderstood my approach to label me as an "economic determinist." On the contrary, I argue that political contestation among organized business interests often determines economic outcomes. Business acts politically. Any theory of the economy that does not recognize this – such as contemporary textbook economic theory – is doomed to fail. If anything I am a "political determinist." Political struggle, public and private, determines much of what happens in the government and the economy.

This is also a book about international political strategy, explaining how broad social forces and interests organize to win their social and political aims. If I am successful, a student of this book will be able to identify major international players, discern their interests, and assess how they might act politically to attain their aims. No one can ever reliably predict exactly what another person, political party, business bloc, or government will do in the future. Anyone who thinks they can will be a poor political strategist, as I explain in Chapter Four. Understanding politics is inevitably a combination of science and art. The science of politics is to define as well as we can the limits of the possible. What can be done? What patterns of behavior can we anticipate? Social science is a realm of probability, not certainty. The art of political strategy is to judge in a moment of imperfect knowledge the most effective course to take given your educated guesses about what is possible according to what others will do. Strategic action is necessarily rife with errors and misjudgments.

Politics is a realm of myths and deception. Exercise of power, to be effective, often must be covert. What is transparent might be more easily countered. Research into political economy can be difficult because much that we want to know is not easy to learn. This is even truer when we try to understand the role of business in politics. First, many business activities are secret and protected by privacy rights. Second, study of business power is neglected within the social sciences today, as Robins suggests above. Therefore, I draw on diverse and sometimes obscure sources not well known to modern mainstream international political economy from a variety of disciplines including political science, sociology, economics, business, journalism, and history. Using such diverse sources, including my own research using business documents, I find there is actually a lot of information about business in international relations that has been neglected.

This book is not a moral treatise. It is not about how the world should be, but how it is and has been. It is not my intent to judge here what is right or wrong, but to try to understand what happens, what is effective, and why. In this regard we follow a tradition in political study that goes back to the sixteenth century and Machiavelli, who was himself reviving the dispassionate method of Aristotle, Thucydides, and the ancient Greek sophists.

This book unfolds in four parts. Part One introduces the major concepts of competing theories of international relations, emphasizing my own approach, corporatism. This part is especially valuable for academic courses guided by a professor, but I hope Chapters Two and Three, at least, are entertaining enough to excite the interest of general readers. Part Two is more crucial to understanding all that follows. It is perhaps the most original part of the book. It introduces the critical importance of dynamic and oppositional analysis of issues as opposed to the comparative statics of much of social science. The first two parts are an introduction to the theories and concepts needed to understand international political economy. Each part has one chapter representing each word of the primary title: chapters one and six are "international" chapters, two and four are "political" chapters, while three and five are "economy" chapters. The first part introduces static concepts; the second part adds dynamics.

The second half of this book applies the corporatist theory of the first half to historical and contemporary problems of international political economy. It is a kind of thematic history of recent centuries, divided into chapters representing major changes in the international system. Part Three traces the rise of the modern world from its incubation during the mercantilist period until the rise of modern corporate organizations and the demise of imperialism in the crucible of World War I. Part Four begins with the origins of the contemporary dominance of business internationalism before and during World War II, then analyzes three major facets of the postwar era: the unification of much of Europe, the industrialization of the Third World, and the Cold War and its aftermath. The final chapter considers the present and future of a fairly peaceful yet economically unstable world.

Acknowledgments

This book is the product of decades of thinking and research. It was all too long in the making. First of all I would like to apologize to my friends and supporters who were so patient during the long period that it took for my ideas to come to fruition. I hope this final product is worthy of the long years I struggled with the ideas. I expect that many who have known me over the years will be surprised by some aspects of argument. Probably some have given up on ever seeing any result.

My intellectual debts are many and varied. I cannot possibly list them all. I apologize to those whom I might neglect to mention. My purpose is not just to thank those who have helped along the way, but also to provide a few elements of intellectual biography that might be helpful to the reader. Perhaps my greatest debt to persons living is to Thomas Ferguson, whom I met only once and barely knew personally. I knew him mostly through his books on business influence in American politics and through several of his students who became friends of mine, introducing me to some of my most valuable sources. I learned liberal international political economy mainly from Robert Keohane and Charles Lipson, and from participants in a seminar chaired by Keohane and Joseph Nye during a year I spent as a dissertation fellow at Harvard's Center for International Affairs. I learned international relations theory and strategy best from one of my favorite teachers, John Mearsheimer. Two more of my most inspiring teachers were Richard Wolff and Stephen Resnick, who taught me a dynamic version of Marx. James Crotty introduced me to post-Keynesian macroeconomics. Sylvia Maxfield challenged me through several years as we struggled to co-author our first publication while we were both still graduate students. Her dedication and thoroughness were a great inspiration. I had the great fortune to co-teach a graduate seminar with Charles Tilly during my time as an assistant professor and program director at the New School for Social Research, now known as the New School University. My greatest direct philosophical challenge and inspiration came from my older brother, John E. Nolt. I expect that none of these will be satisfied with the direction in which my work has evolved. Some of these would likely disavow it. Yet I am grateful for their contribution even though they may not appreciate what I did with it.

I also learned from exposure to the world of business and finance, beginning with many fruitful conversations with Robert Johnson, who first opened my eyes about real financial operations and the political influence of finance. I am grateful to Jai-Hoon Yang for inviting me into the 3/23 Group, a private Manhattan monthly luncheon group of about a hundred bankers who for some years tolerated the participation of me, a non-banker, in their discussions. The group was named for the third floor of the J.P. Morgan headquarters at 23 Wall Street, where it first met. Author, investor, and former banker Eugene Dattel continues to be a friend and encourager who has challenged and stimulated me in many ways. As with my academic inspirations, I do not expect my business acquaintances will all accept or agree with the conclusions of this volume.

I wish to thank several friends from my graduate school days at Stanford University and the University of Chicago and my early years as a professor at Vanderbilt University and The New School, especially but not exclusively David Skidmore, Gary Chapman, Sylvia Maxfield, Raul Hinojosa, Kenneth Thomas, David Steiner, Ian Bremmer, and Sherle Schwenniger. They tolerated and sometimes provoked discussions on many of the topics of this book. Two more acquaintances from my graduate school days who got me involved in this book project in the first place deserve special thanks: David Gibbs and Ronald Cox. I thank my colleague at NYIT Nanjing, Douglas van Wieren, for numerous discussions plus technical and bibliographic help. I am not sure if any of these friends will be satisfied with what I have written, but I am grateful for their patience in discussing ideas with me over the years.

I want to thank the editors and staff of Routledge Press, especially Lisa Thomson, for their immense generosity in sticking with me on this project much longer than was reasonable and for tolerating my many delays and reschedulings. I must thank my wife, Juan Jenny Li, for helping me create a successful joint-venture college in China that I superintended as campus dean for four years. While this distracted me from making much progress on this manuscript for some time, it also gave me a chance to test market my ideas with hundreds of Chinese students. I am grateful to those students for helpful questions and comments. A few of them also assisted me in tracking down source material. Finally, I thank my dear children, Juliet and Bruce, for their patient and competent help accessing my library in New Jersey while I was teaching in China.

James H. Nolt, Nanjing, China
April 2014

Part I

Corporatist theory of international relations

1 Theories of international relations

> In the descriptions of the wars waged by the Florentines with foreign princes and peoples [previous historians] had been very diligent, but as regards civil discords and internal enmities, and the effects arising from them, they were altogether silent about the one and so brief about the other as to be no use to readers or pleasure to anyone.
>
> Nicolò Machiavelli, *Florentine Histories* (1988: 6)

Machiavelli invented modern political science by updating Aristotle and applying his ideas to the world of Renaissance Italy. His approach, like mine, emphasizes politics as a strategic art, not mere administration. The traditions of Aristotle and Machiavelli have been somewhat lost in the textbook versions of the social sciences taught in universities today. Emphasis has shifted from the dynamics of power to the comparative statics of administrative systems, to rule-bound routines. We have lost sight of the strategic exercise of power.

I advocate a corporatist framework for understanding international political economy (IPE) distinct from the two dominant perspectives today: realism and liberalism. Realism is also known as "power politics." Realists argue that broad patterns of international relations (IR) are determined by the systemic interaction of states seeking power to secure their own wellbeing at the expense of other states (e.g., Mearsheimer 2003). Liberalism is a rival tradition that contends that law and economic interdependence mitigate the effectiveness of military power for securing the success and prosperity of nations. Cooperation among states and businesses, for liberals, is often a superior road to wealth and security than the mutual suspicion and armed conflict that realists prescribe. My corporatist approach draws on elements of both traditions, but adds the strategic dynamics of private business power.

At first glance, the subtitle emphasizing the business role in war and peace might seem to place me closer to liberals. Whereas realists focus almost exclusively on state power, liberals admit that non-state actors, including especially business interests, can play a major role in shaping patterns of international relations. However, liberals are too optimistic about cooperation and stability in international relations. While some interests do benefit from international cooperation, it can threaten others. Liberals point to net benefits from cooperation. But they often forget that net benefits do not preclude economic losers. In the real world of politics, potential losers may fight back. International relations involve deep axes of conflict as well as cooperation.

I call my approach "corporatism," a term that embodies two connotations. One, following the modern commonsense use of "corporation" suggests the importance of business corporations as major authors of international relations. The second connotation allies my perspective to the well-known corporatist theories of interest articulation in domestic politics. This second sense of corporatism counters the dominant pluralist perspective in domestic politics. Pluralism says that private interests are so fragmented and diverse that there are no enduring structures of power in the private sphere. Only political institutions like political parties and governmental organs aggregate and articulate broader social interests. Corporatism, by contrast, argues that private interests, such as business associations and labor unions, are so well and broadly organized that enduring structures of power and enduring lines of conflict are common even outside of the formal institutions of politics. In a sense, the first connotation of corporatism suggests my difference from realism, which considers states the key actors in international politics and neglects corporations. The second connotation of corporatism defines my key difference from the main currents of the liberal tradition, which presume pluralism in domestic if not international politics. The distinctiveness of my approach will become clearer as I criticize realism and liberalism in more detail.

Realism and the roots of international relations theory

Realism is not a single unified theory, but rather a broad theoretical perspective that shares several common premises. Realists appeal to evidence to defend the validity of their core premises against rival theoretical traditions. Among themselves, realists debate various specific theoretical propositions consistent with the broad premises they share. Realists were the first to define international relations as a distinctive field of study with its own theories and laws different from those of domestic political life. The core premises of realism originated individually in various contexts by diverse political philosophers before being brought together to constitute the international relations perspective now known as realism. Some of the individual premises of realism are useful and valid outside of realism. Indeed, my corporatist approach draws on some of the same precepts as realism, but takes them in a different direction.

This is especially true of the first premise of realism: that political power is restrained only by opposing power. This is a proposition that many attribute first to the classical Greek historian Thucydides's *Peloponnesian War*. The most quoted phrase from that history occurs in what is referred to as "The Melian Dialogue," when Athenian leaders, besieging the weak island city-state of Melos, justify their draconian demands to the Melians with the dictum, "The strong do what they will; the weak do what they must" (bk. 5, sec. 89, translations vary in their exact wording). This idea, which is sometimes called "the primacy of power," was submerged during the medieval era when Christian theorists emphasized the moral and divine bases of political power. It reemerged most strikingly in the early sixteenth century writings of Machiavelli. My corporatist approach shares this "political realist" precept with IR realism.

The second key premise of realism is that states are islands of law and order in an international sea of anarchy and violence. This notion of international anarchy originates with Thomas Hobbes in his *Leviathan* (1651). Hobbes uses theological arguments from the Protestant Reformation to reject the claim of the Pope to head a universal monarchy of the Catholic Church as a manifestation of the Kingdom of God on earth, an international order superior to secular monarchs. Hobbes thus reaffirmed the conclusion of the Treaty of Westphalia that ended the Thirty Years War (1618–48): government (at this time usually a monarch) is the sole sovereign authority within its territorial realm. Each government is an autonomous power that can rightfully and effectively choose the religious and legal constitution of each state. Whereas each state has its own autonomous legal and political order, the international system of states is not governed by any sovereign law or power, but only by relations of force. It is a realm of anarchy, governed only by the laws of nature, not the laws of man. Of course, this premise, articulated by Hobbes on the basis of Protestant theology, was never popular in Catholic Europe, which continued to view the Pope and the Church as international powers with authority over legal rights in war and peace as in domestic political and religious affairs.

The third premise of realism is the working out of these "laws of nature" of an anarchical international system of autonomous state powers. These laws of nature were seen to be like the scientific laws discovered by natural scientists. They are not laws in the sense of a written code of rules produced and enforced by governments, but regularities in behavior that occur as a natural result of given circumstances, independent of the intent of particular individuals. The specific content of the laws of behavior of the international system is the subject of much dispute within realism. However, all realists believe that there are law-like regularities in international politics that are the proper subject for international relations theory to expound.

The first and most popular of these realist "laws of nature" is the tendency of a system of states to maintain a balance of power. This law was elaborated by the Scottish philosopher David Hume (1752). Hume tries to root this theory in Thucydides, though as I argue in Chapter 6, Thucydides's perspective is in fact very different. Balance of power theory, from its roots in Hume through its modern development by Kenneth Waltz (1979), also draws on the methods of economics. Hume's Scottish friend, Adam Smith, is a key founder of political economy with his notion that even in an anarchic free market society will produce the right amount of goods at the lowest possible prices as if guided by an "Invisible Hand," that is, a natural law based on human nature to be greedy and acquisitive. Hume's argument for a self-regulating international system is similar. Each individual state, though greedy to expand its own territory and power, must be wary of all other states. Any state that becomes most powerful and threatening will elicit a coalition of lesser states against it, each acting in its own self-interest against the greatest threat. The result is that no one state will be able to dominate the others. Thus the independence of each is preserved against the ambitions of all.

Historically the fourth premise of realism is the idea that foreign policy concerns will have primacy over domestic politics. The concerns of domestic politics, realists argue, are relatively petty by comparison with the national security of the state as a whole. This element of realism was last to emerge because it depended on contentious domestic politics, which was not so obvious in the era of absolutist states of the seventeenth and eighteenth centuries. The growth of parliamentary government and episodic revolutions during the nineteenth century made domestic politics seem a highly disputatious realm of shifting interests. Some political leaders, notably Chancellor Otto von Bismarck of Prussia and later unified Germany, argued that international politics was too important to be subject to the whims of domestic politics. Since, in the realist worldview, this international realm is governed by natural laws of power politics independent of the petty and short-sighted concerns of domestic political parties, the statesmen who craft foreign policy must be above party politics, focused only on national security. This realist precept is now ingrained in the rhetoric of American politics whenever politicians appeal to the "national interest" or "national security" as a universal concern against the supposedly more selfish and petty concerns of partisan politics and "special interests."

My corporatist approach to international relations shares elements of the first and third premises of realism, but rejects the second and fourth as general propositions. Corporatism agrees with a broadly Machiavellian approach to politics, expecting that most actors most of the time are motivated by self-interest and restrained only by the power of others. Corporatism also seeks regularities or "laws" of international systems, but disagrees with realism's premise that states are the primary constituent element of an international system. Corporatism considers a variety of international systems constituted by other actors in addition to states. Furthermore, political cleavages within nations can have a profound effect on patterns of foreign relations, contrary to realism's fourth premise. Corporatism argues that there are circumstances in which the second and fourth premises of realism are approximately true, but these premises are too restrictive to form the basis for a general theory of international politics.

Liberalism and the origins of international political economy

International political economy began as a branch of international relations theory concerned with the politics of international economic policy. At its origin in the 1960s and 1970s it also represented a liberal counterattack against the dominance of realism within international relations theory. Realism contends that the security concerns of states trump economic motivations. Liberalism counters that economic interdependence may displace security concerns and that some forms of economic influence may thus be more significant than military power. Whereas realist perspectives have tended to dominate Anglo-American analysis of the World Wars and the Cold War with the Soviet Union, the liberals who founded international political economy were more interested in relations among states where national security was not paramount.

Five main areas of study motivated international political economy at its inception: (1) the international financial order, which became a prominent concern with the collapse of the Bretton Woods system during 1971–73; (2) the international trade system, exemplified by the General Agreement on Trade and Tariffs (GATT) and later the World Trade Organization (WTO); (3) economic development of poorer countries, including the role of international agencies and multinational corporations; (4) international economic integration, of which the European Common Market, now part of the European Union, was the preeminent example; and (5) international cartels, most notably with the dramatic success of the Organization of Petroleum Exporting Countries (OPEC) during the 1970s. All of these issues fell outside the traditional purview of realist international relations theory, although after international political economy was pioneered by liberals, some realists began to dispute with liberals in these topic areas. All of these concerns were arguably instances where force was not as decisive in the outcome as economic incentives and organization. I examine these and other typical IPE topics throughout this book using my own corporatist perspective to criticize and supplement the liberal and realist understanding of these and other key issues.

The roots of the liberal perspective on international relations, including the classic realist issues of war and peace, long predate the emergence of modern IPE. Liberalism as a perspective distinct from emerging realism was already evident during the eighteenth century. Realist and liberal perspectives contended in British parliamentary debates of the nineteenth century. The origins of liberalism can be traced back at least to the French Enlightenment philosopher Charles de Montesquieu and the German philosopher Immanuel Kant. Montesquieu was also a powerful influence on the founders of the USA, who introduced liberal thought in international relations theory to the United States in *The Federalist Papers* and other writings.

Montesquieu wrote in his influential 1752 master work, *The Spirit of the Laws*, how different forms of domestic political regimes influence the behavior of states in their foreign relations. In particular, he argued for three precepts subsequently common, though not universal, within the liberal tradition: (1) law restrains states even in the international realm: "Offensive force is regulated by the law of nations, which is the political law of each country considered in its relation to every other" (bk. X, sec. 1); (2) democratic republics are more peaceable than despotic governments, and thus a league of republican states might legislate peace among themselves; and (3) "Peace is the natural effect of trade" (bk. XX, sec. 2). Montesquieu's principles informed the drafters of the constitution that united the thirteen original American states into the United States.

Kant in his 1795 essay "Perpetual Peace" elaborated Montesquieu's arguments, contending that commercial relations were creating a sort of universal society that would gradually transcend the particularities of individual states. This international society would establish universal rules, interests, and norms that citizens of all states would generally abide. Kant believed that commercial development, the spread of modern business, would make all civilized nations interested in what he called "universal hospitality," peace, and international law in order to secure commercial prosperity. Kant believed that republican states would necessarily represent this sober commercial interest. Thus relations among republican states would be more peaceful than either extreme of democracies or monarchies, which Kant argued are both necessarily despotic. As with Montesquieu and American founders such as James Madison, Kant believed pure democracy, unmediated rule by the majority, would be unstable, driven by the fickle whims of mass emotion. On the other hand, autocratic monarchies might ignore the commercial interests of the majority in favor of their dynastic lust for power through military conquest. Military conquest, Kant argued, could benefit only a few at the expense of most citizens. Only commercially developed republican states will create among themselves a zone of peace. Kant expected that republican states would eventually come to predominate throughout Europe, rendering realism obsolete.

Although liberalism, like realism, is today a broad perspective containing many contentious currents, varieties of liberalism can be identified from their critiques of the core realist premises outlined above. Not all liberals reject all the core premises of realism, but the liberal tradition includes refutations of each of realism's precepts. There are four major branches of liberalism in international relations theory, all of which have also left their mark on international political economy specifically. These are: (1) international law, norms, and culture; (2) liberal institutionalism; (3) liberal transnationalism; and (4) the primacy of domestic politics. Whereas realists tend to be united around the core premises outlined above and divide mainly on their detailed explanations of international system dynamics, these liberal variants do not always share the same set of core premises. Rather, each of these, developing in reaction against one of the core premises of realism, constituted itself as a somewhat independent and perhaps sufficient perspective on international politics. Thus liberalism is more diffuse than realism.

Contrary to the first premise of realism, many liberals argue that there are common values in international society that influence or restrain the actions of states and other international actors. This exception has already been noted insofar as Catholic doctrine never abandoned belief in universal Christian values that govern the behavior of states and statesmen no less than any other individual Christians. Catholic jurists developed elaborate theories of just and unjust war. Monarchs who defied Catholic moral precepts might be punished, in this life or the next. Nevertheless, Catholics also recognized that earthly powers might act in corrupt and sinful ways. Rules of morality are not a guarantee of good behavior. Machiavelli and realists who followed his example argue that even most Catholic authorities, in fact, act according to political interests, not moral precepts. I tend to agree. Protestant lawyers such as Hugo Grotius, Samuel von Pufendorf, and Emer de Vattel further developed the principles of international law, but rooting their arguments in natural law instead of appealing to a supposedly universal theology. The liberal tradition also cites various secular moral and cultural precepts as shaping patterns of international behavior. There are many such arguments, some of which I treat in my historical chapters. Montesquieu and Kant were among those interested in the ways in which differences in law, education, and political culture influence differences in foreign policy.

Liberal rejection of the second premise of realism was also rooted originally in the religious vision of a united Christian Europe or Christian world. Liberals argued that states sharing common values and recognizing the mutual expense, immorality, and futility of war might band together and establish a concert of Europe or league of nations to govern and regulate their mutual relations peacefully. At the center would be some sort of deliberative body representing all the states. Such a governed international order is the antithesis of Hobbesian anarchy. By the eighteenth century, some versions of this vision had been secularized to include even the Muslim Turks in a formal regime for international governance. Instead of each state fearfully arming to defend its own security, liberals advocated collective security provided by negotiations within a global deliberative assembly. Needless to say, realists ridiculed such schemes as unrealistic dreams. Even after formal organizations for collective security like the League of Nations and the United Nations were created to fulfill this liberal vision, realists argue that they function, if at all, only as an expression of temporary alignments of great powers and have no real power or effectiveness of their own. Liberals whose primary focus is on cooperation among states through international organizations are often called "liberal institutionalists" (e.g., Keohane *et al.* 1993), since they study institutions created by states to regulate aspects of their international relations. This approach can also be thought of as "liberalism from above" insofar as states are the principal agents of cooperation in this view.

A third variant of liberalism denies the third core premise of realism that the international system is a system of states. Instead, other actors have come to the fore, including private business and other non-governmental organizations that extend their influence across state boundaries. Recent manifestations of this approach (e.g., Keohane & Nye 1972; Morse 1976) have been called "liberal transnationalism" or "liberalism from below." States are seen as having less and less to do with the ebb and flow of international relations as transportation, communications, and commerce become more and more *trans*national, that is, crossing borders fluidly. Increasingly relations among nations involve particularistic business interests that are too varied and complex to be mediated effectively in state-to-state negotiations. Commercial interdependence of nations leads to diverse and powerful business interests in favor of maintaining peace and avoiding state interference or regulation. Even the residual security problems come increasingly not from wars among states, but from internal civil and revolutionary wars and international non-state terrorist organizations. In extreme versions of this approach, state power is withering away. Today this perspective is included in the concept of "globalism."

Finally, there are a diverse variety of liberal perspectives that reject the fourth premise of realism: the primacy of foreign policy. Instead, these liberals contend that foreign policy is a product of the particular domestic politics of each state. If international politics is determined by domestic politics, then there can be no valid theory of international relations that ignores or subordinates domestic politics, as realism does. There are so many and varied theories in this category, I will not attempt to catalog them all here. However, two of these theories emphasizing the primacy of domestic politics have been particularly influential: capitalist peace and democratic peace. Both derive from Kant and his republican predecessors.

Democratic peace advocates contend that democracies do not fight other democracies (e.g., Lipson 2003). This argument is consistent with Kant only if we understand modern "democracies" as not democratic at all, that is, as not representing popular rule, but as republics ruled mostly by the business class. But with that caveat, explored in more detail in the next chapter, the argument has some empirical validity. Modern representative democracies do rarely fight each other. If they are embroiled in war, it is almost always with autocratic regimes. The idea of a democratic peace has become widely popular not only in academic circles, but even among politicians, political pundits, and governmental foreign policy officials. One of the most enduring of the ostensible reasons that the US went to war against Saddam Hussein's Iraq in 2003 was to install a democratic regime that advocates assume would promote peace in the region.

The idea of a capitalist peace is more fully consistent with what Kant actually argued. According to this view, the transition from feudalism to capitalism changes the nature of the ruling class, changing foreign policy behavior. Feudalism was a system in which the rulers were a hereditary caste that derived its claim to rule because of its presumed superior virtue in war. Feudal states, including the absolute monarchies of eighteenth century Europe, existed principally to uphold the values of this feudal aristocracy, including its profession of war. As capitalism displaced feudalism, it also displaced its values. War, instead of being the principal means of accumulating wealth and power, became an onerous expense and interference with peaceful commerce. Under capitalism, the way to wealth is through business success, not conquest. Capitalism thrives in conditions of stability, including a reliable legal order. Rule by law (not democracy per se) is the foundation of republicanism, which for Kant is the natural political form to institute peace. Thus capitalist states will tend to create a zone of peace wherein mutual commercial interest precludes war. Norman Angell (2012[1913]), a British liberal, was perhaps the most famous and influential proponent of the capitalist peace. He added to Kant's analysis a detailed explanation of why war is becoming less profitable for a capitalist economy, even for the winners. Unfortunately, Angell's cogent arguments were upstaged by the outbreak of World War I among Europe's leading capitalist powers.

Like realism, the liberal tradition includes some insights and elements that are useful for my corporatist approach. I agree with the first variant of liberalism that there are some significant cultural and legal changes that affect patterns of behavior in international relations. However, I choose not to focus on cultural or legal changes in isolation, but instead trace their roots to broader changes in the very constitution of society, such as the transition from feudalism to capitalism. I agree with the second variant of liberalism that international cooperation – not always confined to states – has created powerful institutions and interests, especially within business, that transcend the boundaries of particular states. I agree with the third variant of liberalism that there is much important in the international system that occurs among private actors, though my understanding of the interests and organization of international social forces differs from the common version of liberal transnationalism, as I elaborate in this book. I agree with the fourth variant of liberalism that domestic politics is important for foreign policy, though I do not assume that it is primary. There are indeed many instances in which contending domestic political interests have their own foreign policies and foreign allies. Thus instead of arguing for the primacy of domestic policy, I contend that domestic political-economic struggles routinely extend across borders into the international sphere.

Corporatist international relations theory

My corporatist approach to international relations theory and international political economy aims to restore a central concern of political theory since at least the ancient Greeks: international relations among factionalized nations. I trace the roots of my approach to Thucydides, Aristotle, Machiavelli, Enlightenment-era Republicanism, the American Founding Fathers, Marxism, and corporatism in domestic politics. There is evidence for corporatism even in the Hebrew and Christian Bible. While I draw on some of the same roots and elements as realism and liberalism, I reassemble these elements differently to encompass realism and liberalism both as special cases of my more general theory of international relations.

The social sciences are best understood in historical context. Thus the second half of this book unfolds through historical chapters. Each of these chapters deepens the understanding of contending approaches by showing how each explains and interprets the same historical events. I consider not merely the latest fashions among contemporary academics, but also the historical roots of modern thought, showing the specific contexts that gave rise to each specific theoretical proposition. Along the way I offer fresh interpretations of not only the latest versions of realism and liberalism, but also their historical predecessors, as well as other perspectives within political economy, including mercantilism, imperialism, nationalism, and globalism.

The next two chapters expound my corporatist critique of liberalism by focusing on the differences in my conception of domestic political economy. Chapter 2 develops my concept of "interest blocs" as an alternative to the interest groups of pluralism. Modern liberalism, by adopting pluralism, has largely forgotten the long and fruitful history of understanding politics in terms of broad opposing forces, which I call interest blocs. This concept, under various names, is central to the political thought of Thucydides, Aristotle, Machiavelli, Montesquieu, Madison, Marx, and many more. Pluralism, which became dominant during the twentieth century, replaced the "factions" or "parties" of traditional political theory with a plethora of small, specialized interest groups. In doing so it lost sight of big questions and enduring axes of organization and conflict. Traditional political theory considered factionalized nations. Pluralism assumes fragmented nations. If society is as fragmented as pluralism presumes, then naturally the government appears as the only coherent organizing center of a nation. I refocus attention on how broad social interests are organized in ways that contravene the pluralist assumptions adopted by most versions of liberal theory.

Chapter 3 rejects contemporary economic theory for largely ignoring private power. Liberalism and realism have both adopted a view that segments economics and markets from politics and power. They both adopt the view of economists that the public and private spheres are radically distinct. Corporatism disagrees. All economic relationships are subject to private (and sometimes public) power and consequently there is no autonomous realm wherein only anonymous market forces reign. The Myth of the Market, propagated by economists but believed by most other social thinkers as well, obscures the strategic dynamics of private power.

My purpose in developing corporatist theory is to make it useful for practical political strategy. Therefore Chapter 4 is about strategy, though it is also what social scientists might call my methodological chapter. I choose this method because it focuses on more effective political strategy. Much of modern social science method derives from a positivist understanding of science, which is in fact on the wane within philosophy of science itself. Positivist thinking leads to sterile theory-building that aims to fix the collective behavior of human beings into rigidly predicable formulae. Human beings are always more innovative than the models that try to fossilize their behavior. That does not mean throwing out social science, but rather understanding it from the standpoint of scientific realism and pragmatism. Restoring appreciation for the real practice of political strategy should awaken social scientists to the potential for more effective and relevant science. My principal objection against both realism and liberalism is not so much that they are wrong, but that they are less perceptive and effective for political strategy in most circumstances.

Chapter 5 shows how private interest blocs determine the business cycle by their strategic interaction. It provides a blueprint for creating dynamic theories of political economy based on conflicting private forces. It is simultaneously a critique of textbook macroeconomics, building on the more *strategic* macroeconomics of Keynes, and a critique of the mistaken tendency in political science to defer to economics and markets in anything involving business. By bringing private power, especially credit power, to the fore, this chapter also shows the bankruptcy of the standard textbook accounts of money and banking that so thoroughly ignore the more fundamental role of private credit in what Keynes called the credit cycle.

Chapter 6 considers what it means to talk about international systems. It criticizes the realist and liberal views of what these are, contending that interest blocs, rather than states, are the key actors. Realism has made an important contribution to international relations theory by describing international systems. Within realism, the behavior of states cannot be predicted adequately without reference to the entire system of states, which includes at least the number of states and their relative power. My corporatist approach develops a notion of international systems based on the characteristic factions that divide nations during various periods of history. An international system of factionalized states behaves very differently from one composed of the unified states assumed by realism. Furthermore, whereas realism, at least in its most abstract formulations, assumes that quantitative relations of power are decisive determinants of system outcomes, corporatism pays more attention to qualitative asymmetries in the power and strategies of rival interest blocs. My periodization of historical systems has some parallels with liberalism, but describes their content based on contending private interest blocs rather than liberalism's universal laws, rules, and norms.

2 Polarized politics

> The latent causes of faction are thus sown in the nature of man ... and ... have, in turn, divided mankind into parties, inflamed them with mutual animosity, and rendered them much more disposed to vex and oppress each other than to co-operate for their common good. ... But the most common and durable source of factions has been the various and unequal distributions of property. Those who hold and those who are without property have ever formed distinct interests in society. Those who are creditors, and those who are debtors, fall under a like discrimination. A landed interest, a manufacturing interest, a mercantile interest, a moneyed interest, with many lesser interests, grow up of necessity in civilized nations, and divide them into different classes, actuated by different sentiments and views. The regulation of these various and interfering interests forms the principal task of modern legislation, and involves the spirit of party and faction in the necessary and ordinary operations of government.
>
> James Madison (1787), *Federalist Papers*, no. 10

Madison here introduces the concept of politics that animates this book. It says simply that society is riven by self-interested factions or parties, rooted in concerns about their specific business interests. Politics must contend with this basic social reality. It cannot transcend it. It should not be blind to it. More broadly, politics is the struggle for power in both the public and private sphere. It is not just about what happens in government. Private struggles for power are at least as important as public ones. Business is the key arena for the struggles of private power. The purpose of political economy is to make sense of the struggle for power and wealth in both closely related realms.

Unfortunately, the way the social sciences have developed, private power struggles mostly escape scrutiny. As I discuss further in the next chapter, economics was designed to abstract away from private power. Power was a concern of classical political economy through the middle of the nineteenth century, but "pure economics," now more often known as neoclassical economics, was created, beginning during the 1870s by Léon Walras, Carl Menger, and William Jevons, as an effort to exclude considerations of power from the economy. Production and prices were to be explained only by consumer tastes and producer preferences rooted in market conditions and costs of production. This effort to create economic theory divorced from politics has been a success in theory but a disaster in practice for understanding the very *political* economy in which we live. Likewise, mainstream political science neglects private power by claiming, with the doctrine of pluralism, that power is fragmented among a multitude of competing interest groups rather than concentrated. Large concentrations of private power in corporations and their alliances are largely lumped together as the amorphous "free" or "perfect" market, the purview of economics, not politics.

Corporate power is studied here and there, out of the mainstream, and in a few odd corners of history, sociology, and even anthropology, but otherwise the major loci of private power largely escape social scientific scrutiny. Even those few social scientists who do study corporations and corporate power seldom grasp the major interests and cleavages that motivate and divide business. When attention is turned to private power, the focus is usually on ways of conceiving power that highlight unity rather than division, process rather than conflict. This chapter argues against both pluralism and the analogous theoretical dispersion of private power under the rubric of the free market. I also argue against the opposite extreme that views power as singularly concentrated in a unified government or governing elite.

Madison is often called a pluralist, but this is inaccurate. He saw political struggle as typically bifurcated or polarized into two broad factions, as I do. His political ideas and mine are rooted in a long tradition of political realism that includes Thucydides, Aristotle, Machiavelli, Montesquieu, and Hume. Thus it includes many of the greatest and most celebrated thinkers in Western political thought. Modern pluralism, on the other hand, does not much predate Alexis de Tocqueville's famous *Democracy in America* of 1835–40. De Tocqueville originated the pluralist view that society is divided into myriad competing and overlapping groups and thus includes no great agglomerations of power. In fact, he did argue in one chapter (1840, sec. 2, ch. XX) that an "aristocracy of manufacturers" is the greatest potential danger to democracy in America, but that it did not (at his time) yet exist as an effective political force because, although manufacturers do rule despotically *within* factories, he wrote, their mutual competition makes it difficult for them to coordinate sufficiently to rule outside of the workplace. He was wrong about this, even for his own time, as argued by detailed studies of elite organization such as Dalzell (1987). By contrast, Madison contends, in the next paragraph after our opening quote:

> No man is allowed to be the judge of his own cause, because his interest would certainly bias his judgment, and, not improbably, corrupt his integrity. With equal, nay with greater reason, a body of men are unfit to be both judges and parties at the same time; yet ... what are the different classes of legislators but advocates and parties to the causes they deter-mine? Is a law proposed concerning private debts? It is a question to which the creditors are parties on one side and the debtors on the other. Justice ought to hold the balance between them. Yet the parties are, and

must be, themselves the judges; and … the most powerful faction must be expected to prevail. Shall domestic manufactures be encouraged, and in what degree, by restrictions on foreign manufactures? are questions which would be differently decided by the landed and the manufacturing classes, and probably by neither with a sole regard for justice and the public good. The apportionment of taxes on the various descriptions of property is an act which seems to require the most exact impartiality; yet there is, perhaps, no legislative act in which greater opportunity and temptation are given to a predominant party to trample on the rules of justice.

The rival private factions Madison identifies are those that predominate in this book: those with and without property, that is, wage earners and business owners; debtors and creditors; and protectionists (manufacturers in Madison's example) and free traders (often, as he says, including landed or farm interests). Tax incidence is an issue for all of these. Understanding the power and interests of such private factions is the foundation of any realistic study of political economy. I say *realistic* because Madison, like me, insists on understanding politics as it is really fought out, not merely according to what would be ideal or just in some legal, abstract, or utopian sense. Political realism and idealism have been contending perspectives since ancient times. Idealism is generally more prevalent and popular because it is the more reassuring view. But it also obscures so much about what is real in the world of power.

Conceptual clarification

Idealism and realism, two broad traditions in the study of politics, are rooted in the contending philosophies of the ancient Greeks and also have parallels in other systems of thought, including Indian and Chinese thought. Idealism emphasizes that societies are united around common principles of justice or righteousness or morality or religion or natural self-regulating equilibrium. Realism presumes that politics – and indeed, political economy – is about the struggle between rival forces. The idealist tradition originates in the works of the Greek philosopher Plato, and in Chinese tradition, Confucius. Most of modern social science, including neoclassical or equilibrium economics, falls within this tradition. Economics and liberal IPE considers the public good to be unitary, incontestable. The realist tradition derives in Western thought from Aristotle; in China from Taoism and strategists like Sun Zi; and in India, from Kautilya (Boesche 2002). Considering modern political economy, political realism is congenial with disequilibrium economics and the strategic deployment of private power, as in oligopoly theory. The fundamental number for idealists is one, since "the Good" is singular; the fundamental number for realists is two. It takes two sides to fight. Vulnerabilities invite opposition. For political realists, social science is the study of the evolution of societies through broad political struggle. Each of these two traditions has engendered a vast corpus of social scientific thinking.

Aristotle developed categories of regime types reflecting both realism and idealism. Those associated with realism he calls corrupt, perverse, or degenerate (depending on how the Greek term is translated), meaning those with power rule in their own self-interest, as Madison argues, rather than for the social good. Those regimes associated with idealism Aristotle labels as ideal or perfect forms. He also distinguishes regimes according to the scope of the ruling or sovereign power, that is, whether the rulers are one, few, or many. We can adapt his schema somewhat for modern categories that distinguish the number of major concentrations of power or cleavages in the society or the number of independent business firms in an industry or line of business, as shown in Figure 2.1. In each case there are three levels to indicate the scope of sovereign power or the divisions of power within a polity or industry. These abstractions help us use terms more precisely. Aristotle's terminology influenced political discourse until modern times, although, as we will see, with some obfuscating drift of meanings.

Modern readers often miss distinctions such as Aristotle makes between democracies and republics. What Aristotle calls democracy, clarified by Madison as *pure* democracy, is rule by the many. This might not be the majority of people, but at least a large number of them. For example, in classical Athens democracy never included slaves or women. Democracy literally means "the people rule." Oligarchy means "few rule." Monarchy means "one ruler." But for Aristotle, as for Madison, democracy is a corrupt form, wherein the many, the people, rule in their own self-interest, *against* the few. Aristotle is explicit that in actual political practice "the many" are the poor and "the few" are the rich, so democracy means for Aristotle what pure democracy means for Madison: the poor (those without property) ruling in their own interest against the rich. Madison argues in favor of the US Constitution because what it creates is *not* a democracy, in Aristotle's sense, but a republic that safeguards against any majority faction, such as the poor, oppressing the rich, for example, by redistributing their property to the poor. Modern readers, because of our confusion of terms, typically lose this key distinction. But Madison is also a little less strict than Aristotle, because although he believes a republic with checks and balances against factional domination is more virtuous than a pure democracy, in which the poor majority will rule in a self-interested way, a republic for Madison is not really an ideal form because it can seldom reconcile opposing interests; at best it can only mitigate their struggles and channel them into legitimate politics rather than rebellion.

At least since De Tocqueville and the rise of the Democratic Party under Andrew Jackson, the meaning of "democracy" has changed. For De Tocqueville, interests within society are not grouped into broad factions, as in Madison, but fragmented into myriad small interest groups. Once this pluralist vision of democracy replaces the realist tradition from Aristotle through Madison, "democracy" loses its pejorative meaning. The distinction between democracies and republics is lost. An example of the consequences of this comes in an otherwise superb book on the history of the US Constitution (Amar 2005:

| Rulers | Aristotle's Constitutional Forms | | Modern Interest Bloc Theory | | | | | Corps./ Factions |
	Unified/Perfect	Conflicted/Corrupt	Domestic Politics	International	Private Power	Industry Organization	
ONE	Monarchy	Tyranny	Power Elite	Realism	Unified Public Interest	Monopoly (and Public Goods)	ONE
FEW	Aristocracy	Oligarchy	Corporatism	Corporatism	Polarized	Oligopoly	FEW
MANY	Republic	Democracy	Pluralism	Liberalism	Fragmented	Perfect Competition	MANY

Figure 2.1 Modern faction or interest bloc theory mapped to Aristotle's constitutional forms

5–9, 14–19) that considers the issue of democracy solely from the standpoint of formal procedure and legal theory, not actual political power, and thus conflates democracies and republics. My aim is to challenge the pluralist vision and thus revive consideration of the broad factions that, for Madison as for Aristotle, almost inevitably corrupt politics. Although Aristotle did distinguish ideal forms in theory, following the usage of his idealist teacher, Plato, Aristotle distinguished himself from Platonic idealism by contending that in practice only the corrupt forms exist. The tradition of political realism agrees.

Figure 2.1 also helps us distinguish corporatism, the perspective of this book, from pluralism and the "power elite" theory, a term coined by sociologist C. Wright Mills (1956), but more broadly applicable. Corporatism is a term commonly used in comparative domestic politics to distinguish a system characterized by the broad organization of social interests, often labor and capital, into two or a few "peak associations" representing the common corporate interests of each private bloc. This use of corporatism also directly contrasts it with pluralism, wherein social organization is much more diffuse and diverse. I adopt the term to talk about broad interests that are not necessarily organized into formal peak associations, but which nonetheless constitute loosely aligned factions, which is how Madison uses the term. Because Madison's terms "faction" and "party" are commonly used in so many diverse senses, when I wish to emphasize my distinctive meaning I will often use the phrase "interest blocs" instead. Power elite theory emphasizes the essential unity of the rulers. As discussed in the previous chapter, this is also the view of politics advocated by the international relations theory also called "realism." Corporatism argues that the dominant powers in society are usually polarized, not unified, but they are not as fragmented as in pluralism. I do not contend that there are not diverse and pluralistic interests in society. Certainly there are. But pluralism is blind to the broadest private interests in society, those listed by Madison, that *are* typically polarized. Below I explain why.

International relations theories may be situated within these broad traditions. IR realism believes in a unified power elite. Liberal international relations theory assumes a pluralist understanding of political power. This is especially evident in Robert Keohane and Joseph Nye's (1977) influential concept of complex interdependence, which is a version of pluralism applied to international politics. Corporatism argues that power is generally bifurcated into broad rival interest blocs. Understanding politics as a polarized struggle between rivals is more descriptively accurate than pluralism as well as more parsimonious. It emphasizes that politics is about struggle, rather than politics as mere idealized administration, aiming at some fairly consensual common good, as in the Platonic tradition, or legal and legitimate process of bargaining, as in liberalism. Corporatism is about bifurcated power. In corporatism there is not one right answer as to what is most socially desirable, because it depends which side you are on.

Figure 2.1 also helps keep two meanings of "realism" distinct: *political* realism contrasts with idealism, and is shared by two international relations theories, corporatism and realism. As if to add to the confusion, the international relations theory, liberalism (a term also used in many other senses), is often referred to by international relations critics as "idealism," to emphasize one aspect in which liberalism and realism differ sharply.

Some might wonder where I would fit Marxism. Generally, Karl Marx is a political realist colored by an idealist teleology that derives from Hegel. His theory of history, for example, is too idealist for my taste. In addition, Marx, at least in some of his writings, has a different view of elite politics from mine. His idea that governments in capitalist countries are merely the "executive committee of the bourgeoisie" is consonant with power elite theory, not corporatism. Yet at other times, as he analyzes the political struggles of his day, he does emphasize struggle between contending elites, though he never adequately grasped the central importance of credit power or its strategic dynamic. Furthermore, his broader view of society as polarized between opposing classes is compatible with corporatism, although I would not always put the primary emphasis on social class, as he does. The struggle between rich and poor, or, more specifically, workers and capitalists, may, at some junctures, become the primary polarization of politics, but usually it is not. It is indeed, however, always *one* issue in political economy, as, for example, in the ubiquitous struggle over wages and working conditions, although this is often local to workplaces or specific industries rather than the animating issue of politics writ large, as Marx expected.

Finally, Figure 2.1 shows that the "one, few, many" distinction is also used in economics to distinguish different industry structures that give rise to different theories about price determination. The most common textbook discussions of neoclassical economics and the major conclusions it draws about the economy being fair, stable, and efficient (discussed further in the following chapter), depend on the (often implicit) assumption that every industry and every market approximates their perfectly competitive ideal. Thus by assuming that the perfectly competitive case is the normal case, neoclassical economics is the counterpart of pluralism in politics. Both typically assume away major concentrations of power, except for the government. Government provides, among other things, public goods, discussed more in Chapter 6. The "public" is singular, a Platonic idealization. Economists will doubtless object that they do have a theory of what happens if oligopoly or monopoly exist, but most textbooks treat these as exceptions, rather than the rule, and most formal models typically used by economists ignore them, especially when it comes to finance. Furthermore, in their congenital enthusiasm for market solutions, economists typically ignore the important caveat that the markets they are extolling are the idealized perfectly competitive ones, not the real world markets chronically subject to private power. If my approach had to be expressed in textbook economic idioms, it would be a system in which oligopoly predominates at the highest levels and monopoly power, typically in the form of cartels, is common within many specific industries. Generalized free markets in the textbook sense do not exist now and never have, except in the minds of economists.

Private or business power

Private power comes in many forms, but most decisive throughout the centuries is the power to advance or withdraw credit. Credit itself comes in many forms. Most people equate credit with loans, which are indeed one form, but usually not the most common one. Another kind is paper money. Many people associate paper money with governments, but few governments got into the paper money business before the twentieth century. Before then, nearly all paper money was a form of circulating notes issued by merchants or banks. Even when governments did get into the business of printing paper money, they have typically left in the hands of private banks the power to issue it as credit. Private businesses have also always issued other forms of circulating credit that we do not often think of as money, but which function in much the same way, called by various names, including bills of exchange, letters of credit, commercial notes, and bankers acceptances. These forms of private credit have financed trade and commerce for centuries, and still do. All businesses, not just financial ones, issue credit to each other and to customers in the form of what accountants call accounts receivable. This means goods or services have been sold and delivered but payment has been deferred. It is yet another form of short-term credit. Modern consumer credit cards function similarly. Other forms of credit are longer term, of which bonds, debentures, and annuities are the most important kinds. Bond markets were the decisive innovation that enabled Europe to dominate world trade for five centuries and colonize the world. As we shall see, bond financing utterly transformed international politics.

The power to issue credit is an enormously significant power in domestic politics as well. For example, the origin and development of the two-party system in the United States is intimately connected with the origin and development of banks that were created by a specific political party and then financed that same party and its supporters. A wonderful book by banker Bray Hammond (1991) tells the story.

The first large American banks, including the Bank of the United States and the Bank of New York, were created by Alexander Hamilton and his supporters, who became the Federalist Party. These and subsequent Federalist banks were capitalized by the richest and most powerful merchants, like earlier banks in Britain, Italy, Sweden, and the Netherlands, and financed primarily two things: large-scale trade – foreign and domestic – and government debt. Later they added financing of long-term infrastructure projects such as harbor development, canals, and eventually railroads. Federalist banks supplied the credit for the very same business strategies that the Federalist (and later, Whig or Republican) Party supported in politics.

The opposing party, the Democratic-Republican Party (called the Democratic Party consistently since the 1820s) formed around Thomas Jefferson, James Madison, and their supporters, at first opposed banks in principle as corrupt instruments of the aristocratic Federalists. However, unable to destroy the

Federalist banks, Democrats found that banks were such an indispensable tool of political power that they created their own in whichever states they governed. This illustrates Madison's political theory of checks and balances at work to prevent either party from utterly dominating at the expense of the other. At that time each bank was created by a separate law of a specific state legislature. Different parties ruled in different states, so each party's banks could be secure in the states they dominated. Democratic banks operated differently from Federalist ones. They gathered their founding capital from rich Democrats and then gave credit to those neglected by Federalist banks, especially "farmers," often real estate speculators, and "mechanics," which are what we would today call industrial manufacturers. Democratic banks also financed infrastructure projects, especially those in Democratic-controlled cities and states that enriched their supporters by enhancing the value of the real estate and other business investments they had made. Banks in all countries operate as great strategic centers of business and political organization, so I discuss them throughout this book.

The second major form of private power is market power, or, more aptly, pricing power. Economists define market power as the ability to influence price. Neoclassical economists contrast idealized "perfect" markets, wherein no buyers or sellers have any influence over price, with oligopolistic and monopolistic markets, wherein either the buyers or the sellers or both are large enough in relation to the market as a whole to influence price according to the quantity they are willing to buy or sell. Most neoclassical textbooks claim that many if not most markets are close to being perfect markets, but they do not provide proof. I argue throughout this book that nothing close to perfect markets has ever existed. All or nearly all markets for all goods and services throughout history have had powerful players on either the buying or the selling side or both. Since perfect markets do not exist, all market relations are infused with private power. This power helps large merchants, financial companies, and corporations earn disproportionately high profits, influence the direction of investment and thus economic development, and determine what goods and services get produced. Furthermore, pricing power is, as we shall see in Part II, a strategic asset in competition with other businesses. Since market power is so valuable, private businesses interested in securing it often invest in politics to help gain or defend it.

The third major private power is employment power: discretion over wages (a form of pricing power) and working conditions. In most countries in modern times most people depend for their livelihood on being hired by private employers. Employers set wages and salaries and determine working conditions. Neoclassical economists tend to minimize or ignore this power by assuming labor markets are perfect markets in which power does not impinge, but clearly this has never been true. Before the rise of neoclassical economics in the 1870s, classical political economists asserted that wages were determined not only by the cost of the means of subsistence but also by the struggle between workers and employers, both within workplaces and in the broader society, for example, in shaping the specifics of labor, welfare, vagrancy, and other laws. For example, in Britain during the rise of capitalism, the infamous "Poor Laws" essentially criminalized poverty and vagrancy, forcing destitute people into the workshops and factories to work for low wages. The universally honored founding father of both political economy and economics, Adam Smith (1976, Bk I, ch. 8, sec. 12–13), contrary to modern economists, argued that it is the power struggle between workers and "masters" (capitalists or business owners) that determine wages, not the "Invisible Hand" of free markets:

> It is not, however, difficult to foresee which of the two parties must, upon all ordinary occasions, have the advantage in the dispute, and force the compliance with their terms. The masters, being fewer in number, can combine much more easily; and the law, besides, authorizes, or at least does not prohibit their combinations, while it prohibits those of the workmen. We have no acts of parliament against combining to lower the price of work; but many against combining to raise it. In all such disputes the masters can hold out much longer. A landlord, a farmer, a master manufacturer, or merchant, though they did not employ a single workman, could generally live a year or two upon the stocks which they have already acquired. Many workmen could not subsist a week, few could subsist a month, and scarce any a year without employment. In the long-run the workman may be as necessary to his master as his master is to him, but the necessity is not so immediate.
>
> We rarely hear, it has been said, of the combinations of masters, though frequently those of workmen. But whoever imagines, upon this account, that masters rarely combine, is as ignorant of the world as of the subject. Masters are always and every where in a sort of tacit, but constant and uniform combination, not to raise wages of labour above their actual rate. To violate this combination is every where a most unpopular action, and a sort of reproach to a master among his neighbors and equals. We seldom, indeed, hear of this combination, because it is the usual, and one might say, the natural state of things which nobody ever hears of.

There are other kinds of private power, including important choices over the direction of investment, what private business alliances to make, what to produce and how much. All of these are important for understanding international political economy, but the first three above most of all. Economists pretend that individual private choices are determined by their idealized "perfect" market, thereby obfuscating every form of private power. This book restores choice to the realm of power, where it belongs. As Thucydides, one of the founders of political realism, argued, "The strong do what they will; the weak do what they must." This is the realist theory of "rational choice"!

Capitalism as a two-party system

Political scientists often argue why political systems tend toward two parties. They typically do not consider that the main reason this happens is because the economy, capitalism itself, has two-party tendencies. Instead, the most frequent answer given is that since a bare majority is required to win, a winning party needs to strive to represent at least half of the voters. Only two parties (or in some systems, two coalitions of parties) can realistically strive for this at the same time. Whichever interests are neglected by one party will naturally gravitate to the other. This answer is not wrong, but it is only part of the reason.

Madison gets closer to a more complete answer in the polarities he highlights. First of all, capitalism is inherently a credit-driven system. Credit is the lifeblood of the economy. Competition over its expansion or contraction causes the boom-and-bust business cycle. As Madison's list implies, a credit system necessarily creates opposing parties, debtors and creditors, with broadly irreconcilable interests. Similarly, it creates the closely related parties of bulls and bears, terms commonly used to designate investors who are betting that an economic boom will continue (bulls) or falter (bears). These two parties have opposing interests regarding inflation, debt, and money or credit supply. This critical polarization figures in every chapter that follows. It is also nearly always one of the primary issues of politics. The direction of the economy and the distribution of wealth is strongly influenced by which way it falls.

Second, Madison mentions disputes between manufacturing and landed interests about whether to protect domestic industry, using policies like tariffs. We shall see that this issue does not always break neatly the way Madison characterized it, based on his own time. More generally, it is the contest between economic nationalists, who favor protection of the national market from foreign competition, and economic internationalists, who are internationally competitive and thus generally favor lower barriers to international commerce, in other words, free trade. I prefer the terms nationalist and internationalist to protectionist and free trader because, as we shall see, there are some specific circumstances when business internationalists support protectionism, without, by virtue of their international competitiveness, losing their unique interests as internationalists.

American party politics for much of its history has been organized around these two cleavages, debtors versus creditors and nationalists versus internationalists, plus the issue of slavery and its aftermath of racism. The modern political economy of most other countries revolves around these concerns as well. Conditions for war and peace are shaped by them.

Although Madison lists first the perennial struggle between those with property and those without, I put it third here because, although it is certainly always an issue in the workplace, it is not always as salient an issue in national, let alone international, politics. Except in times of extraordinary popular mobilization, major national parties in most countries, even those called "labor" or "socialist" parties, despite their electoral rhetoric, often neglect the concerns of less powerful ordinary folk. Yet even self-styled leftist parties can seldom win or maintain power without taking a stand on the first two issues, which are so central to the private business interests that continually contend for wealth and power, and so will adhere to one or another political party, regardless of what political label it uses, according to its policies regarding trade and credit.

In particular societies at particular times, other issues may on occasion overshadow these, but seldom do these disappear entirely. Pluralists might object that since I have already outlined, as Madison did, several issues, not just one, cross-cutting alignments among these various issues will produce a system more akin to pluralism than polarized corporatism. This is indeed possible and sometimes happens. There are also specific times and circumstances, which I will discuss in several later chapters, when all dominant interests tend to align the same way on each key issue, producing something like a unified power elite. Both of these are limiting cases. However, the general tendency toward polarization in the economy, no less than in elections, occurs because having a realistic chance of winning depends on having a preponderance of power. Only two interest blocs can have a fighting chance of such preponderance at any one time. Schattschneider (1935) brilliantly enunciated this principle in his study of interest group politics, specifically over US tariff policy. Furthermore, there are tendencies in the nature of capitalism, as we shall see, for interests on each of these questions to line up roughly the same way. The objective of corporatism is to investigate in particular societies at particular times how private interests are aligned, and, for political strategy, whether any significant political realignment is possible.

Interest blocs are not always coincident with formal political parties, such as Democrats and Republicans. Sometimes private interests realign faster than political parties adapt, so that both parties are split into factions favoring one or the other interest bloc. Sometimes the reverse is true, parties realign faster than private interests, with a similar consequence. At other times one interest bloc, for example, business internationalists, may be striving for predominance in both political parties, and thus be well represented in both, whereas their opponents, business nationalists, might organize almost entirely within one of them. In multiparty political systems, each interest bloc must typically court more than one party, perhaps hedging its bets. In other systems, political parties are weak, nonexistent, or banned, in which case interest blocs might cultivate particular powerful political leaders, cliques, bureaucracies, military branches, or other bases of power, which of course they may also do in party-dominated political systems. Likewise, some private organizations are expressions of a particular interest bloc, as, for example, the Council on Foreign Relations has been for US business internationalism. Other organizations may be contested by factions representing rival interest blocs or might be irrelevant to such interests. The complexity of real politics is not easily reducible to simple formulas – which opens the door wide to the complex *art* of political strategy – despite the fact that similar economic systems do tend to give rise to similar interest bloc cleavages. Furthermore, the dynamic of the business cycle sometimes promotes rapid realignments and strategic surprises, as I explain in Chapter 5.

Political realism and idealism

My perspective is rooted in political realism. Since its foundation in ancient Greece, political realism does not view the struggle for power as occurring only within governmental institutions, but perceives struggle as rooted in the distribution and types of private property. Gaining state power is one of the means by which property is secured and increased, but it is never the sole locus of political struggle. Political economy studies the ways in which private power is exercised both within the private sphere – the economy – and within the public sphere – the government. It recognizes that the two are intimately related. Arbitrarily divorcing them by creating separate and distinct academic disciplines of economics and political science in place of a unified political economy has only served to obscure the intimate connection between public and private power.

Yet I am enough of an idealist to believe that law, even though inevitably corrupted by wealth and power, is at least some restraint on power. It is better than lawless anarchy. It is as a student of politics and as a political strategist that I am primarily a political realist. Politics should not be understood only in terms of law or idealized administration. One must also take into account actual power, especially the often veiled private power. Libertarians excoriate most government. Yet government is the author of law. This simple truth, so obvious throughout civilized history, is today increasingly obscured by fashionable anti-government tirades. Curtail government, and only private power reigns. Private power does not dissipate when government is minimized; it dominates even more. There are plenty of examples around the world today and throughout history that clearly show that the antithesis of lawful government is not individual freedom, but rather rule by warlords and gangsters.

3 Political economics

By the nature of the subject, in social studies the various and general objects are, quite necessarily, mutually inter-connected and inseparable in reason, so that the one aspect can only be adequately explained by the consideration of the others. It is certain that the economic and industrial analysis of society cannot be *positively* accomplished, if one leaves out the moral and political analysis: and therefore this irrational separation furnishes an evident indication of the essentially metaphysical nature of the doctrines based upon it.

John Stuart Mill 1843 (Mill 1987: xiv)

British political economist Mill, one of the last and greatest of the classical political economists, here echoes one of those who inspired him, the French founder of sociology, Auguste Comte. Like me, Comte and Mill were determined to study social science without cutting it up into isolated academic disciplines, such as economics. Comte proposed sociology as that general social science he sought, whereas for me it is political economy, with a full dose of politics included. Both Comte and Mill, by their time in the middle of the nineteenth century, noted that political economy was already tending to drift toward what it would become more fully by the 1870s with the invention of neoclassical economics: *pure* economics, divorced from consideration of private power. Mill and Comte both ridiculed this tendency as "metaphysical," or what I would call "idealist," in the Platonic sense. That is, the core economic precepts, like Plato's forms, are idealized as truths more fundamental than the confusing and misleading empirical reality. The world of appearances is messy and complicated. Only by abstracting away from the confusing reality, economists believe, can we reach an understanding of the deeper essence. Unfortunately, this sort of metaphysical view tends to render the ideal forms or precepts impervious to correction or revision: knowing the truth conceptually, economists do not let reality intrude.

All prices are political. This claim flies in the face of 140 years of efforts by neoclassical economists to establish a separate science of economics distinct from politics and power. This enterprise has failed, I believe, as science, but triumphed as ideology. Economists posit an idealized perfect market system in which all prices and quantities of goods and services produced in the private sector of an economy are determined by supply and demand. Private power has no place in this imagined world. Before the rise of "pure" or neo-classical economics during the 1870s, economic conditions were studied by classical political economists, including Adam Smith, David Ricardo, John Stuart Mill, and Karl Marx, who allowed for both private power and markets to determine economic outcomes. This is obvious, for example, in Adam Smith's appreciation of the role of private power in determining wages, as quoted in the previous chapter. If, as Smith argues, wages are a product of private power struggles, then so are prices, since all prices are influenced by wages, at least. Classical political economy never lost sight of this. Furthermore, as I shall argue throughout this book, private credit and pricing power also influence prices and competitive dynamics.

Elements of political economy have continued to exist and sometimes flourish alongside the dominant paradigm of neoclassical economics. However, neo-classical *pure* economists dominate the conceptual definition of the field. Yet the foundations of their neoclassical economics are fundamentally flawed. Economies can only be adequately understood if private power is system-atically restored to a central place in our understanding of all economic phenomena. This cannot be done without debunking neoclassical economics and allied fields, such as modern finance theory (Keen 2011; Adler 2010), and replacing them with the older tradition of *political* economy reformulated for greater conceptual richness and scientific precision. Throughout this book, when I say "economics" with no qualifier, I refer to neoclassical economics, aka marginalist or equilibrium economics. The alternative corporatist conceptuali-zation of the economy developed here I refer to as "political economy" to indicate the centrality of private power and to connect with the more nuanced and interdisciplinary tradition of classical political economy. As Mill (1987: xxvii–xxviii) says on the very first page of his 1848 preface:

> Except on matters of mere detail, there are perhaps no practical questions, even among those which approach nearest to the character of purely economic questions, which admit of being decided on economical premises alone. And it is because Adam Smith never loses sight of this truth; because, in his applications of Political Economy, he perpetually appeals to other and often far larger considerations than pure Political Economy affords – that he gives that well-grounded feeling of command over the principles of the subject for the purposes of practice.

Whenever the term "politics" is used in this book, it refers not just to what goes on within and among governments, but more importantly, to the ubiquitous realm of private power. Private power derives from control over the economic resources of a society, including credit. Corporations and business owners control most of the productive and investable wealth of most societies. (We shall defer until Part IV the problem of the nature of power under socialism, in which the government owns much of a society's productive wealth.)

Businesses set most prices, determine what to produce and how much, and decide how to develop capacity for producing more and different things in the future. Workers and employees also have some power, especially if their skills are scarce and valuable or they are strongly organized in unions or professional associations. Private power involves many struggles, including over the division between owners and employees of the profit from what is produced, and between businesses competing with each other to attract investors and sell to consumers and other businesses. Private actors also struggle to influence government policy to favor their interests. Thus it *should* be a commonplace idea that all prices are political, that all economic outcomes are influenced by these private power struggles, yet economics tries so hard to displace this commonplace conception in favor of an independent realm of "the market" where power, public and private, does not extend. This myth of the market is one of the most powerful ideas of our time, but it prevents us from discerning and investigating the real dimensions and effects of private power.

Neoclassical economics and the myth of the market

The key propositions of neoclassical economics are designed to show that markets, when allowed to operate without government interference, are stable, efficient, and fair – the three golden pillars. But in order to derive these attractive results, neoclassical economics requires assumptions that are far from reality, sometimes even bizarre. No matter how unrealistic the assumptions necessary to demonstrate these three golden results, most economists are loath to employ more realistic economic models if they do not guarantee the golden results under normal circumstances. This commitment to specific results a priori is why I claim economics is more ideological than scientific.

The one major challenge within mainstream economics to the modern dominance of the three golden pillars began during the Great Depression of the 1930s, when they seemed most obviously implausible. A new branch of economics was created under the leadership of the British economist, John Maynard Keynes. This new branch is called "macroeconomics," the study of the economy as a whole, or sometimes simply Keynesian economics. This is, however, a misnomer because several of the key ideas of Keynes have been suppressed in trying to reconcile Keynes with neoclassical economics, which remained dominant within the realm of "microeconomics," the study of individual markets. This reconciliation effort is called "establishing the microfoundations of macroeconomics," in other words, trying to make the new ideas of Keynes as consistent as possible with the neoclassical perfect market ideals. The result is the neoclassical-Keynesian synthesis, the foundation of modern mainstream economics, divided into two realms. Microeconomics retains the traditional three golden pillars of neoclassical economics, under "normal" perfect market circumstances. Macroeconomics implicitly retains these neoclassical pillars, except that "stable" is replaced by "manageable." That is, macroeconomics concedes that bad government policies and other "exogenous shocks" may occasionally drive market economies away from stable equilibrium, however, competent macroeconomic management by governments, directed of course by economists, should restore stability. Economies are at least reassuringly manageable, if not perfectly stable. The comforting ideological message of neoclassical economics is restored.

However, the neoclassical-Keynesian synthesis is only reassuring at a serious scientific cost: large and persistent arenas of private power are neglected in the process. The Keynesian revolution was a good start, but it is unfinished. What Keynes pointed toward, but did not accomplish, was to undermine the neoclassical conception of markets altogether. The foundations of this task were also laid by several contemporaries of Keynes, including Piero Sraffa (1926, 1960), Friedrich von Hayek (Keen 2011: 445–49), and Joan Robinson (1981). These three and their allies launched three alternative schools of economics still struggling for influence outside the mainstream, respectively called neo-Ricardian, Austrian, and post-Keynesian economics. These awkward labels suggest the central problem of each of these schools: each attacked core propositions of neoclassical theory from a different direction without establishing a new core. I bring this missing core back into focus. The missing core is the systematic analysis of the dynamics of private power.

What is needed to complete the Keynesian revolution and restore sense to the important insights of Keynes is not the neoclassical agenda of establishing the microfoundations of macroeconomics, but rather, establishing the macrofoundations of microeconomics. This is a huge task. It starts conceptually with a new analysis of the strategic dynamics of private power, but will be consolidated only by empirical work in new directions. This endeavor is so vast that this simple text can at best provide only initial signposts of the direction of the road and the tasks ahead.

Economic stability

The first golden pillar of neoclassical ideology is its argument that market economies tend toward stability, even in the absence of government intervention. Stability means that prices fluctuate to adjust rapidly to changes in supply or demand, and that most if not all productive resources in the society, such as labor and capital, are thereby efficiently employed. Individual markets for various particular goods and services are stable in the sense that supply and demand tend toward equilibrium as long as prices are sufficiently flexible. Conservative economists also believe that the overall economy naturally tends toward stability near full employment of all labor and capital. Liberals or Keynesians, as mentioned above, believe that some degree of government economic management may be necessary to stabilize the macroeconomy, but that government does have the monetary and fiscal tools to achieve overall stability if it has the political will to use them correctly. Liberals generally agree with conservatives that many if not most individual markets are self-stabilizing.

My corporatist approach is very different. Pure capitalist economies are inherently *un*stable. When they enjoy periods of stability, this is only a temporary phase in a larger business cycle that is driven by competition in credit markets to experience recurring boom-and-bust. Whereas neoclassical economics builds its foundations beginning with supply and demand for particular products in individual markets (microeconomics), political economy begins with credit conditions that produce the economy-wide business cycle and frame the individual decisions of business leaders and consumers about how much to invest, produce, buy, and save. Since all these "micro" decisions are strongly shaped by the overall economic mood as reflected in the stage of the business cycle, economic analysis must begin with the big picture, the macroeconomy. It colors everything else.

Corporatist political economy differs from both liberal and conservative economics in seeing the source of economic instability within the competitive process itself. In neoclassical economics, free competition leads to stability. In fact, competition in credit markets is inherently destabilizing, creating a boom-and-bust business cycle. Producers of most kinds of goods and services struggle to escape the vicissitudes of credit-induced disruptions to supply and demand by *avoiding* free markets as much as possible through regulation, public or private. Private regulation includes contracted prices and cartels, which became ubiquitous by the later part of the nineteenth century as a defense against the increasingly disruptive influence of credit-driven business cycles. Thus whereas neoclassical economists have convinced the general public to talk about modern economies as "market economies," free markets are the exception, not the rule. Modern economies are properly called "capitalist economies," because they are driven by the central role of credit in the accumulation of capital, which is the predominant means of gaining wealth for corporations and individuals. Where there are islands of stability within a rather chaotic capitalist economy, this is largely because private power successfully *resists* market influences. Economists obscure this by assuming that all private economic transactions are market transactions even though many of them are in fact private *deals*, executed by strategic arrangement or long-term contract.

Corporatists should be more skeptical than Keynesians about the ability of governments to manage the economy to avoid instability. The reasons for this will be developed throughout this book. Whereas nearly all economists are Platonists and therefore view the economy as having one ideal state, political economists follow Aristotle by understanding that no state of the economy satisfies everybody. In fact, which direction the economy should move is always an issue of heated struggle between rival forces. Among the most important and enduring of these contending forces I call "bears" and "bulls," extending the meaning of common terms used in discussing financial market players. Bulls believe the economy will continue to expand as asset prices rise. Bears believe prices will fall, typically causing the economy to stagnate or contract. However, the importance of bears and bulls goes far beyond mere belief. Since the most powerful bears and bulls are also major investors, they position their assets, their capital, to profit if their beliefs become true. In business this is called "taking a position." For an economy to be relatively stable, bears and bulls must have roughly equal power, hence the polarization of the economy discussed in the previous chapter, but any such balance is typically transitory.

The strategic competition between bulls and bears determines the business cycle. Bulls tend to thrive on easy credit and rising prices. If they are too powerful, expansion will overheat, resulting in chronic inflation of product and/ or asset prices. If the latter, a speculative bubble inflates. Less debt-addicted bears thrive when credit is tight, even during price deflation. If bears are too powerful, economic growth will slow or even turn down. If economic expansion continues, bulls will grow faster and outcompete bears. In other words, during booms, bulls trample bears. If expansion reverses, bears eat bulls. When economies go bust, many excessively indebted bulls are bankrupted and their assets often taken over cheaply by bears. I discuss this competitive dynamic in more detail in Chapter 5, following a necessary interlude on strategy in Chapter 4. Because bulls and bears also struggle to influence governments in their favor, governments, which are seldom insulated from private power, will not necessarily promote the Keynesian ideal of economic stability, even if they have the policy tools to do so. At any particular moment, bears or bulls may have the upper hand in national politics. Capitalism is a two-party system. This point is being driven home with a vengeance during the present worldwide economic difficulties.

Economic efficiency

The second golden pillar of the neoclassical ideology of market economies is the claim that free markets are efficient at allocating resources. This is such a fundamental article of faith among neoclassical economists that they systematically refuse to consider economic models that do not embed this result in their starting assumptions. Economists do consider exceptions to efficiency, but only by using, as their metric for efficiency, models that rest on impossibly arcane free market assumptions. For instance, economists say that socialism, or government allocation of resources according to political priorities, is necessarily less efficient than free (perfect) markets (except in the case of public goods, which we need not define yet). Part of the argument for this rests on the contention that government bureaucrats cannot have nearly as much information about the relative scarcity of various things in the economy as free market prices convey. But the assumptions required to prove that market prices are accurate indicators of relative economic scarcity include: (1) that there is no private market power (all producers and consumers are small relative to the total market), (2) that all economic transactions occur at equilibrium prices (there is never any excess supply or demand), (3) that all producers and consumers are rational, and (4) that all producers and consumers have perfect information about the prices and qualities of all goods and services. In other words, free markets allocate resources more efficiently than governments *if* we assume everybody is perfectly brilliant *except* government bureaucrats! The conclusion is embedded in the assumptions.

It is not my purpose to prove that either governments or markets are more efficient in principle. The entire exercise is a useless game among Platonic idealists. In any case, as mentioned above, I argue that private power often subverts markets anyway. Furthermore, there is no valid universal standard of economic efficiency. Economists themselves admit that efficient allocation of resources depends on the initial allocation of those resources. In other words, what is "efficient" when the richest one percent owns 50 percent of a nation's resources is not the same as what is "efficient" when the richest one percent owns 20 percent. Efficiency as economists define it is always relative to distribution of wealth. There is no absolute standard. In fact, what is "efficient" to most people who are rich and powerful is whatever makes them richer and more powerful, and this differs among them. There is no one Platonic ideal. Bears and bulls, and other ways of differentiating invested wealth, do not share the same interests. Any presumed Platonic ideal does not matter one iota to anyone with any real wealth and power. What matters is their own particular interest and advantage in striving against rivals to secure their wealth and power. Platonic idealism may seem plausible to intellectuals without much wealth at stake, but it is useless for those striving to win.

Theoretical and empirical critiques of economists' notion of efficiency are legion, but few economists are capable of *seeing* any of these because their heads are stuck in the Platonic sand. If reality contradicts their core precepts, reality is at fault, not the Platonic ideal types they uphold. Various critics attack each of the four neoclassical perfect market assumptions listed above. The central critique of this book and of political economy in general is that all universal notions of economic efficiency fail because private power so effectively subverts the first assumption on which they are based: that economies are free of private power. Post-Keynesian economists, among others, focus their attack on the second assumption of neoclassicals: market transactions do not necessarily take place at equilibrium prices. This is sometimes called disequilibrium economics (Leijonhufvud 1968). Excess supply or excess demand is relatively common and empirically demonstrable, not the least in the labor market, where chronic excess supply of labor is experienced by millions of people as involuntary unemployment. Furthermore, I will show that capitalists, acting strategically, lack consistent incentive to employ their capital fully or to strive toward equilibrium. Behavioral economics, which has flourished brilliantly in recent decades (Shermer 2009; Kahneman 2013), uses psychological research techniques to prove how much the behavior of real economic agents departs from the third neoclassical assumption of economic rationality. Neoclassical assumptions of perfect information have been challenged, often from within the neoclassical paradigm itself, by information economics (Birchler & Bütler 2007). All these critiques are necessary and valid. However, in this book I focus most on private power because it has been, surprisingly, among the most neglected of the critiques of the neoclassical myth of the market. Bringing private power systematically into the picture also enhances our understanding of the other three: the effect of power on the stability of markets, how psychology and behavior vary with power, and how private power enhances and exploits asymmetric distribution of information.

Fairness and fundamental flaws in the neoclassical theory of distribution

Perhaps no proposition of neoclassical economics is more important politically than the claim that free markets are fair, the third golden pillar. Fair means that everybody gets what they deserve. Any injustices exist because of distortions to the market introduced by politics and government. This is one of the principal foundations of modern political conservatism. Economists' doctrine of fairness derives from their marginal product theory of the distribution of income. According to this theory, goods and services are produced using a mix of various factors of production that are grouped into three broad categories of labor, capital, and land (which includes natural resources). Each of these factors receives payment commensurate with its marginal contribution to the value of the output. Labor receives wages and salaries. Capital receives profit, interest, and dividends. Land receives rent. However, the first curious thing to notice about these categories is that labor is the only one that represents the work of people. Payments to capital and land are payments merely for *ownership* of a resource. Though what someone owns may indeed be valuable for producing more things, the mere fact of owning in itself does not produce anything. Yet the *owners* get paid, not the productive thing they own. According to marginal product theory, in any particular state of the economy, there is only one possible distribution of income that is efficient and fair. Any deviation from this ideal distribution is less fair and efficient.

The neoclassical account is unworkable in at least two major regards: the theory of returns to capital and to labor. (I defer the problems of the neoclassical theory of rent.) The theory of returns to capital (profits, dividends, and interest) is hobbled because the neoclassical economists have such confused conceptualization of what capital is. No other topic of neoclassical economics is so muddled. Neoclassical labor market theory also suffers because one half of the labor market, the capitalists who hire labor, is mistheorized. Of course, the neoclassical understanding of the income of both labor and capital suffers from the common problem we have highlighted throughout: neglect of private power.

Neoclassical economics' confusing treatment of capital stems from their habitual conflation of its dual nature. Capital is both liquid investable wealth *and* already invested means of production and distribution. The former may earn interest or analogous returns such as dividends; the latter returns profits. The fundamental economic problem for neoclassicals is allocating scarce resources among alternative uses. Since their focus is on choice, capital must be in its liquid form, which I will call "money capital," even though, strictly speaking, liquid wealth may be held in various assets that are not normally considered money, including non-monetary credit. Before money capital is committed to buy any particular means of production, such as productive machinery and raw materials, it can potentially be used to produce anything. Choice among alternative uses is indeed possible, as neoclassical theory emphasizes. But once society progresses beyond mercantile or financial capital to industrial capital, more and more of society's total capital is in the form of physical means of production, like factories, shipyards, productive machinery, and railroads. This already invested capital I will call "physical capital" or sometimes "means of production." Some physical capital is highly generalized, for example, computers and electric motors, and thus might have a range of alternative uses, though never as broad as money capital. However, other physical capital, such as an automatic loom or a cement factory, is highly specialized and thus must be used to produce only one specific product or it is virtually useless. Perhaps scant value could be recovered by scrapping it. Yet almost all economics textbooks and mathematical models treat physical capital as if it can be seamlessly reallocated to produce whatever changing consumer tastes and relative prices indicate. In fact, neoclassicals typically assume that all factors of production are useful, to some degree, to produce anything, so that given any specific mix of desired output within any economy, all factors will be employed. This is absurd. Neo-Ricardian theory is useful for considering the consequences of a more realistic theory of physical capital.

Neoclassicals treat all forms of capital as equivalent since the process of competition supposedly creates one common profit and interest rate. Actually, as a slight complication, there is one common spread of rates from short-term to long-term, which is called the term structure of interest, illustrated by what is called the yield curve. Furthermore, some borrowers will be charged a risk premium. Any individual firm should, in the neoclassical world, borrow if its rate of interest is lower than the profit it could earn by using the borrowed money to buy and operate physical capital with the term of the credit and the service life of the physical capital matching. In actual fact, competition never equilibrates profit rates across all invested capital or interest rates across all borrowers, even if there were some non-subjective way to adjust for relative risk. Actual profit and interest rates differ widely because of variations in credit relationships and market power. Credit relationships are rich with power. No process of competition has *ever* been able to equalize private power throughout a capitalist economy. Throughout history, there have always been powerful or prescient businesses that earn far more than average profits. Such highly profitable businesses are indeed some of the most interesting places to observe private power at work.

Beyond the problem of private power, two logical problems with neoclassicals' concept of capital render it useless as a general explanation of profits. The first is the circularity inherent in defining the quantity of physical capital. The second is the general impossibility of separately defining the marginal contributions of physical capital and labor to output. If these quantities cannot be defined consistently in the real world, then the marginal product theory of income distribution fails, even if somehow private power could be assumed to be equalized, for example, if all firms throughout the economy were very small. Both problems are obscured by economists' misleading tendency to treat capital as if it were always in its fluid form as money capital, always available for diverse investment but never yet instantiated in productive use.

Piero Sraffa (1960), an Italian economist teaching at Cambridge University, pioneered a critique of neoclassical capital theory using linear algebra to develop a more sophisticated presentation of the theory of capital used by the classical political economist David Ricardo. Thus this approach is usually called "neo-Ricardian." Sraffa then debated his findings with Paul Samuelson of MIT in Cambridge, Massachusetts, then one of the most prominent neoclassical economists. This debate has been labeled "the Cambridge capital controversy," since its most prominent protagonists had a "Cambridge" affiliation. The debate is well reviewed in Keen (2011: 142–57). Sraffa proved that the neoclassical definition of profit as a percentage return to a stock of capital is circular and thus illogical, since the only way to measure the quantity of various kinds of physical capital is to aggregate capital using some universal measure of price or value, but that all such measures would themselves vary as the profit rate changed. Measuring the quantity of capital depends on the rate of profit so the quantity of capital cannot be the explanation for the rate of profit without a hopelessly circular argument. This criticism has been evaded and ignored by neoclassicals, but never adequately answered.

Neoclassical economics defines the marginal product of a factor of production, such as capital, as the output it would produce if it alone were increased while all other factors of production are held constant. This concept was applied in classical political economy only to land and natural resources. Neoclassicals extended it to labor and capital. David Ricardo, like many classical political economists, considered that labor and capital were often employed in fixed ratios, based on the technology of production, in which case marginal productivity of either would be undefined. Ricardo referred to each increment of labor and capital together as a "dose." During Ricardo's time the quintessential technologies of the industrial revolution were the automatic loom to weave yarn into cloth and the spinning jenny to spin fibers, such as cotton, into yarn. Later the sewing machine was invented to speed the sewing of cloth into clothing. All three, like many machines, are designed for a single operator. Add another machine and you must add another operator. Adding, for example, a sewing machine without adding a worker to operate it makes no sense. In many offices and design companies today, the basic capital equipment is a computer. Each worker needs one and only one. Adding a computer workstation without adding an additional worker to operate it is nonsensical. Thus in very many instances, it is not possible even to define the marginal productivity of capital apart from that of workers. The fact that there are *some* instances when this *is* possible is not enough to make it the universal measure of the value of an increment of capital, as neoclassicals insist.

Some might imagine that the marginal productivity idea could be rescued by adding increments via improving the quality of the single machine in use by a worker by buying a more advanced machine. However, this would usually involve an improvement in the technology of production, which is different, according to neoclassical theory, from simply adding an increment of the same kind of capital. There are some increments of physical capital that do potentially illustrate the neoclassical case, for example, adding spindles to a spinning machine without otherwise changing the technology. Also, today's computer-controlled spinning machines are so reliable that one worker can tend several at the same time. The ratio of machines to workers is not fixed in such cases, so marginal productivity could be measured by adding an additional machine to one worker's responsibility and measuring how much additional output results. Presumably, giving the neoclassical law of diminishing marginal productivity, the more machines that are added, the lower the marginal productivity when adding each additional machine since the chance increases that two or more will have a problem or breakdown at the same time and therefore simultaneously demand the attention of the overtaxed worker. But since this sort of variability applies to only some forms of physical capital and not to all, marginal productivity cannot be defined for all forms and therefore cannot be the universal explanation of the profit rate.

Neoclassical economists explain wages in exactly the same way: keeping capital fixed and increasing the number of workers to see what is the marginal increment produced as each new worker is added. According to the neoclassical theory of the firm, capitalists will hire additional workers until their marginal product just matches the current wage rate. If wages increase while everything else, including the firm's physical capital, stays the same, neoclassical theory expects the firm to employ fewer workers. Therefore the number of workers hired depends on the wage rate. The lower the wage rate the more are hired. The wage depends on the marginal product of labor throughout the economy. Of course, this theory of wages suffers from the same problem as the theory of profits: if increasing or decreasing workers does not make sense without changing the physical capital stock, then the marginal product of labor is undefined. Historically, the theory was used by American economist John Bates Clark to argue that it was fruitless for workers, widely protesting during the 1880s and 1890s for a legal limit of an eight-hour work day, instead of the then typical 12 hours, at the same pay, to make such a demand, since, Bates assumed, if they win their demand fewer would be employed. Neoclassicals since Bates have tended to assume the truth of this case deductively rather than testing it empirically, though in a few instances when it was tested it was found to be false (Adler 2010: 143–50).

In fact, the neoclassical theory of wage determination includes two rival explanations, though these are not reconciled. On the one hand, there is the microeconomic theory at the level of the individual firm, which is most certainly false, given the relatively fixed nature of most capital-labor doses. On the other hand, more reasonable, though still problematic for failing to account for bargaining power, is the economy-wide or macroeconomic determination of wages according to the marginal productivity of the least productive in the economy as a whole. These two, in practice, give highly divergent predictions of what wage and employment levels should be. Neither is accurate, but the microeconomic explanation is the most deficient.

I have personally inspected scores of operating factories in three countries, the USA, the Philippines, and China, including especially textile factories. I have read about many others. I have never been able to square the neoclassical theory of the firm with what I have observed. For example, although wages in China are a small fraction of those in Germany, Chinese textile factories using the latest German automated spinning machines do not employ significantly more workers per machine than in Germany. This is not in fact surprising from an engineering perspective. The machine is designed to conserve labor and does so just as effectively operating in China as in Germany. I am sure the machine and the workers produce similar output in both places too. If output is perhaps a little higher per worker in Germany, it is in any case nowhere near as different as the enormous difference in wages. Thus the marginal productivity of the workers does not determine either their wages or the number of workers employed by the firm.

Instead, it is the macroeconomic explanation of wages that works somewhat better. Most factory workers in China are migrants from the poor agricultural interior, where their marginal productivity is quite low. There are generally plenty more willing to migrate and take jobs in the city at low pay, as long as it is higher than what they would earn back home. Their pay is thus not at all according to the marginal value of their output when they work with the latest productive machinery, but according to the situation of the most desperate migrant workers willing to take their place (Lewis 1954). This can be easily seen along the US–Mexico border. The same workers using the same capital equipment with the same productivity do not earn the same pay on both sides of the border; not even close. This is why so many people are willing even to risk their lives to cross it. Yet neoclassical textbooks often gloss over the great difference between productivity in an economy as a whole and in an individual firm.

An interesting study of this was done of workers at McDonald's restaurants around the world. Regardless of the country, McDonald's work process and technology of production are virtually identical. There may be small variations in the productivity of workers from restaurant to restaurant according to location and customer traffic, but not so drastic as to justify the fact that the value of McDonald's workers' wages in Japan, measured in terms of the number of hamburgers they could buy from their own restaurant, is about 13 times higher than the value of the wages of the lowest paid McDonald's workers in India and Indonesia (Adler 2010: 149). It is not the value of their own work product that determines the low wages of McDonald's workers in the poorest countries, but the low marginal productivity of the least productive agricultural workers that keeps other workers relatively poor unless they have rare skills or greater power through union organization.

Conclusion

Perhaps no economic diagram is more widely used than the supply and demand curves that intersect to determine the equilibrium price. As ubiquitous as this sort of analysis is, few textbooks warn users that these curves, even by the analysis of neoclassical economists themselves, are not defined except in conditions of perfect competition, that is, when no private power exists. Introduce private power in any market, and the demand curve for any individual firm is vague. Demand for the output of any one firm depends on whatever choices its competitors are making. The firm's supply curve is similarly ill-defined when the competitor's behavior matters. Yet I doubt if there has ever existed a market that was even close to perfectly competitive, in the economists' sense of that concept, on both sides (buyer and seller). Why build a general theory on an idealized fantasy? Real world competition involves strategic interaction, as even economists admit when they are being careful, as in specialized studies of oligopoly. Whereas economists are experts in fantasy world of equilibrium through perfect competition, I prefer to start with a methodology centered on strategic competition, rather than adding it as an afterthought. Strategic interaction should be at the foundation of political economy.

Modern neoclassical economics is a degenerative research paradigm. It is so rife with logical inconsistencies and empirical absurdities that it cannot be reformed (Keen 2011). It is more useful and direct to simply bypass it by restoring and developing the more broad-minded and interdisciplinary traditions of classical political economy, supplemented by careful study of the dynamics of private power. Much of the great use was lost when neoclassical theorists took the wrong turn toward creating "pure economics" and thereby propagated the myth of the universal market, an autonomous realm of freedom unsullied by power. Neoclassical analysis of credit and financial operations, in particular, is blinded by their obsession with free markets to the utter neglect of private power. In fact, it is in the financial arena that private power manifests itself most decisively. Without understanding this, the business cycle is incomprehensible, as we shall see in more detail in Chapter 5. Indeed, neoclassicals have avoided developing an endogenous theory of business cycles because they cling so strongly to the ideological notion of market economies as self-stabilizing. For them, any disturbances of the brilliant promise of stable markets must come from outside the market realm itself, from what they call "exogenous shocks." No sensible progress will ever be made in political economy until the theory of business cycles is endogenous and central to our concerns.

Other contemporary critics of neoclassical economics are also striving to develop endogenous theories of the business cycle, but most of them have in common with neoclassicals a mechanical model of the economy devoid of strategic interaction and intentionality. While such "toy" models may be useful heuristically to illustrate in highly simplified ways how economies could develop boom-and-bust cycles using assumptions somewhat more realistic than those at the core of neoclassical macroeconomics, this approach has its limits. To better understand both specific economic events and general trends, more useful and certainly more interesting than any mechanical model is realistic understanding of political economy as a realm of strategic interaction among powerful players with rival interests. This approach reconnects political economy with concrete history, practical business, and political strategy. It brings political economy closer to the realm of Machiavellian politics and war.

My approach to political economy, taking private power seriously, requires a different methodology; different not only from neoclassical economics, but even from most critics who retain the basic neoclassical methodology of modeling economic processes as if they were as devoid of human intelligence and intentionality as are atoms and hydraulic systems. Social sciences do not become more scientific by aping physics, but less. Processes involving power and strategic intent cannot possibly be treated scientifically if we treat them as if they were as random and non-intentional as subatomic particles. Thus in the next chapter we introduce our strategic method and show how much more of reality appears comprehensible when we admit the possibility that human beings do not behave like billiard balls or quarks.

Part II
Dynamic political economy

4 Strategic methodology

War does not belong in the realm of the arts and sciences; rather it is part of man's social existence. War is a clash between major interests, which is resolved by bloodshed – that is the only way in which it differs from other conflicts. Rather than comparing it to art we could more accurately compare it to commerce, which is also a conflict of human interests and activities; and it is *still* closer to politics, which in turn may be considered as a kind of commerce on a larger scale. Politics, moreover, is the womb in which war develops ... In war, the will is directed at an animate object that *reacts*. It must be obvious that the intellectual codification used in the arts and sciences is inappropriate to such an activity.

Carl von Clausewitz (1976: 149)

Empiricism is not about having theories, beliefs, and causes and effects: it is about avoiding being a sucker ...

Nassim Nicholas Taleb (2010: 311)

Taleb is one of my favorite contemporary philosophers of methodology. He is both an accomplished financial trader and best-selling author. This definition of empiricism, though appearing only in a footnote, is his best. My methodological approach is inspired by an attitude reminiscent of Taleb's. Part II of this book is about the strategic dynamics of business competition, or private power. Like Clausewitz's view of war, I view political economy as a psychological and strategic contest of powers. Like both, I am highly skeptical of economic and statistical models that claim scientific virtue, but in practice are too remote from real-world behavior to be of much use. Some simplifying assumptions are necessary to hone in on what is most essential to avoid being a sucker. But some assumptions, such as those at the root of neoclassical economics, seductively enlist you in the ranks of the suckers. In the world of business, the only way to avoid being a sucker is *not* to be an economist. In other words, you must understand private power dynamics, not the "perfect market equilibrium" economists prattle about. The only equilibria in business competition are the episodes – short or long – of apparent calm that interrupt bouts of intense conflict. Clausewitz (1976:

82–83, 216–19) understood this kind of "equilibrium" far better than economists do. In Chapter 2 I argued that capitalism is typically a two-party system. In epistemology too there are two parties. In keeping with my animal metaphors, instead of suckers and con artists, I shall refer to them as sheep and wolves. Sheep move and think in herds. Wolves hunt sheep in packs, with strategy.

Although I studied the classics of strategy since I was a teenager and understood their application to political economy while I was writing my PhD dissertation, it was only with the world financial crisis that began in 2007 that I grasped the universal applicability of the strategic methodology. On the one hand, because of the crisis, I was studying financial derivatives in some detail. I noticed that the much-touted Black–Scholes formula for pricing options (one kind of financial derivative) depended on many of the same perfect market assumptions that I already knew were flawed in economics. I wondered why the powerful financiers who ran major investment banks would subscribe to such an obviously bankrupt way of measuring anything when there were trillions of dollars at stake. At the same time, I was rereading Clausewitz, who writes (1976: 111), "A major gulf exists between the commander-in-chief ... and the senior generals immediately subordinate to him ... subjected to much closer control ... and thus [given] far less scope for independent thought." Then it hit me.

The highly paid traders who staff the trading desks of financial companies do not need to know the big picture to be useful. In fact, it is better for the moguls of finance if most ordinary traders are blinkered. Staff traders have a lot in common with eighteenth-century Prussian grenadiers. What they need, to be useful, is not truth, but *training*. Black–Scholes, and other such formulas, are not so much about divining the truth as they are about training most market participants to behave in ways that are broadly regularized and thus predictable. They become part of the ordinary rules of the game, standard operating procedures. Like well-drilled troops, traders are a more useful instrument of power when they respond to orders in orderly ways. This creates a kind of inertia or regularity in financial markets that is indeed a prerequisite for strategic financial maneuvers by those with real power. An army acting chaotically is no longer a useful instrument of strategy; nor are traders acting chaotically or idiosyncratically a useful instrument for financial strategists. Wolves hunt more successfully because they understand how sheep will move as a herd, as sheep are taught in textbooks.

Neoclassical economics, and its applications such as the efficient market hypothesis taught in corporate finance textbooks, is more about training than truth. It is about training generations of mid-level employees and investors to believe in the myth of the market so they are more effective instruments in the hands of those who wield financial power in defiance of that myth. I am not sure anyone consciously set out to do this, but this is effectively what has evolved as dissident currents of economic thought were pruned away and textbooks standardized, like army drill manuals.

Ordinary and extraordinary action

One of the most striking failures of economics as science is its extraordinary adherence to the ordinary, positive, routine, public, and bureaucratic aspects of economic life to the almost complete neglect of the extraordinary, negative, extreme, private, strategic, and utterly disruptive aspects that appear most evident during crises. Ben Bernanke, the chair of the Federal Reserve Board during the recent global financial crisis, says this unapologetically:

> Standard macroeconomic models ... did not predict the crisis [of 2008], nor did they incorporate very easily the effects of financial instability. ... Most of the time, including during recessions, serious financial instability is not an issue. The standard models were designed for these non-crisis periods ... (Bernanke 2010: 16–17; quoted in Keen 2011: 16)

In other words, economics is the "science" of the economy when nothing much is happening. It predicts "nothing much" pretty well. It cannot predict anything unusual. Indeed, many routine economic phenomena are fairly easy to "predict," or at least extrapolate, when change is not abrupt. It is like writing a history of war without the decisive battles. My corporatist political economy is more ambitious in aiming to understand dynamics of crises, which are far more important for changes in wealth and power than the routine interludes that economists "explain." In fact, both the periods of seemingly routine growth and the intermittent crises are aspects of a single strategic business cycle that can be best understood as separate stages of a common process.

The dialectic interplay between the ordinary and extraordinary has been a feature of the best strategic thinking since ancient times. It is central to the Taoism of Chinese philosopher Lao Zi, which likely inspired China's most famous strategist since ancient times, Sun Zi, whose book, *The Art of War* (1993) remains on many people's short list as one of the best books every written on strategy. Sun Zi gives considerable attention to the interplay of the routine, ordinary, and expected forces and the extraordinary, surprising, and ultimately decisive forces. He does not say to employ only one to the exclusion of the other. Both are needed. The ordinary force distracts the enemy's attention and lulls him into a sense of complacency by presenting him with an expected threat that confirms his prejudices, while at the same time the extraordinary force appears suddenly, at an unexpected place and time, at a weak point, when the enemy is overextended, to utterly confound his ability to resist. Collapse follows quickly.

Nothing like this is ever imagined in economics textbooks. Yet in the exercise of financial power, such extraordinary operations are often moments of great profit and loss. They are likewise more effective because so many investors are lulled into complacent expectations by routine times, and by textbook formulas. This is why Sun Zi remains popular in some financial circles and is quoted in films about financial operations such as Oliver Stone's *Wall Street* (1987). Financiers understand aspects of the exercise of power unknown to most economists, absorbed as they are in their world of dull gray averages.

The economists' viewpoint is not only dull, but recklessly misleading. For example, a popular introductory macroeconomic textbook, co-authored by the same Ben Bernanke, illustrates the power of compound interest by saying that if your ancestor had invested $10 at 4 percent interest in the year 1800, by 2005, assuming the interest rate never changed, it would be worth over $31,000 (Frank & Bernanke 2009: 193). While mathematically correct, this is a social absurdity. First of all, many of the banks that existed in 1800 have since gone bankrupt, so most of the balance might have been lost that way. Second, because of the business cycle, 4 percent nominal return does not always represent a real return on wealth. Money, our measure of value, itself varies in value. During times of high inflation the 4 percent return would have been effectively negative whenever the value of money was falling faster than that. Losses are not symmetrical with gains in percentage terms. Thus if you have $100 and lose 50 percent, you have $50 left, if you subsequently gain 50 percent you are not back where you started, but have only $75. That is why smart investors, like the fictional Gordon Gekko in *Wall Street*, "hate losses." They are hard to recover from.

Nearly all long-term illustrations by economists smooth everything out using average rates of growth that hide the fact that within those average gains were many losers who never recouped their losses. Economic cycles define winners and losers. Throughout history, besides war, there are two great destroyers of financial wealth: bankruptcy and inflation (including asset bubbles). Over decades, given periodic business cycles, what seems extraordinary becomes ordinary and should be expected to recur, including the dire effects of crises. This is why Taleb focuses attention on seemingly rare "Black Swan" events, like financial crises, that may nonetheless have momentous or even catastrophic impact. A macroeconomic model that focuses entirely on the routine and ignores the extraordinary promotes not prudence, but reckless complacency. It is for leading sheep to the slaughter; for duping suckers.

The myth of market applied to finance

The "efficient market hypothesis" (EMH), the foundation of most of modern mathematical finance theory, is an extension of the neoclassical myth of the market into the realm of the financial markets. It abstracts away every aspect of real, successful financial operations to leave only a desiccated corpse, called an efficient market. Left out are conflict, strategy, deception, credit rationing, and, of course, private power. Contemplating this corpse, many economists have convinced themselves that financiers who make money are just luckier than average. Ignoring all the tools of real credit power, most economists and finance professors have lost the ability even to *imagine* how someone could get rich *deliberately* by strategic exercise of credit power. Useful tactics for strategic action are largely invisible in textbook economics and finance. Effective action is often the opposite of the platitudes textbooks teach. But, as I said, from textbooks you should expect only training, not truth. The extremely unreal assumptions of the EMH are the antitheses of the strategic methodology.

The EMH assumes that asset prices change because of the random arrival of news that impacts the price. Like everything important and interesting in economics, news is exogenous according to the textbook theory; it arrives from outside the business system itself. This basic proposition is absurd to anyone who knows the news business, like my father, a former newspaper editor, and me, who worked for him for six summers. Most news is created by the public relations departments of business firms and released to news agencies at the time of the issuer's choosing. Even when reporters and publishers are honest and not bribed to print news that profits a particular business operation (which does happen often enough in history), business secrets are protected by privacy laws and therefore businesses themselves decide if and when to release internal information as news or when to create rumors about their competitors. The arrival of news is neither random nor exogenous. Much of it is coordinated as part of the strategic design of business leaders. Again, Oliver Stone's film *Wall Street* illustrates this key point that textbooks ignore. In this instance, art trumps "science" as a source of wisdom. Contemplating this non-random generation of news, I have invented the political realist adage, "corruption is a constant, but scandal is a variable."

Sun Zi says (1993, Ch. 1, sec. 18), "All warfare is based on deception." The same could be said about business and politics. His final chapter is about spies. Clausewitz too emphasizes the importance of deception and uncertainty in creating "the fog of war," a term he popularized. Because of this, intelligence about the enemy is critical but always suspect:

> Many intelligence reports in war are contradictory; even more are false, and most are uncertain. ... In short, most intelligence is false, and the effect of fear tends to multiply lies and inaccuracies. ... This difficulty of accurate recognition constitutes one of the most serious sources of friction in war, by making things appear entirely different from what one had expected. ... Ordinary men, who normally follow the initiative of others [i.e., sheep], tend to lose self-confidence when they reach the scene of action; things are not what they expected, the more so as they still let others influence them. But even the man who planned the operation and now sees it being carried out may well lose confidence in his earlier judgment. ... War has a way of masking the stage with scenery crudely daubed with fearsome apparitions. ... this is one of the great chasms between *planning and execution*. (Clausewitz 1976: 117–18)

Commerce is no different, except, as Clausewitz emphasizes, for its relative lack of mortal danger. Yet the EMH, as with other perfect markets myths, assumes ample information. All that is knowable about factors that affect the value of any security is already reflected in its price. Or, in a weaker but equivalent version, if there were any secrets known only to insiders, those insiders would already be taking advantage of their knowledge to trade the security and therefore would have moved the price to what they (correctly!) believe is its fair value. Either way, current prices of securities always reflect the collective wisdom of all traders in the EMH myth.

As a first approximation, this sounds like a plausible working hypothesis for routine conditions, but it ignores power and conflict, the essence of strategy. Traders in the process of executing a strategic financial operation try not to tip their hand or telegraph their intent. Nor do they aim at a fair market price. They may drive prices to extremes before cashing in and locking in their profits. Surprise is essential. Without surprise, opportunists could jump on the bandwagon and steal some of the profits of the intended price movement and adversaries might be able to counter the plan.

When Richard Fuld, the CEO of Lehman Brothers investment bank, rushed home from India in March 2008 to confront the rapid decline of the stock price of his firm, his instincts were *not* those taught in textbooks. He did not assume that the falling price of his stock reflected the collective wisdom of an efficient market. He assumed what was occurring was a repeat of one sort of financial operation that has occurred thousands of times in the history of financial markets, a bear raid. He cursed the bears, powerful investors that he assumed were using market power to drive down the price of his stock and destroy his company. He vowed to defeat them by a counterattack: using Lehman's liquid reserves to buy back its own shares, raise Lehman's stock price, and force losses on those loathsome bears, to induce them to give up their short positions and retreat (Sorkin 2009: 10, 13–17). We shall see shortly how this is done. His actions were not those of a mere trader, but of a general of finance, locked in mortal combat with his adversaries. He correctly understood that the very survival of his 160-year-old firm was at stake. None of his strategic wisdom is taught in textbooks of economics or finance. Unfortunately for him, he used up Lehman's remaining liquid reserves without staunching the fall of its stock price. This time the bears won. Their resources, including surprise, were greater than his. Lehman Brothers was destroyed. A worldwide financial crisis ensued, during which all short positions were richly rewarded. The bears drank champagne.

Fuld's defeat points out another flaw in the EMH: the absurd assumption that unlimited credit is available to every investor at the same constant interest rate. This assumption is logically inconsistent even within neoclassical economics itself, which otherwise emphasizes the scarcity of all resources, yet, because this is a convenient way to simplify the model, the assumption is made. In real business, credit is the critical reserve asset and there is never enough (Chancellor 2000). In war, armies lose battles when their reserves run out before those of their opponents. It is not just the total size of armies that matters, but the availability of uncommitted reserves at the critical place and time. This was the decisive factor, for example, in the rapid defeat of France in 1940. Business is similar. The business that runs out of credit is the one that goes bankrupt and is destroyed. This is why control over credit is the decisive power in capitalist economies.

Most glaringly, EMH assumes that all investors have similar expectations. It assumes markets enjoy some sort of idealized Platonic unity of thought instead of Aristotelian conflict. This is why I find it so useful instead to distinguish bears and bulls. There are several related senses in which I use these concepts. At the simplest "micro" level involving individual asset trades, there are always two sides to every trade: sellers, bears, who expect the asset's price has peaked and buyers, bulls, who anticipate that its price will increase further. "The market" is never of one mind. During most routine business periods, the same investors are simultaneously or alternatively bearish or bullish, buying those assets whose price they expect to rise and selling those whose price they expect to fall. In this tactical interplay of bears and bulls in myriad individual transactions, for long periods of time no discernible patterns might emerge. This is why conventional finance theory can indeed gain some insight into normal trading patterns that occur routinely during ordinary times, which do *appear* to be quasi-random much of the time. However, human action is not random, but motivated by intent.

At any moment any particular asset, say, Enron stock or Russian government bonds or oil futures, can, as investors say, "come into play." This means that major investors with market power to move the price are doing so deliberately in an effort to achieve some strategic effect. They may act because they detect some vulnerability or opportunity as yet unknown to the general public. As soon as an asset comes into play, textbook financial theory is useless since it is based on the notion of efficient markets wherein nobody has enough power to move prices. Of course, in general, market power is inevitable, because any corporation is obviously big enough to influence its own stock and bond prices, at least, and any government is big enough to influence the prices of its own bonds, not to mention the fact that large corporations (e.g., the Dutch East India Company and the Bank of England) and the largest investors have had the power to move the price of any particular asset since the inception of capitalism. Therefore, although strategic manipulation of asset prices is not always occurring, it is always possible.

Privacy and deception

There is a critical methodological consequence to economists' assumption that the price system contains all the information that is necessary for understanding economies: their blindness to all things private, which includes private prices. Markets are, by definition, public. Market prices are public prices. The *myth of the market* includes the naïve perspective that everything interesting about the economy occurs in public view. Yet vast areas of economic life are hidden from public view by privacy laws, including the prices at which non-market business deals are made.

Wages, for example, are usually public information when made by union contract or when advertised to attract employees. But unions are weak in many places and there are many workplaces where what people get paid is secret. Some companies will even fire employees who are overheard speculating about who gets paid what. Control over salaries is a power managers prefer to keep secret, if they are able.

Credit has always been allocated in secret. All loans are private contracts. The Law of One Price is not enforced in private contracts. Discrimination is widespread. Economists will object that although individual loans may be secret, they reference – approximately – interest rates that are determined by bond yields in public markets. While it is true that secondary markets for bonds are public, these are *not* markets for credit, but markets for existing assets. The primary "markets," aka initial public offerings or IPOs, where new marketable credit originates, are usually not markets at all, but private deals first negotiated between a borrower and an investment bank that are then offered selectively, by invitation only, to brokers and the initial investors. Economists largely ignore IPOs, as they neglect all arenas of private power, and instead focus on the public secondary markets as if they constitute the market for credit. IPOs are priced in relation to public markets, but are not solely determined by them.

Furthermore, most large business-to-business sales are private deals made at negotiated prices that may be different from customer to customer. The goods and services most commonly sold in public markets are those sold to consumers – and thus most obvious to students of economics – and even these are not so public in cultures where haggling over price is customary. Because market prices of commodities are today so often manipulated by speculators, large buyers who actually need the commodity, such as oil, often sign long-term contracts with suppliers fixing their price in order to avoid the vicissitudes of the market price. Market prices, far from being universal, are exceptions. This is why I say it is inaccurate to call modern economies, where in fact private deals predominate, "market economies." This label only helps validate the myth of the market.

IPOs are largely ignored in standard textbooks, because they are a key arena of private power. IPOs apply to both stocks and bonds. Although IPOs create securities for sale in public markets, and so may be subject to more stringent legal reporting requirements than private placements, not all details are made public, including who is allowed to buy first, which is a strategic decision. The initial price at which any new security will be offered to the public is decided by the investment bank that underwrites it. Since an IPO sells something new, its exact market price is not yet known. Although powerful governments sometimes insist on conducing IPOs through auctions, investment banks avoid auctions with most IPOs because these would rob them of some of their credit power.

What investment banks do instead is use their expert knowledge of secondary market conditions to negotiate an initial price with the issuer (the borrower).

Bankers do not target the initial price exactly at the expected market price. They aim instead at a price a little lower. Their purpose is to create excess demand for the IPO. If they issued the IPO at the expected market price, then demand would exactly match supply of the new security. Instead, investment banks prefer to develop a reputation of rewarding their IPO investors with instant profits when they buy at the IPO price and then immediately see the price rise as secondary market trading begins and excess demand drives up the price. Successful new issues all have this initially positive performance. Therefore investors eagerly jump at the chance to buy into IPOs from successful investment banks. This gives the investment bank the power to award instant profits to whomever they choose, a power they use strategically to win big clients among top investors and to influence journalists and government officials who may be included among the lucky few who are offered a "taste" of a juicy IPO. Investment banks typically operate through multiple brokers, who are eager for IPO business and thus may pander to the suggestions of investment bankers as to who should be offered a first taste. Issuers and investment banks may also reserve some of any issue for themselves or their favored clients. Brokers who are favored with the best business from the best investment banks can also attract the richest and most powerful investor clients. The world of the IPO is a pyramid of power, not a free market.

Even the secondary stock and bond markets, trumpeted by neoclassicals as examples of efficient markets, contain hidden reservoirs of insider power. First is the fact, mentioned above, that large investors always have the power to move the price of any security, and such intent may not be reflected in its current price until their position is established, using methods described below. Even without strategic intervention by major investors, brokers, especially the largest ones, have systematic information about future prices that is hidden from ordinary investors. This is possible because many investors do not place orders simply to buy or sell as soon as possible at any price, but instead place standing orders with their broker to buy or sell some specific quantity at a specific price, anticipating that the market may move to their favored price. Such standing orders are logged in a broker's "book." Because a broker can see in his book many standing orders that have not yet been executed, he has a better idea than the public does about which way prices are likely to move in the near future. If there are many standing sell orders but few buy orders near the current market price, the broker expects that the price must decline a lot before the aspirations of the sellers can be met by willing buyers. Potential sellers will only discover this gradually as their sell orders remain on the book longer than they expected and as they revise their offer price downward without getting many bids from potential buyers. Panic selling can result as sellers discover that the book is very thin on the buy side. But brokers can anticipate this before their customers do, since each individual investor will not necessarily know what other investors are thinking until the market price finally does move. Thus brokers systematically benefit from inside information.

Contrary even to the weak version of the EMH, insiders can prevent their own price bets from moving the current market price and thus tipping off others to their intent by lending (if expecting the price will rise) or borrowing (if betting the price will fall) securities. How this works is detailed in the next section. Like all loans, these are private deals, unknown to the general public and not yet reflected in the market price. The existence of a private loan market in assets, or its equivalent, using financial derivatives, makes spot prices a poor guide to investor expectations, since it facilitates and rewards insider deception of public markets. It is usually legal too. Brokers may use their insider information about price trends to tip favored investors and investment banks as a way to gain the best connections. The biggest financial groups today have made this even easier, since most now own their own large brokerage firms. Now all key insider information is in-house.

There are some economists who, if confronted with arguments like mine, will hurl the charge "conspiracy theory!" This charge tries to associate arguments based on careful research and the greatest thinkers in history with the wild claims of the most paranoid people. Though if in fact by "conspiracy" is meant not the legal definition, but any self-interested secretive action, then indeed even Adam Smith, let alone Sun Zi, would agree that "conspiracy," in that sense, is commonplace. Smith (1976: bk. I, ch. 10, part 2) famously wrote, "People of the same trade seldom meet together, even for merriment and diversion, but the conversation ends in a conspiracy against the public, or in some contrivance to raise prices." The charge of "conspiracy theory" is often merely a defensive reaction by people too lazy to research difficult questions for themselves. One great benefit for economists of propagating the myth of the market, of pretending that everything important is reflected in public prices, is that it makes research so much easier. Economists can assume the economy is much simpler than it is in fact and thus save themselves a lot of trouble that would come from divining the truth. That is why I must rely for much of my information on historians, journalists, sociologists, political scientists, my own archival research, and real business people, rather than economists. Economists who should know better do not. Too many economists have given up researching any part of the real world that is not embodied in public prices, thus saving themselves a great deal of effort and making the academic rules for research and publishing so much easier, though the results are so much more dull.

Long and short financial strategies

Most people understand how to make money from the rise of the price of an asset, this is known in financial circles as a "long" strategy. However, few people outside the financial world grasp how easy it is, and often faster, to make money from falling asset prices, a "short" strategy. People and firms that have a short position in an asset are known as "shorts." Generally, long and short positions are being taken all the time as some prices rise and others fall without much correlation. But when a business cycle is close to a turning point, many more prices may become correlated and move in tandem, in relation to general credit conditions. When the time is close for a boom to end and prices to turn down, many bears take a strong short position in the most vulnerable asset classes and may make quick returns if their timing is right. We explore this occasional broader polarization of bears and bulls in more detail in the following chapter.

Short selling is as old as financial markets. It was certainly practiced in Amsterdam by the seventeenth century and indeed figured in the first famous bubble and crash in history during that city's Tulip Mania of 1637. Many of the most successful investors in history made their fortunes primarily from short selling, including Jesse Livermore during the half century ending in 1940 (Smitten 2001) and John Paulson, who made tens of billions of dollars for himself and his hedge fund clients during the 2008 crash (Lewis 2010). Remarkably, textbooks in finance and economics have very little to say about short positions. They advocate, for the ordinary students who believe in textbooks, the sucker play, the "buy and hold" strategy of investing. This common strategy relies on a diversified long position with no effort to avoid what is supposedly impossible to anticipate, that is, major downturns in the market. However, it is a characteristic of asset markets throughout history that they rise much more slowly than they fall. Therefore the patient "buy and hold" investor who is rewarded by modest gains during an economic boom witnesses these gains wiped out or worse during every downturn. Since, as mentioned above, losses are not symmetrical with gains, this strategy is not an effective way to conserve wealth, let alone to gain it. Few people ever get rich by using the sort of consistent, diversified long position advocated in the textbooks. Great fortunes in finance are made by investors who know how to make quick returns from a well-timed short position and by using credit, that is, other people's money, to leverage their gains. Most people's savings are not actually for themselves, but merely provide the capital for the real players. You save money to make others rich.

The original method of short selling works with any type of asset, including commodities as well as financial securities. An investor borrows not money, but an asset, say, for example, 2,000 shares of East India Company stock, from a broker or another investor. (Some unscrupulous brokers even lend securities that they may possess for the moment but do not themselves own.) Typically the asset is borrowed for some fairly short fixed term, say two months, and the borrower pays a small fee representing interest on the loan. Let us assume the fee is 1,000 guilders and the stock was selling at 50 guilders per share on the day that stock was borrowed. Thus the total value of the loan on the day that stock was borrowed was 50 x 2,000 = 100,000 guilders and the fee represents 1 percent interest for the two month loan, which would be a simple annual rate of interest of 6 percent, a little high for seventeenth century Amsterdam, but perhaps about right for a loan of this type. Rather than retain the borrowed stock, however, the short seller immediately sells it at the current market price for 100,000 guilders. Since the short seller borrowed stock though, and not cash, sometime later, within the two month term of the loan, during which time the price of the stock hopefully moves lower, the short seller will buy back 2,000 shares to return them to the lender. The lower the price at the time he buys, the more profit he makes. For example, suppose 45 days after the original loan the market price of Dutch East India stock hits 40 guilders per share. The short seller could buy back the 2,000 shares for a total of 80,000 guilders and thus net a profit of 19,000 guilders, after deducting the 1,000 guilder loan fee. Note that all the investor needed up front to make this trade was the 1,000 guilder fee. For that small initial fee, he can potentially earn a very much larger return, but only if he is right that the asset price will go down. If instead the asset price only climbs, the short seller will lose money. Therefore a broker will typically lend assets only to those rich enough to afford the loss if the price moves against them. Otherwise borrowers might be bankrupted and default on the deal. Short selling is a rich person's game. This is one reason why the rich and powerful have a systematic advantage in gaining wealth. It is also makes money fastest when overall economic conditions appear most dire. No wonder the textbooks neglect it! It certainly weighs against the notion that free markets are fair.

Anyone owning any asset is taking a long position in it. The owner will gain wealth whenever the price of the asset increases. Most people understand this more readily than the short position. However, just as with the short position, if you have good credit it is not necessary to have cash to buy an asset. If an investor were able to borrow the full value of an asset price, in our example, 100,000 guilders, at the same fee as our short seller borrowed the stock, then for 1,000 guilders interest he could own a long position in Dutch East India stock for two months. In this case the short and long positions are mirror images of each other. One will profit and the other will lose, depending on whether the price goes up or down. Both could profit if during some days within the loan term the price goes above and on others below the initial price and both investors time their trades well. In fact, some investors will take both a long and short position at the same time in the same asset, which is called a straddle. This could be used to hedge against losses or to profit from a bubble, as we shall see in Chapter 7.

Long and short positions can also be established using financial derivatives. These are contracts that allow investors to bet on the future price of almost any underlying asset. The major forms of derivatives are summarized in Figure 4.1, which also shows their strategic uses. Options apparently originated around the same time as stock markets, in Amsterdam during the seventeenth century, if not earlier. Futures contracts seem to have originated among commodity traders many centuries ago, but certainly high-volume commodity futures markets existed in Chicago during the post-Civil War decades. Stock and bond futures were eventually offered as well. Swaps seem to be much newer. They are discussed in Chapter 14. Options and futures are similar in many respects. Until the final chapter, whenever I use the term "derivatives" I am referring only to these two types.

type	contract	right to	underlying asset	until (American) or **on** (European)	at	strategy
	call	buy				long
option			stocks, bonds, etc.	maturity date	strike price	
	put	sell				short
		obligation to				
	long	buy				long
future			commodities, etc.	maturity date	strike price	
	short	sell				short
	CDS	insure	bond			short
swap	interest	exchange	fixed/floating interest			contingent
	currency	exchange	foreign currency			contingent

Figure 4.1 Types and strategic functions of financial derivative contracts

All derivative contracts have two sides: a buyer and an issuer. Just like a bet between two people, one side of the contract will always win exactly the opposite of what the other side loses. Thus derivatives contribute to the polarization of business interests. Derivative winners and losers will exist in equal measure, given the movement of any asset prices either up or down. The more volatile are asset prices, the more valuable are derivatives. While derivative contracts allow the owner to either buy or sell the underlying asset, the vast majority of derivative bets are never settled by an actual exchange of the underlying asset, but simply settled between the two parties as if the asset had been traded. That is, most derivative trades are virtual trades.

Another important aspect of derivatives is that they are typically very cheap relative to the value of the underlying asset, so that bets can be placed on future of asset prices without requiring nearly as much capital as would be required to own the underlying. In other words, for the same quantity of capital, investors wishing to make a long bet could either buy the asset or buy call options on the asset for a small fraction of its price and with limited downside risk, therefore allowing them to make a bullish bet on a much larger quantity of the asset than they could afford to own. Derivatives thus provide a powerful form of leverage. The upper limit on the quantity of trades is also not restricted by the total quantity of the underlying asset, especially in the case of virtual trades. As an extreme example, a stock that has only 5,000 outstanding shares could have tens of thousands of outstanding derivative bets on its future value. This is not unheard of. Since derivatives can be bought on credit, which is in fact what most hedge funds and bank trading desks do today, this allows the erection of almost unimaginable pyramids of leveraged positions, limited only by the availability of counterparties willing to take – or, worse, unknowingly taking – the opposite side of these ballooning bets.

It is one thing to take a position, long or short. It is another to make sure that position pays off. If all business players were small and weak in relation to the total market, as is assumed in the EMH and in economists' concept of perfect markets, then these positions would be little more than gambling. Yet those who criticize derivatives as dangerous gambling are seeing only half the problem. When positions are combined with the power to move prices, which economists refer to as market power (but then largely ignore), then it is possible, absent a more powerful or prescient strategic adversary, to create a self-fulfilling prophecy, making money fairly reliably by manipulating price. Understanding this is so important for understanding the business of war and peace because both create huge price swings. If you can anticipate or even cause war or peace, after positioning your assets accordingly, large profits are possible and, let us not forget, *legal*. It is little wonder then, as we shall discover in the chapters to come, that the foremost investment bankers are routinely involved in foreign policy and international affairs. Lending to governments is part of their business, and thus, by extension, so is the business of governments: war and peace.

Bears and bulls in non-financial business strategy

I broaden and generalize the concepts of bears and bulls to apply them to all business, not just financial operations, following the example of how strategy is taught in some business schools and consulting companies (but ignored by economists). The standard micro-economic theory of the firm routinely assumes that all companies in an industry are the same. In fact, companies in the same industry may have very different capabilities, vulnerabilities, and strategies. The famous consulting company, Boston Consulting Group (Stern & Deimler 2006: 259–62), popularized a way of categorizing firms using a two-by-two diagram (see Figure 4.2). On one axis are companies with a high or low growth strategy. On the other axis is high or low income (profits). As often happens with two-by-two diagrams, the most interesting cases are the mixed ones. Of course a high income high growth "star" company is ideal, but rather rare. A low income low growth company, a "dog," is rather more common but obviously undesirable. Of the mixed cases, the "cow" or "cash cow" is high income but low growth; the "bull" is fast growing but with low or no profits. Now to translate these into my simpler dichotomy, we need only introduce credit. Cows typically need not borrow since they are slow growing and usually generate enough cash for their own needs. Bulls need a constant infusion of credit to sustain their fast growth, especially insofar as they lack enough profit to expand their capital without external funds. Thus cows tend to be bears (an unfortunate mixed metaphor) and bulls are aptly named. Stars and dogs are less clear cut, but become easier to classify in relation to the business cycle. Dogs usually have failed at whichever strategy they were

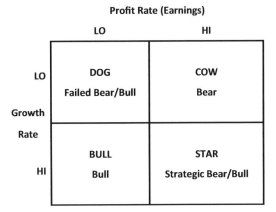

Figure 4.2 Performance and strategy of firms

attempting. Stars may either be bulls during a boom or bears during a bust. Either way, they timed their strategy right.

During a boom, every bull is hungry for credit. The demand for credit is never in equilibrium with supply, but always in excess. Therefore credit is always rationed by those who control it. This is the basis of credit power. Ironically, neoclassical textbooks sometimes admit that credit rationing occurs (e.g., Mishkin 2011: 238), but at the same time maintain the inconsistent fiction that all markets are in equilibrium. Any firm that can borrow can grow at the expense of its competitors. Any business that can be done at a profit can be done on a larger scale if credit is available. Typically it is credit rationing rather than rising marginal cost that limits the growth of firms, as Sraffa (1926: 550) argued against the standard neoclassical theory of the firm. Economists who have unlimited faith in free markets may counter-argue that if credit is in such high demand, new financial firms will start up and existing ones will expand until the excess demand for credit is eliminated. This does not happen because the excess demand for credit exists by design. Large financial firms periodically use their strategic market power to clip the wings of potential competitors who become too bullish. Bears eat young bulls. This argument is elaborated in the next chapter as we explore the strategic determination of the business cycle.

On the other hand, when economies crash, many bulls find that their excessive growth and debt, so irresistibly tempting during the boom, become a yoke if not a noose. Again credit is rationed as financial firms doubt customers' ability to survive and instead retain more capital reserves to avert their own demise. Some heavily borrowed firms can no longer roll over their debt and thus go bankrupt, often taken over by bears who are not so indebted. Bearish strategies, which looked so stodgy during the boom, appear wise during the crash. Bullish strategies that worked so well during the boom fail during the crash, exposing the vulnerability of over-expansion. The first ones now will later be last.

Limited efficacy of modeling in the strategic method

Most economists equate theory with formal modeling. If you do not have a mathematically specified model you cannot have a theory in their view. I disagree, as does Clausewitz (1976: 136), a genius of the strategic method:

> It is only analytically that these attempts at theory can be called advances in the realm of truth; synthetically, in the rules and regulations they offer, they are absolutely useless. They aim at fixed values; but in war everything is uncertain ... They direct the inquiry toward physical quantities, whereas all military action is intertwined with psychological forces and effects. They consider only unilateral action, whereas war consists of a continuous interaction of opposites ... Anything that could not be reached by the meager wisdom of such one-sided points of view was held to be beyond scientific control: it lay in the realm of genius, *which rises above all rules.*

Not all economic models are absolutely useless. If they are sufficiently realistic, for example, including the effects of credit and an endogenous business cycle, they can help train our imaginations as to what could be possible under various circumstances. That is, the best economic models (not those of neoclassicals) have heuristic if not predictive value. Among the economic modelers who are on the right track are post-Keynesians like Steve Keen. However all models, including those that attempt to model strategy, such as game theory, impose rules and regularities on reality that do not bind real entrepreneurs, real strategists. The essence of strategy, like entrepreneurship, is innovation, doing something new or surprising. Anything routine enough to be widely modeled is merely an ordinary force, in Sun Zi's terms. Extraordinary force cannot be so easily modeled, as Clausewitz understands. If it could it would no longer be extraordinary.

Clausewitz understands the term "theory" in a broader sense than mere mechanical modeling. Theory includes a robust understanding of what exists and what might be possible, what philosophers call ontology. Good theory trains the imagination rather than imprisoning it. Recognizing the extraordinary, Taleb's Black Swans, good theory does not reduce economies to some clock-work mechanism. It recognizes uncertainty, as Keynes did, that is not calculable and therefore not reducible to quantifiable risk. Clausewitz (1976: 86) understands our discomfort with such an uncertain social world:

> Although our intellect always longs for clarity and certainty, our nature finds uncertainty fascinating. ... Unconfined by narrow necessity, it can revel in a wealth of possibilities ... Should theory leave us here, and cheerfully go on elaborating absolute conclusions and prescriptions? Then it would be no use at all in real life. No, it must also take the human factor into account, and find room for courage, boldness, even foolhardiness. The art of war deals with living and with moral forces. Consequently, it

cannot attain the absolute, or certainty; it must always leave a margin for uncertainty, in the greatest things as much as the smallest. … Even in daring there can be method and caution; but here they are measured by a different standard.

Pretending the world is more mechanical and predicable than it is in reality does not lead to good social science, but rather to the sucker's strategic blindness. Inability to see the world realistically prevented nearly all economists from anticipating the likelihood of a severe crash in 2008, except for some anti-neoclassicals who understand the key role of credit, not to mention hundreds if not thousands of leading bankers and investors who maintained aggressive short positions. The blindness of economists is most evident in their lack of an endogenous theory of the business cycle, one of the most obvious and important facts about credit-based economies. Because it is so hard for economists to imagine that their perfect markets in stable equilibrium could generate periodic crises, any crises that do occur must to them be unforeseeable, caused by random exogenous shocks. It is another remarkable inconsistency that the same neo-classical economists that are so apt to assume perfect information and rational expectations in their economic models are quick to proclaim that everything extraordinary that happens in economies is unforeseeable in principle. Obviously it is not just economies that fail, but also the imaginations of economists! In the next chapter we apply the strategic method to understand how the business cycle is generated by the strategic competition between bears and bulls.

The best social science is disquieting. It suggests more questions than answers. Good social science must not rest complacent within a specific model, for the simple reason that any system that can be modeled can be gamed. Strategic players will find a way to beat it, changing the social system in the process. If social science teaches anything it must be that human beings are relentlessly innovative. They cannot and will not be contained within the confines of any system, anarchic or orderly. They organize anarchy and disrupt order. When you reach the conclusion of this present book, it is my sincere wish that you do not remain complacent with my own conclusions. My conclusions represent the present limit of my imagination, but do not let the limits of my imagination limit yours.

5 Strategic determination of the business cycle

> The total amount of the Financial Circulation depends ... mainly on the magnitude of the "bear" position ... being likely to be phenomena of rapidly *changing* prices rather than of an absolutely high or low level. ... there are altogether four possible type of speculative markets:
>
> (i.) A "bull" market with a consensus of opinion, *i.e.* security-prices rising but insufficiently so that [savings deposits are] falling, and "bears" are closing their positions on a rising market.
>
> (ii.) A "bull" market with a division of opinion, *i.e.* security-prices rising more than sufficiently so that [savings deposits are] rising, and "bears" are increasing their positions on a rising market.
>
> (iii.) A "bear" market with a division of opinion, *i.e.* security-prices falling more than sufficiently so that [savings deposits are] falling, and "bears" are closing their positions on a falling market.
>
> (iv.) A "bear" market with a consensus of opinion, *i.e.* security-prices rising but insufficiently so that [savings deposits are] rising, and "bears" are increasing their positions on a falling market.
>
> John Maynard Keynes (Keynes 2011[1930]: vol. I, 252–53)

> Banks mean credit, and credit means power.
>
> Charles W. Morse, banker (Bruner & Carr 2007: 40)

Neoclassical economics, by arguing that market economies are inherently stable, permanently marginalized the study of the real boom-and-bust business cycles of credit-driven economies. Keynes, despite the hopeful start he made with bears, bulls, and the credit cycle in his 1930 book (2011[1930], vol. I, Chs 18–20), dropped this complication in his more famous work, *The General Theory* (1936). For most economists the credit or business cycle is created by external shocks, exogenous to the otherwise stable economy. In much of popular political discourse today, economic downturns are unfortunate accidents to be blamed on the government in power. But in fact the business cycle is the outcome of the perpetual competition between contending bulls and bears. Credit-fueled bulls profit from booms. Unchecked, they would trample the bears. According to the strategic judgment of bears, when bulls are sufficiently overextended, bears withdraw much of the credit that fueled the boom and curtail if not bankrupt many bulls. When economies crash, bears eat bulls.

This is the dynamic strategic dance that has animated economies even before the rise of capitalism, but it is more decisive under capitalism when virtually all production and commerce are mediated by money and credit. Bears and bulls are not confined to the financial sector. The credit system extends throughout business. Industrial firms may be heavily leveraged bulls or largely self-financing bears. Credit is extended by all types of businesses as accounts receivable, at least, not just financial companies. Understanding this is essential to understanding the dynamics of political economy, yet it is largely unknown outside the consciousness of practical business strategists. Textbooks largely ignore it. Neoclassical economists fail to grasp these basic macroeconomic foundations of microeconomic behavior.

I am one of the few to use the common Wall Street slang, "bears" and "bulls," in such a broad sense. I do this to show the link between credit policy, monetary politics, business strategy, and the business cycle. It is a further application of my Aristotelian or polarized view of the economy, as opposed to the naïve neoclassical Platonic view that presumes there is an ideal economic state for everyone. Every state of the economy is good for some and bad for others. Every change in direction favors some and hurts others. The reason is that investors are always taking contrary positions.

Keynes, in his *Treatise on Money*, quoted above, explained the relationship between money, credit, and prices of both goods and assets in a polarized way, using the concepts of bears and bulls, much as I do. Unfortunately, this element of his thought has been neglected and virtually lost ever since. I only "rediscovered" it after developing my own similar concepts. Part of the reason for its neglect is probably his somewhat awkward exposition, frequently delving into dynamics and disequilibrium without an appropriate mathematical framework to express interrelationships concisely (he would have needed differential equations). But Keynes's exposition of a polarized credit cycle often in disequilibrium also is incompatible with the Platonic harmony and equilibrium that neoclassicals embrace.

The major difference between Keynes and me is that Keynes is trying to craft an ideal policy for a central banker that would just balance the economy, even in the face of contradictory pressures, such as in cases (ii) and (iii) above. On the other hand, Keynes (2011[1930]: vol. I, 255) does admit that such a precarious balancing act may be "beyond the wits of man." Mine is an easier task. I am thinking less as a central banker than as a strategist of private power. I wish to consider how the bears and bulls that Keynes describes may struggle to advance their own position at the expense of their adversaries, regardless of its effects on the overall economy, and thereby swing the business cycle into a new phase. In particular, the cases of broad polarization between bears and bulls, cases (ii) and (iii), represent culminating points during which the economy might tip one way or the other, depending on the relative power of the bears and bulls. Such culminating points are like decisive battles in war. Keynes (2011[1930]: vol. II, 195–96) analyzes September 1929 as one such a culminating point of type (ii). September 2008 was another, which we examine in Chapter 14. In both instances, opposing bull and bear positions were built up to such heights that massive losses were likely to one side or the other whichever way the chips fell. Keynes wanted to be a referee or mediator, above the fray, but I first wish to understand the game.

The typical textbook treatment of business strategy seldom takes the business cycle seriously, unfortunately. True strategy takes into account the dynamic possibilities of business cycle, recognizing that there is no "one size fits all" strategy. Every strategy has a counter. "Rock, paper, scissors," the common game many people use to select among two or more people, illustrates this principle simply. More specifically, firms following a bullish strategy that succeed brilliantly during an economic boom are often the first to fail when the economy goes bust. On the other hand, bearish firms that look unnecessarily stodgy and conservative at the height of a boom will appear prescient and prudent when credit seizes up and the economy crashes. Most importantly, power over credit gives large financial firms strategic power to influence the timing of the cycle, and the balance of forces at the critical culminating moments, potentially creating a self-fulfilling prophecy for their favored position.

When several large firms tighten credit at what Keynes calls a culminating point in the credit cycle, either in collusion or mutual imitation, they can engineer a crash. If they have taken a short or bearish position, it will be in their interest to do so. They often profit enormously from the ensuing downturn. Similarly, powerful firms expanding credit in concert can initiate a boom. Booms and busts need not be accidental. Government policy is not the only or typically the primary influence on their timing. They typically result from coordinated strategic action by the leading capitalists. Although Keynes considers bear/bull credit strategy from a purely financial perspective, I apply these terms to broader business strategy, influencing industrial and commercial firms as well as financial ones.

Credit over the course of the business cycle

Bears and bulls are general categories representing opposing forces. Exactly how they position their assets at any particular moment varies with their assessment of the opportunities and dangers of the current situation, especially in relation to the business cycle. Bears may employ a short strategy, but this is not what defines them as bears. When they do employ a short strategy, it is often because they believe a "Type ii" culminating point is approaching and therefore the economy is ripe for a downturn. At other more normal times they might simply use less leverage or more liquidity than bulls, sacrificing potential income for greater flexibility and reduced vulnerability. Keynes (2011[1930]: vol. I, 250) describes this:

> The second category of Savings-deposits comprises what, in language borrowed from the Stock Exchange, we call the "bear" position, – including, however, as bears not only those who have sold securities "short", *i.e.* have sold securities they do not own, but also those who would normally be holders of securities but who prefer for the time being to hold liquid claims on cash in the form of Savings-deposits. A "bear", that is to say, is one who prefers to avoid securities and lend cash, and correspondingly a "bull" is one who prefers to hold securities and borrow cash – the former anticipating that securities will fall in cash-value and the latter that they will rise.

These terms, "short" and "long," probably come originally from the terms of loans. Short sellers almost invariably take short-term loans of financial assets, typically one to three months, since nobody can expect to see a price crash coming very far ahead of time. On the other hand, those who own assets might hold them for years or even generations, so owning tends to be long term, though it need not be. Likewise credit is either short term or long term. Short-term credit is usually for a term of days or months. Long-term credit extends for years. Historically short-term credit developed to finance local and regional trade. Its term represents the time required for merchants to carry goods from the place of manufacture to the place of sale and also to market them. During the time merchants' capital would otherwise be tied up in unsold inventory, they often prefer short-term financing instead, conserving their capital by leveraging other people's money. Short-term credit also finances working capital for many manufacturing companies. Finally, through history short-term capital is vital for financing speculative positions. Long-term credit developed to finance primarily three things: wars, overseas trade in the age of sail, and eventually durable industrial investments such as railroads, ships, and factories.

Consider first the anatomy of a boom. For whatever reason, investment is stimulated to higher than usual levels. Examples include the successive waves of railroad booms in the last two thirds of the nineteenth century and the internet or "dot com" boom of the 1990s. Increased real investment in productive equipment for business, such as railroad equipment or computer servers, increases demand for output of industries that produce such capital equipment. If these industries have excess capacity at the start of the boom, output can increase quickly. If they do not, first prices will increase and then businesses that produce the desired investment goods will respond by increasing their own capacity to produce, increasing their factory size, for example. Either way, they will be hiring more workers and buying more raw materials, thus increasing demand in other industries in the process. As firms become more bullish at the prospects for growth, they want to beat their competitors and grow as quickly as possible. They need to buy lots of machinery and raw materials and hire many more workers. Typically they lack the liquid resources to grow as fast as possible without adding debt. Therefore as the boom accelerates, not only does demand for physical capital increase, so does demand for money capital to pay for expansion in the form of bank loans, bonds, or new issues of stock. The more aggressive and fast-growing the bulls, the faster they accumulate debt. Interest rates may also begin to rise in response to the increased demand for credit, especially as the demand tends to outpace the supply of loanable funds.

In any boom, not every company or every industry benefits equally. New and leading industries grow the fastest. Often newer and more innovative firms in an industry grow faster than older, established ones that already have large market share. Older, larger firms and firms in less dynamic industries are often cows, as defined in the previous chapter. Large size and established market niches may enable them to earn high profits, but they are no longer fast growing, if for no other reason than they already dominate a large share of existing markets. On the other hand, newer firms and those in more dynamic industries typically take advantage of the boom to borrow and grow. The faster they grow, the easier it is for them to borrow more as long as the boom continues, since they appear competitive and successful. The faster they grow, the more they foreclose opportunities for other potential competitors and steal market share from any large cows already dominating industries they enter.

A boom will also affect asset markets. Stock prices tend to rise, especially in those industries that benefit from expanded demand. Companies seeking to raise additional capital sell new issues of stock into this rising market. Companies may also meet their capital needs by issuing bonds or borrowing from banks. Interest rates are often low during the early stages of growth, meaning bond prices are high, so firms can more easily raise funds by issuing new bonds at relatively high prices. One of the first signs of a maturing boom is interest rates creeping up as demand for credit strongly outstrips the supply of loanable funds. Bond prices often start to fall before those of any other asset, thus as a boom matures among the earliest attractive bear strategies are short positions in bonds. If bears also include major creditors, as is often the case, then they can create self-fulfilling prophecies for their short bond positions by tightening competing forms of credit, like bank loans. Forcing up loan rates tends to depress bond prices and thus validates short positions in bonds. Credit becomes more expensive, but bulls may continue to be enticed to borrow even at these higher rates to invest in still rising stock and/or real estate markets. Heavy borrowing by bulls to buy into rising markets contributes to their continued rise, as demand remains strong. During the famous bull market of the late 1920s, bulls continued to borrow at higher and higher interest rates to buy stocks as their prices continued rising to dizzying heights.

Financial firms often choose sides during a boom, allying their own strategies with those of their main customers. Some lenders, often the most profitable and fastest growing during the boom, are funding primarily the bulls. They are often newer firms with less access to more established customers. On the other hand, the largest and most well-established banks that already have top customers, including the largest cows and some stars, often lend less aggressively and expand their loans slower than their most bullish competitors.

Sometimes there is an institutional difference between the financial bears and bulls. For example, in the run up to the Panic of 1907, the bulls were mostly fast-growing new trust companies whereas the bears were larger and more established banks. Sometimes the bulls are exploiting a less regulated segment of the financial business, where risk and leverage are less restricted by law. Regardless of why financial firms differentiate, once they do their interests diverge. The most bullish investors want expansion to continue to validate their own investment bets. The more conservative firms, often larger and more powerful as well, watch carefully for signs that the boom is stretching the limits of growth. Two typical signs are rising real interest rates, especially short-term rates, and rising prices. As loan demand outstrips the supply of loanable funds, new credit can be created, but whenever there is dis-equilibrium between savings of consumers and investment in physical capital by businesses, excess demand tends to increase prices of goods in highest demand. Excess credit also tends to drive up some assets prices, perhaps stocks or real estate.

As the culminating point of the boom approaches, bears build up short positions rapidly. Now a crisis must come quickly or the shorts will lose money. Since shorts may be borrowing assets to sell them immediately, as shorts build up their positions their asset sales create downward pressure on prices, validating their short bets. Yet short positions are potentially very costly to maintain if prices continue to rise because bullish expectations remain strong and well-funded. Losses in a rising market may even bankrupt premature shorts. Interestingly, short strategies inherently create a floor on price drops because many shorts must eventually buy back the asset they sell short before they can close their position and return the borrowed asset (unless the short position is entirely based on derivatives without any trading of the underlying), so strong short positions also represent a massive reserve of buying interest that will sustain prices in the near future, perhaps driving them higher whether or not the short bets pay off. Shorts must win quickly or lose heavily.

As soon as rival long and short positions are rising fast, as Keynes notes, when they approach equal weight, a culminating point is reached and the battle begins in earnest. The winners will get richer and many of the losers will be bankrupted. Bulls are frequently at a structural disadvantage because it often happens that the source of their short-term credit is the very same bears that have now built up large short positions against them.

During the 1929 stock market crash, the bulls were borrowing less from banks than directly from the bears, often brokers and investment bankers (Keynes 2011[1930]: vol. II, 196), who could cut off their credit at a moment's notice, and eventually did, bankrupting many bulls and cashing in their lucrative short positions on the resulting distress sales that crashed prices.

During the 1927 crash in Japan, which I researched as part of my PhD dissertation, the bulls among what the Japanese called the *shinko zaibatsu*, or new financial-industrial combines, depended for much of their capital on revolving overnight loans from the five biggest banks, four of which were the central institution in the Big Four *zaibatsu*, which were older, more established combines that could afford to be bears. Several of the *shinko zaibatsu* quickly collapsed, allowing their component companies to be acquired cheaply by the victorious Big Four, especially the largest, Mitsui. The five biggest banks quickly doubled their deposit assets as panicked savers moved their accounts to the safest large banks. Many smaller banks collapsed. The *shinko zaibatsu* and their supporters eventually took revenge with a spate of assassinations of wealthy and powerful business and political leaders whom they blamed for their downfall, which intensified political polarization within Japan, contributing to the subsequent aggressive turn in its foreign policy (Nolt 1994).

During the financial crisis of 2008, J.P. Morgan was among the least bullish of the leading banks. Goldman Sachs had taken a strong bullish stance until the eve of the crisis, when it heavily shorted vulnerable markets. Both firms emerged from the crisis stronger and richer than ever. These are just a few examples of scores that could be told if only more researchers understood and investigated private power and strategy. Both bulls and bears create self-fulfilling prophecies at critical moments in the business cycle: bulls by investing in growth and in rising prices that their own feverish buying bids higher; bears by tightening credit and thus pulling the trigger on their heavily leveraged bearish competitors, driving many to bankruptcy.

The public tends to despise shorts – insofar as they even perceive their existence – and feel more affinity toward bulls, since bulls represent growth and rising employment, whereas bear raids are associated with economic crashes and bankruptcy, but in fact, as the "Austrian school" of economists has emphasized, the "creative destruction" of bears opens the way for a new cycle of growth, rather like occasional forest fires in a healthy natural forest cycle. Without the restraining threat of bears, the greed of bulls would push economic bubbles higher and higher on ultimately unsustainable pyramids of debt. Debt is irresistibly attractive whenever asset prices are rising and profitable investment opportunities exist. If money can be borrowed at 4 percent and invested to earn 5 percent, what is the limit on the desire to borrow? Effectively there is none. Of course economists emphasize that diminishing marginal returns to capital investment will eventually emerge, since there are not infinite opportunities to earn 5 percent, but until asset prices stop rising, such limits may not appear. Asset prices may be propelled upward, bubble fashion, whenever there is enough new credit continually available to fuel asset demand. Most economic models miss this possibility by downplaying both credit and assets. The most effective antidote to a frenzy of bullish greed is a cabal of bearish greed.

Excess demand for credit is seldom fully equilibrated by new banks entering a bullish market. Some potential new entrants are deterred from entering or attacked when they do by powerful bear raids. In the early development of the banking systems of Britain and America, the biggest bear on the block was the government-sanctioned but privately owned Bank of England and Alexander Hamilton's similar institution, the Bank of the United States, ultimately destroyed by President Jackson because of its bear raids on the bullishly over-issued notes of various state banks gleefully financing Democratic Party supporters and land speculators. Even though Jackson managed to kill this one giant federally sanctioned bear, other private bears took its place, especially those closest-linked to the greatest British bankers and their bearish gold-standard policy, such as J.P. Morgan, in the later part of the nineteenth century. Bray Hammond's (1991) wonderful book, *Banks and Politics in America*, shows in intimate detail how closely related bank strategies and competition were to the emergence of a two-party system in American politics.

The paramount power of big bearish banks

The biggest banks, throughout the centuries, are the only ones capable of doing that part of the financial business most relevant to international political economy: the long-term bond business. This business was invented by Italian merchant bankers during the medieval period to finance especially the expensive naval wars against the Ottoman Turks and each other. Until the nineteenth century long-term bonds and annuities were almost exclusively used to finance wars. The only large-scale private business that required long-term financing before the nineteenth century was global trade, but this capital was mostly raised by selling shares of joint-stock companies like the British and Dutch East India Companies, only occasionally supplemented by long-term bonds. The war bond business is the origin of the bearishness of the biggest banks.

Bonds are debt instruments with a fixed face value defined by some quantity of currency, say 10,000 dollars. Specific details of annuities are explained in Chapter 7. The issuer (borrower) promises to pay the face value to the bond owner on the stated maturity date, which, for a long-term bond, may be many years in the future. Some early bonds, often called annuities, were even perpetual, never maturing. Many long-term bonds for war finance have terms of 10 to 30 years, giving the government ample time to win (hopefully) the war and subsequently build up budget surpluses to gradually pay back (retire) the war debt before the next major war. Most long-term bonds pay a coupon rate, which is a fixed interest payment made by the issuer in regular installments to the owner at the moment. Bonds may be traded from one owner to another prior to maturity at a variable market price.

Bonds create a bearish interest because bond owners, indeed, the owners of any loans at fixed interest, such as most mortgages, suffer losses with either price inflation or rising interest rates. Most booms, especially prolonged ones, produce one or the other or both. Price inflation represents the falling value of money. If money is worth less, then the value received by the bond holder when the bond matures will be worth less than the money originally loaned to the issuer. Rising interest rates cause bond prices to fall (unless they are close to maturity) because their coupon rate and implicit yield between the current market price and the maturity value of the bond are worth less whenever investors have the opportunity to earn a higher rate of interest another way. Thus bond holders hate inflation and rising interest rates. Short-term rates may sometimes rise without much affecting long-term rates, but usually toward the end of a boom the burgeoning demand for credit raises all rates. Banks in the business of issuing new bonds do their best business at the start of a boom when interest rates are still low, thus bond prices are high, and demand for credit is growing. Later in a boom they may switch emphasis from bond to stock IPOs, chasing the hottest asset market, while becoming bearish on bonds.

On the other hand, the interest of debtors is opposite. Debtors, including governments who have financed a war with bonds, often would prefer inflation so that their business or tax revenues rise while the real value of their debt falls. Thus early bond markets developed mainly in Italian, Hanseatic, Flemish, and Dutch merchant republics where governments were run by the big merchants who were also the major bankers and bond holders. As long as they could control government finances themselves, they could insure that an indebted government did not become too profligate with their money and either default or repay with a currency devalued by inflation. England was not able to develop an efficient bond market until the "Glorious Revolution" of 1688 deposed the last native king of Britain, enhanced the power of the merchant-dominated Parliament, and invited a Dutch merchant prince, William III, to be the first of a long-line of foreign monarchs, king by the grace of Parliament. Soon after, the new Whig merchant rulers of England formed the Bank of England, patterned after a similar Dutch bank, to stabilize and consolidate bond financing (Homer & Sylla 2005: 147). Sovereign bond lending is far riskier when the borrower is an absolute monarch over whom the merchant lenders have little power. The kings of France and Spain, for example, defaulted on their debt numerous times, ruining some leading merchant bankers in the process. Their currencies were also more inflation-prone than the conservatively managed British pound (Reinhart & Rogoff 2009: 86–88). Countries without a powerful bearish bank interest tend to be more inflation prone than those with it.

From its beginning, the long-term bond business has always been dominated by a small number of banks, sometimes even a legal monopoly within one country. Whenever multiple banks compete for the same bond business, they often form a cartel to share the loan business among themselves rather than allow sovereign borrowers to play them off against each other, to borrow from Peter to pay Paul. Competition sometimes occurs, but it both lowers the profits and increases the risk of the sovereign lending business. Whenever possible, unity in a single international consortium (as bank cartels are called) is better for bankers. Occasionally rival financial consortia line up as lenders to rival powers, as happened in the decades before World War I. As in that case, prolonged war between rival powers can debilitate both consortia and numerous investors.

Industrial competition through the business cycle

Money capital, reliable sources of credit, and other liquid resources are strategic reserve assets for financial and non-financial firms alike. Controlling such reserves gives companies flexibility whenever business conditions are changing rapidly. In a boom they enable firms to quickly make new investments in new directions. During a bust they help avert bankruptcy and allow takeovers of other distressed firms. Industrial firms potentially have another important reserve asset, however, which is excess productive capacity. Neoclassical economists generally assume all productive resources are fully employed since it would be inefficient and less profitable to leave some assets idle. They believe if some productive resources are idle, their owners should be willing to reduce output prices so they can sell more and thereby employ whatever is idle. In the real world this does not usually occur. On average significant amounts of productive capital are idle. During recent decades in the US idle capital has hovered between 15 to 30 percent (Keen 2011: 114). Neoclassicals do not consider why capitalists would deliberately leave expensive capital equipment idle. This is because most economists lack a strategic perspective on business competition.

I first began to understand the strategic perspective of industrial firms when as a graduate student I read a memo by the US Ambassador to Turkey about his conversation with an executive from General Electric Corporation who explained that GE was building a light bulb factory in Turkey with output capacity considerably greater than all existing demand for light bulbs in the Turkish market. Since Turkish and neighboring countries' tariffs were high, GE did not expect to export from the new plant to markets outside Turkey, but GE did anticipate producing at a low enough cost to destroy or deter any competition to their Turkish light bulb business (Maxfield & Nolt 1990: 70). Once they were established, no other firm would dare enter the market because GE could use their excess capacity and low cost of production to drive new entrants out of business. However, absent of any competitors, they could sell their low-cost output at high prices and therefore enjoy high monopoly profits. Significant excess capacity also allowed GE to expand its production substantially without much further fixed investment as the Turkish light bulb market grew.

Whenever the business cycle favors growth and interest rates are relatively low, businesses will tend, like GE in Turkey, to over-invest, to develop excess capacity, for several reasons. First, they expand when long-term interest rates are low, that is, when bond prices are high, so that the cost of borrowing to buy capital equipment is currently at a discount. Second, anticipating a developing boom, they buy enough capacity at the start to avoid having to buy more later in the boom when interest rates typically creep up. Third, as the GE executive explained, excess capacity may give a firm a jump on potential competitors, deterring others from expensively investing in even more excess capacity to compete with it. Fourth, excess capacity enables firms to expand output easily if a price war is necessary. The purpose of a price war is to expand capacity rapidly even at the cost of lowering prices and one's own profits. A firm might even be willing to lose money for a time if by doing so it can force its competitors to lose money too, it might bankrupt them before it bankrupts itself, especially if it has ample reserve productive capacity and reliable reserves of liquid funds or credit. As in real wars, the loser is often the one who runs out of credit first. This last sort of competition is modeled abstractly by a few economists who study oligopoly using game theory, but insights gained cannot be applied to microeconomic theory because it generally assumes perfect markets and static equilibrium. Understanding private power requires dynamic analysis.

When an economy reaches a culminating point in a business cycle, not only financial firms, but also industrial and other firms will align with either the bears or the bulls, according to their assets and vulnerabilities. If they have loaded up on debt in order to expand during a boom, bulls are vulnerable to a downturn and so push for the boom to continue. If bears do not expand rapidly at the start of a boom, bullish competitors may overtake them. On the other hand, first movers who emerge as dominant in an industry during a boom may become bears by the end of it. Once they have secured their own dominance and reduced their credit needs, they are well placed to destroy smaller, fast growing, but more indebted competitors rising in their wake by aligning with a broad bear challenge to the boom. No one strategy is ideal throughout the business cycle, but firms do not move in lockstep either. Whenever their strategies diverge, strategic competition emerges sharply. Since banks typically finance many different industrial firms, they naturally become headquarters for coordinating strategy among firms whose interests are similarly aligned at a culminating point. We will see instances of this in the coming chapters.

The myth of the money supply

The popular media follow neoclassical economists and textbooks in recent decades by giving inordinate attention to something called the "money supply." Its importance is exaggerated all out of proportion to its actual role in the economy. The myths about money and the money supply are a major element of the broader myth of the market. The myth of the money supply effectively obscures the far more significant role that private credit, and thus credit power, plays in our economy. As soon as one learns the truth about money and credit, the world appears as a far different place from the one portrayed in the textbooks. Strategic conflict between bears and bulls becomes inevitable. Governments may be players in this private drama, but they are not its authors.

The myth of the money supply is promulgated in all standard textbooks on macroeconomics, money and banking, international finance, and so on. The textbook story starts by proclaiming money as the alternative to barter. Primitive people exchanged goods they possessed in excess, say goats, with goods someone else had in excess but which they lacked, say fish. However, such transactions were hard to arrange, as the fable asserts, until money appears, some third commodity convenient to hold as an intermediary store of wealth in between selling your surplus and buying what you really want. In fact, the only instance where barter and money stand as alternative states of the world is in the formal mathematical models of neoclassical economists, many of which still, for "convenience," ignore money and credit even today!

This imagined "history" of the transition from barter to money utterly ignores the vast research of economic historians and anthropologists that illustrates the real variety of exchange and redistributive systems in human history (e.g., Graebner 2011). More pertinent to the modern world, it ignores credit. Already in 1976 Adam Smith (bk. IV, Ch. 1) understood that private credit can easily substitute for money:

> If the materials of manufacture are wanted, industry must stop. If provisions are wanted, the people must starve. But if money is wanted, barter will supply its place, though with a good deal of inconveniency. Buying and selling upon credit, and the different dealers compensating their credits with one another, once a month or once a year, will supply it with less inconveniency. A well-regulated paper money will supply it, not only without any inconveniency, but, in some cases, with some advantages. Upon every account, therefore, the attention of government never was so unnecessarily employed as when directed to watch over the preservation or increase of the quantity of money in any country.

This idea was commonplace throughout classical political economy. It was only forgotten when neoclassical economics replaced the classical tradition. The pinnacle of the classical tradition is John Stuart Mill, whose 1848 *Principles of Political Economy* was widely used as a textbook until the twentieth century. Mill (1987: 514) echoes Smith, but is even more explicit:

> In a state of commerce in which much credit is habitually given, general prices depend at any moment much more upon the state of credit than upon the quantity of money. For credit, though it is not productive power, is purchasing power. ... The forms of credit which create purchasing power are those in which no money passes at the time, and very often none passes at all.

Private credit is almost certainly much older than money. In ancient Mesopotamia, among the earliest written documents (on clay tablets) are numerous debt contracts. These often specify the local god, represented by the temple high atop the city's prominent ziggurat and its priests, as the creditor. What was lent – at interest – was not money, but usually grain or other goods stored by the temple. The penalty for defaulting was often both supernatural, a curse by the god, and more down to earth, debt slavery. Ancient Near Eastern societies, even before the appearance of coined money (likely in Lydia about the seventh century BCE), evidently experienced boom-and-bust cycles, perhaps, as in modern times, credit driven. One solution to excessive debt was rebellion. Another was debt jubilee, or forgiveness, as attested in the Hebrew Bible and other ancient law records (Homer & Sylla, 2005: 17–31). Credit is so ancient and ubiquitous that the two most fundamental concepts of accounting, credit and debit, are, obviously, derived from credit and debt, that is, what we own and what we owe. It is only a very short step to creditor and debtor and therefore to bipolar power, bear and bull, and short and long strategies.

Credit comes in two forms: bilateral and circulating. Bilateral credit need not involve money at all. Economists arbitrarily define some forms of circulating credit as money, while ignoring others, but there are many forms of circulating credit that are never counted as money by neoclassical economists. Thus even circulating credit may not involve money, as economists define it.

The simplest form of bilateral credit is when a friend lends another friend something of value. This may have an effect on output. For example, if a farmer lends a horse to other farmers in order to help them plow their fields, these farmers' output will increase, but this transaction, a common one throughout much of history, need not involve any money or payment. Whether the lending farmer expects compensation does not much affect the expansionary impact of this loan. Typically, the lender at least expects the borrowers to feed and care for the horse during the time they make use of it. This sort of bilateral credit takes myriad forms in modern business life.

The most ubiquitous form of bilateral credit is what accountants measure in accounts receivable. These record customers who have received something of value, but not yet paid for it. The custom of delivering goods or services without receiving immediate payment is widespread in business throughout history. Naylor (2006: vol. II, 13–15) describes a clear example of this in his superb book on Canadian business history. During boom times, when many are bullish, such credit is freely extended to make it easier for customers to buy and to win customers away from the competition. When economies crash and all forms of credit dry up, more and more businesses demand immediate cash payment for sales. Thus accounts receivable may shrink rapidly and drastically, contracting demand without any influence from the money supply.

Extending credit in this way conserves scarce currency and capital, stimulating economic output independent of the money supply. This allows merchants to sell more using less capital in the process. For example, medieval fairs flourished using a similar form of credit. Fairs attracted merchants from all over Europe to gather at a specific place for several weeks to trade their wares. Carrying lots of cash to the fair risked robbery and in any case merchants profited from investing more of their limited capital in tradable goods and less in coin. During the weeks of the fair, merchants would trade back and forth various goods without paying in cash, but merely adjusting their balances in ledger books. Only at the end of the fair would cash finally change hands, and then only to reconcile net balances. These were much smaller than the gross volume of transactions undertaken over the course of the fair. Both currency and money capital were thus greatly conserved and a larger transaction volume facilitated without using money as the means of payment for most transactions. This way of conserving cash in business transactions has increased over the centuries, culminating in modern credit cards, accounts receivable, and various forms of deferred payment used in business-to-business transactions. Whereas economic textbooks emphasize money as *the* means of payment, it is only *one* possible means of payment. Contrary to the textbook version, the quantity of money need not significantly constrain the quantity of transactions.

Economists might object at this point that they capture all this in their concept of "velocity" of money. They have a notion that there is a fixed stock of money that circulates at a certain velocity, measured as the number of times each year that the stock of money turns over. But this concept of velocity merely conceals the greater and independent role that credit plays. Velocity is a residual category, and an arbitrary one. It is calculated merely by dividing the GDP by the money stock (variously measured) to get an arbitrary number for velocity. But this ignores the fact that money is used for many transactions that are *not* included in GDP – such as buying and selling assets and inter-mediate goods – and money is not used as the means of payment for many transactions that *are* included in GDP. The so-called velocity of money measures nothing definite or concrete, but it obscures much that could be seen more clearly if the focus were instead on the private credit system.

Non-commodity money (i.e., other than specie) is one form of the general category, circulating credit. There are so many myths about money, many of them perpetuated by economists. First of all, anyone can create money legally, though governments, banks, and other financial companies are typically doing it most successfully on the largest scale. What is not legal is to fraudulently impersonate another issuer's notes, such as a Federal Reserve Note (US paper money). How can you create money legally? Just write on a piece of paper: "I promise to redeem this note on demand for $100" and sign it. If someone accepts this note as payment for a used textbook, it is bilateral credit. If the recipient passes your note on to someone else as the means of payment for another transaction, say, to buy a used bicycle, it has become circulating credit, effectively money. It may or may not ever return to you to be redeemed. As long as it keeps circulating, you have effectively increased the money supply.

The amazing thing about this, and this is fundamental to how banks make money, is that you have created this note from nothing, it is backed by nothing but your creditworthy reputation, and you may never have to pay it back as long as it continues to circulate! With bilateral credit, there is a presumption that the debt will be repaid. With circulating credit, it might not be. Whether and how quickly a note returns to its original issuer depends on two things: how much people trust the issuer, which makes it easier to keep a note in circulation, and how buoyant is the business cycle. During boom times notes will circulate longer and faster than when economies crash. This is why banks are most often bankrupt when economies slow down, because various forms of circulating credit return to them to be redeemed for whatever currency is the official legal tender, but banks may lack enough capital or credit at that moment to honor all of their notes. Banks keep as little capital idle as possible to keep their circulating credit creditworthy. Though in theory, if they are solvent, liabilities like circulating notes should be balanced by assets, but few of a bank's assets are liquid. Most may be in the form of loans that are hard to redeem quickly. How much liquid reserves are enough depend on circumstances, such as the business cycle, that are somewhat beyond the control of any one bank.

This general explanation of circulating credit is independent, and indeed, historically prior to, any specific laws or regulations. Textbooks start with the idea that government regulation controls the quantity of money, but this is never entirely true. It is only partially true because economists arbitrarily designate one part of circulating credit as money – typically the part governments are most apt to try to regulate – and ignore the rest. Which part of the circulating credit should be counted as money is debated among economists, but they never include all of it. Yet, as Mill contends, all circulating credit does stimulate supply and demand for real goods and services, as well as assets. Thus all of it should be considered when we consider whether the supply of credit is stimulating expansion of the economy or contraction. Even non-circulating credit counts too. Economists may not be conscious of the reason why they ignore some circulating credit and measure only a subset, but I believe it derives from their obsession with government as the sole regulatory agency in free economies and their consequent neglect of private power over credit.

On the other hand, financiers, and especially the most bullish sort, often devise new forms of circulating credit that is outside of government regulation and restraint. Many economic booms throughout history were facilitated by the propagation of new forms of circulating credit or new institutional loci for issuing credit. We shall see examples of this throughout this book. Capitalism is more relentlessly innovative than typical textbook authors imagine. Even today, money and banking textbooks are still stuck with a 1930s view of money that was inadequate even when it originated.

Neoclassical textbooks emphasize three functions of money: means of payment, store of value, and unit of account. Only the latter is unique to money. It means that money is our measure of value, though, as I have said, always an imperfect unit of account since the value of money itself fluctuates. As a means of payment, money has always been supplemented and sometimes virtually replaced by credit. Economists try to rule out credit as a means of payment by emphasizing that only a money payment can finally settle a transaction if it is first conducted by credit. This may be true in the long run, but, as Keynes famously said, "In the long run we are all dead." What Keynes meant is that in a dynamic economy it is not the final resolution of a transaction that matters, but the rates at which various things happen, economic dynamics. When transactions can occur faster because credit substitutes for money as a means of payment, bullish growth in demand is possible even with exactly the same supply of money. Likewise, when credit is bearishly curtailed, whether or not the money supply also changes, demand will fall. The effect of expansion and contraction of credit might be indirectly reflected in the textbook conception of velocity of money, but it is simpler and more illuminating just to study the private credit system directly.

Money as a store of value has many rivals, as all economists admit. Wealth may be held in many forms, including real property, productive capital, loans, bonds, stocks, derivatives, and money. Each of these has advantages and disadvantages as assets. Keynes recognized that liquid assets, such as money, are especially useful in times of uncertainty when an investor is not sure which way the economy will go or whether his credit lines might suddenly fail. Liquid assets like money thus have strategic importance in a dynamic credit-driven economy. But his neoclassical contemporary and critic, Jacob Viner, characteristically rejected this, saying money

> is a store of wealth. So we are told, without a smile on the face. But in the world of the classical economy, what an insane use to which to put it! For it is a recognized characteristic of money as a store of wealth that it is barren; whereas practically every other form of storing wealth yields some interest or profit. Why should anyone outside a lunatic asylum wish to use money as a store of wealth? (quoted in Minsky 1982: 77)

Viner is quite correct. In the perfect equilibrium world of the classical (what we now call neoclassical) economy, money as a store of wealth would be nonsensical, but that imaginary world does not exist. In the real world, cash reserves are often a vital resource. It is no wonder that neoclassicals like Jacob Viner and his equally famous contemporary, Irving Fisher, both lost significant wealth during the stock market crash of 1929 and the Great Depression that followed, whereas Keynes, using short strategies, added to his. The neoclassical view is a suckers' play, though I might not be as impolite as Viner and echo it as "lunatic."

The only unique role of money is as a unit of account. That is, money units are our measure of the value of everything else. Unfortunately, unlike other quantitative measures, such as meters or tons, money itself does not have a constant value. We often think of inflation as when prices on average increase. But sometimes a more useful way to think about inflation is that the value of the money unit is decreasing. Not only the money unit itself, but all financial contracts, including loans and bonds, that are denominated in money also decrease in value along with it. Prices of goods can change. Inflation-adjusted contracts can also be written, but throughout history the vast majority of financial contracts have been fixed in nominal money terms. This is what makes the value of money vital to the distribution of wealth in the society, which divides the interests of debtors and creditors.

Many economists say flat out that governments control the money supply and thus largely influence the value of money. Others are more careful and claim that government is only one player among several in determining the money supply. Private banks play a role too (e.g., Mishkin 2011: 347). In fact, I would argue that central banks, such as the US Federal Reserve (Fed), that purport to regulate the money supply using open market operations, are doing so very indirectly, if at all. The process does not work at all like money and banking textbooks describe. Open market operations are the common day-to-day operation of central banks involving buying or selling short-term government bonds. Supposedly, when an investor purchases bonds from the Fed the money supply decreases because "money" is transferred from the hands of private investors into the Fed account, where it ceases to be defined as money because it stops circulating among the public, buying things. Yet in fact few investors buy bonds using either currency or checking accounts, which are what economists define as money, specifically, M1. Most bond trading is done using brokerage accounts which are not counted in either the M1 or M2 measures of money supply. Thus the most frequent means by which economists claim the money supply is regulated merely changes the form of wealthy investors' assets, but not the money supply, which, in any case, is fairly trivial compared with the privately controlled credit supply. Government tinkering to control the money supply is both a myth and largely irrelevant even if it were true.

That is not to say that the government has no influence on the financial economy. It does. Just not in the way textbooks claim. Government central banks, as large buyers and sellers of short-term bonds, do influence short-term bond yields, which are a reference interest rate for many short-term loans as well. But short-term bond yields and indeed short-term interest rates have little direct or unmediated effect on the general public or the broader economy. Demand for houses and cars are affected by long-term interest rates. Credit card interest rates are so high they barely register the short-run movements of short-term interest rates either. Short-term interest rates are of significant interest only to business. Short-term credit is largely used to finance trade, the working capital of companies, and asset speculation. Loan demand for asset speculation is the most volatile component of demand for short-term loans. It is this demand that fuels asset bubbles. When it is curtailed, bubbles burst. Thus former Fed chairman Alan Greenspan was being disingenuous when he claimed that asset bubbles, such as the two that the Fed stimulated with extremely low interest rates during the late 1990s and again until 2007, are not the Fed's concern or responsibility. While he is correct regarding the legal mandate of the Fed, in practice its day-to-day influence is much greater over the cost and ease of financial gambling games than it is over the real economy. Wall Street keeps a close eye on the Fed because it influences, as do any large private banks acting strategically, the delicate balance between leveraged bear and bull positions.

Central banks like the Fed do have one decisive power that was evident in 2008: lender of last resort. If authorized to do so, they are able, by tapping into the taxing power of the state, to inject liquidity back into a financial system in general crisis. Large private banks have also undertaken this role in the past, so this power is not unique to central banks, but they are especially suited to wield it.

However, during ordinary times, modern central banks are arguably less powerful than the leading private banks. As strategists teach, power comes from flexibility, deception, and surprise. Central banks, by following policy rules and announcing their objectives in advance, surrender the element of surprise during their ordinary operations. Their attempts to influence short-term interest rates using open market operations might be unsuccessful if there are large private banks determined to influence national currency values or interest rates in a different direction for whatever reason, perhaps because they have established a long or short position opposing the central bank policy, and commit greater resources in the opposite direction. The central banks of smaller countries, with more limited balance sheets, are especially vulnerable in this regard. A ring of investors led by George Soros even managed to defeat the Bank of England this way in 1992. The power of central banks is not derived entirely from their legally granted mandate, but also limited by the extent of their assets and strategic ingenuity.

Government or private economic regulation

Neoclassical economists propagate the myth that the only power capable of regulating modern economies is the government. Conservatives generally argue that most government regulation is bad or unnecessary since the "invisible hand" of the free market maintains sufficient stability without it. Liberal economists loosely follow Keynes in advocating some government regulation through fiscal and monetary policy to smooth out the occasional – presumably exogenous – disturbances in the free market economy's natural balance. Neither has any adequate endogenous theory of why business cycles occur. Corporatist political economy aligns with the financial instability hypothesis of Hyman Minsky and Steve Keen, which has its roots in Keynes. This perspective does not argue that the economy is utterly chaotic, but to the extent there is any stability it is more as result of a balance of private power rather than a free market equilibrium of powerlessness.

Throughout the chapters that follow, as we examine historical issues of global monetary policy, I contend, contrary to many neoclassical textbooks, that governments never *control* the money supply, but at best merely have some *influence* on it. Furthermore, even influence over what economists define as the money supply is a rather weak power, since it is the credit cycle, the fluctuations in the supply and demand for credit, that drives the business cycle. Expansion of credit is independent of the money supply. No capitalist governments have ever controlled the credit supply. Creation of credit is a private power. Government may have some limited influence over the price of credit, but private interests also act strategically and thus may have significant influence over government policy, so it is never proper to consider government policy in isolation as the sole regulating power in capitalist societies. Many prices of all kinds are regulated by private contracts and cartels. Credit creation, to the extent it is regulated at all, is only stabilized by the balance of contending powers and the collusion of large lenders in financial consortia or cartels. By the nineteenth century, such financial cartels emerged globally, and hence became a proper subject for international political economy.

6 International system dynamics

> The interstate system is not the only international system that one may conceive of. Wallerstein shows in many interesting ways how the world economic system affects national and international politics. … But saying that a theory of international economics tells us something about politics, and that a theory of international politics tells us something about economics, does not mean that one theory can substitute for the other. … In international politics the appropriate concerns, and possible accomplishments, of systems theory are twofold: first, to trace the expected careers of different international systems, for example, by indicating their likely durability and peacefulness; second, to show how the structure of the system affects the interacting units and how they in turn affect the structure.
>
> Kenneth N. Waltz, *Theory of International Politics* (1979: 38, 40)

Kenneth Waltz had one brilliant idea: that the international system is something distinct from the nation-states that comprise it. In other words, the whole is greater than the sum of the parts. This one great idea revived the realist theory of international relations that was reeling under attack from liberal political economy. In fact, Waltz's idea was not so new, he just radically simplified older versions of systems theory. But his systems theory was hobbled by two realist assumptions: that nation-states act as unified entities and that economies, business, and private power are subordinated to this unified state power. Corporatism recasts international systems theory to account for bifurcated nations, true endogenous dynamics – as opposed to the comparative statics Waltz borrowed from economics – and the international conflicts and alliances of private interest blocs. Waltz's international system is populated only by a few great powers interacting through war and the threat of war. A corporatist international system understands that the substance of most international relations is business relations, that most wars are financed – or not – by private business, and that international business interests are highly organized and often polarized.

For Waltz, the international system is constituted by the distribution of power – largely military – among major states, known as the "great powers." Great powers are each roughly equal in power. During most of modern

European history until 1945, there are several great powers, typically five or six. This is called a multipolar system. After 1945, the world system became a bipolar rivalry between the two remaining superpowers and their allies, the US and the Soviet Union. Bipolarity still pertained, Waltz believed, when he wrote his major work during the 1970s. Waltz's major concern was which system is more stable and peaceful. He concludes it is bipolarity.

Multipolarity also brings into contention another major area of realist concern: alliance behavior. Having multiple powers means that security depends not only on one's own efforts, but also on securing allies. Realists have generally argued that other great powers will ally against the most powerful or threatening state, which is the main argument of the balance of power theory. Weaker states might also do the opposite and ally with the strongest power for their own safety, which is called bandwagoning. In general, realists emphasize that alliances are not a matter of culture or sentiment, but purely for the security of the state. Today's friend might become tomorrow's enemy and vice versa, according to the national interest.

Most realists accept bipolarity and multipolarity as concepts, though not all accept when each existed or agree on the consequences of them for system behavior. For example, when Waltz was writing the book quoted above, Henry Kissinger, first as an influential academic realist and then the chief foreign policy advisor to President Richard Nixon, argued for five major powers: the US, the Soviet Union, NATO Europe, Japan, and China. Kissinger considered – wrongly in retrospect – that the Soviet Union was the fastest rising and thus most dangerous power. Therefore, it would be wise for the US, already allied with Europe and Japan, to gain China as an ally in order to counterbalance the overweening power of the Soviets and maintain peace. Waltz and Kissinger were both realists, but they could disagree within the overall framework of the realist perspective.

Other realists emphasize the hierarchy of states in a power system rather than considering great powers to be roughly equal and largely autonomous, as Waltz does. A.F.K. Organski (1958), for example, developed an elaborate system of hierarchal powers polarized between status quo powers that support the rules and norms of the existing state system and revisionist states that oppose the existing world order. Rules and norms are maintained and enforced by the strongest of the status quo powers, the hegemon. System-wide wars or world wars occur during what Organski calls a power transition when a rising power, championing the cause of the revisionist powers, challenges the hegemon. The problem with testing the validity of the theory is that there are very few instances in history to illustrate it. Even for those few it is arguable whether they fit his model.

Organski's notion of a hegemonic power has been adopted by many liberals since economist Charles Kindleberger (1973) first popularized it in a book explaining what he saw as the systemic failures that contributed to the origin of the Great Depression of the 1930s. Whereas many liberals put their faith in international law, international organization, and eventually even world government, others, recognizing the difficulties of collective action and the free rider problem identified by economists, have come to believe that international cooperation cannot always succeed spontaneously. For some issue areas, notably, free trade and a stable international monetary system, it may be necessary, at least to get the ball rolling, for there to be a powerful hegemon that has the incentive and capability to enforce new rules. This view is called hegemonic stability theory.

The difference between Organski's power transition and the more liberal version, hegemonic stability theory, is that Organski starts with a polarization between opposing visions of what is an ideal world order. Hegemonic stability theory, in typical liberal fashion, believes there is only one ideal world order; the same order is good for everyone. The only problem is how to create and enforce cooperation in the first place, since there are potential benefits to cheating or free riding on the rules of any cooperative order.

The economic foundation of hegemonic stability theory is the theory of public goods. Public goods are things that benefit "everyone" but that will not necessarily be efficiently produced in a pure market system. For example, cleaner air is a public benefit, but private interests alone are not likely to provide it because those who bear the cost of preventing pollution (say, the chemical industry) are a small subset of the public. They might not be willing to bear high costs for a benefit that accrues to everyone unless forced to do so by government regulation or subsidized to make it profitable for them to do so. Yet the international system has no single government to represent the global public, so public goods will be neglected unless all parties can agree in some way to enforce and pay for the requisite cooperative solutions. A hegemonic power might substitute for the lack of world government, providing solutions to public goods problems.

The two issue areas that have attracted the greatest attention within international political economy in recent decades are international trade and finance. Liberals argue that the public goods for these two are free trade and stable, easily convertible currencies. These are supposedly public goods, so that all nations benefit from them if they are available, but if some nations do not expect them to be available or adequately enforced, they may be tempted to cheat or free ride and manage their national economies autonomously to protect their narrow interest at the sacrifice of the collective interest of all.

Corporatism takes a position closer to the realist Organski than to liberals on these key international economic issues. Real and powerful interests are, as Madison argued, perennially divided on issues of trade and finance. However, contrary to realists like Organski, corporatists understand that divisions of interests occur *within* states and not just between them. At any particular moment, one or another interest may be predominant in the government of a particular state, but the opposing bloc still exists and can cooperate with like-minded interests abroad, and perhaps come to power through defeat in war, revolution, or merely an electoral victory of an opposition party. This is why, for example, although the economic nationalists who led Germany and Japan into World War II were diametrically opposed to business internationalist policies emanating especially from the US and Britain, as soon as these nationalists were defeated and overthrown, Germany and Japan could become leading members of the postwar world order under the leadership of their own business internationalists who favor and benefit from the new world order. Organski does not explain how and why a country can rapidly switch from being a revisionist to a status quo interest. This depends on interest bloc politics. National power alone does not explain it, though revolution or defeat in war can facilitate a reversal of the interest bloc in power.

Thucydides and polarization

The first obvious difference between realism and corporatism has already been outlined in Chapters 1 and 2: realists like Waltz and Organski treat states as unified actors within the international system, whereas corporatism recognizes that states are often internally polarized by conflicting interest blocs that may operate internationally or at least ally with congruent interests abroad. There is no single "national interest" or common foreign policy that unites opposing interest blocs in most circumstances. I first understood this clearly when during graduate school I read a book usually claimed as a foundation of international relations (IR) realism, *The History of the Peloponnesian War* by the Classical Greek historian Thucydides. Shortly after that I read Aristotle's *Politics* to learn more about the contest between democratic and oligarchic parties that appeared so central to Thucydides. These two works provided the foundation for my conception of international systems composed of polarized polities. Subsequently I applied this approach to modern political economy.

Thucydides was not an IR realist, but he certainly was a *political* realist, like Aristotle. Both perceived most Greek city-states as riven by opposing democratic and oligarchic parties, each striving to gain power to resist the other. These were not the pure or idealized republics of Plato, but violently polarized polities in which each party ruled not in the "national interest," whatever that might be, but only in the interest of maintaining the governing party's rule. Foreign policy too aimed at securing not some abstract state interest, but only the interest of one party against the other. There are many lines of evidence supporting this (Nolt 1997c), but here I will briefly mention only a few.

Waltz and other realists believe that international systems are characterized by the configuration of power among the great powers. In the Greek world of the fifth century BCE, there were two leading powers, Athens and Sparta, but neither became a great power mainly because of its own size or predominant power. This international system therefore did not become bipolar because the power of either leading pole was overweening on its own. It was polarized instead because of the chronic struggle between democrats and oligarchs in so many states. Democrats, upon taking power in any state, allied with democratic Athens for their own self-preservation. Likewise, oligarchs aligned with oligarchic Sparta against the subversive threat of Athens and its allies. During the war, many states switched sides, but only when internal revolutions reversed the party in power. In several instances, when a city was under siege, it was betrayed to the attacker by members of the party out of power. Although Athens lost the war when Persia joined the Spartan side and an oligarchic coup, after previous unsuccessful attempts, finally overthrew Athenian democracy, democracy regained the initiative early in the fourth century after the Spartan garrison of Athens went home and the democrats regained power. Democrats destroyed Sparta's power only a few decades after that when the former oligarchy of Thebes switched sides after a democratic revolution and joined Athens against its former ally, Sparta. Consideration of state power alone cannot, as Waltz (1979) says, "trace the expected careers of different international systems," because the power dynamic of that time was so deeply wrapped up with what each contending party was fighting for.

Aristotle argues that democracy and oligarchy are not just contrasting regime types without any substantive policy differences. Since political rights are so much more broadly allocated by democracy (certainly more broadly than what we call democracy today), the foreign policy objectives and strategies varied characteristically between the two. Aristotle referred to Athens as a "naval democracy" because, like most Greek city-states, Athens' *hoplite* (heavily armored infantry) army of about 10,000 men was composed of those rich enough to supply their own expensive bronze armor and weapons, a defined tax class. On the other hand, the Athenian navy comprised 200–300 triremes during war, each with a crew of about 170 men plus a few dozen soldiers, altogether much larger than the army. Many of the men who rowed these ships were from the poorest classes of Athenian citizens, but they had political rights, including the right to vote for their military leaders and to vote for or against war. Most of the rest of the rowers were citizens of democratic states allied with Athens. Aristotle argues that democracy is rule by the poor, in this case, the large navy, in their own interest, whereas oligarchy is rule by the rich, generally the large landowners who dominated the armies of most oligarchic states. Navies of oligarchic states were not as well trained as the Athenian and did not perform nearly as effectively, ship for ship, since they were manned by polyglot mercenary crews assembled only during wartime and lacking political rights. Aristotle even argues that various elements of strategy differ between states according to the party in power. Even the policy of fortification differs. Monarchies tend to build a strong central citadel for the ruler. Oligarchies build fortifications scattered across their territory to secure the agricultural land and slaves of the landed oligarchs. Democratic Athens did not defend the extensive property of its landed oligarchs, so that their property was plundered and thousands of their slaves escaped during the war. Instead it fortified only its connection to the sea through its port.

Although Aristotle has less to say about this, I believe that democracy was also supported by rich merchants and ship owners who advocated an active overseas strategy rather than defense of the home territory. Thus during both the first and second Peloponnesian Wars between Athens and Sparta in the course of the fifth century BCE, Athens ignored the Spartan armies plundering its hinterland and instead launched far-flung naval expeditions that widened the war to engage powerful new adversaries that were not originally involved. During the first war Athens invaded Egypt and during the second it launched an expedition against rich but distant Syracuse on the island of Sicily. Both expeditions ultimately ended in disaster. From a strictly military standpoint these diversions seem outrageous, but they make more sense taking into account that these prospective expeditions were rich with promise of plunder for both the poor majority and a few rich leaders, known as demagogues, a word used pejoratively ever since. One wonders if some of the oligarchs cynically egged on the democratic masses to send them as far away as possible and then reveled in their defeat. Thucydides characterizes the debates between the demagogues and the conservative oligarchic opposition, which argued for defeating Sparta more directly or making peace. The democratic majority were swayed to elect the demagogues as war leaders, but when their Syracuse expedition was defeated, oligarchs, clearly despairing about Spartan forces ravaging their rural property, tried the first of several coups to end the war on Sparta's terms.

The rich detail I found in Thucydides and Aristotle showed that, contrary to the state-centric view of realists, Greek city-states were radically and chronically divided on issues of foreign policy and strategy, and this division affected all elements of international system behavior, including the alignments of city-states, their strategies, and even the constitution and training of their military forces. There was no unified national interest. For many Greek partisans, even defeat by a foreign power, if better aligned with their own partisan interests, was preferable to domestic defeat by their party opponent, according to Thucydides's account. Realism is wrong to assume nation-states are necessarily unified actors, but liberalism is also wrong to imagine that there is one universal public good that will benefit all if only cooperation can be attained.

Polarization around global monetary and trade policies

Liberal international relations theory conceives of international system characteristics quite differently from how realism does. With the exception of hegemonic stability theory, discussed above, liberals do not consider the distribution of power among states to be the most important characteristic defining systems. Instead, liberals focus on the specific laws, rules, norms, and international institutions or organizations that shape international relations. Since these are complex and diverse, liberals, like pluralists in domestic politics, seldom consider over-arching power structures, but instead focus on the specific configuration of rules and power in each specific issue area. Issue areas are diverse, but among those most discussed within liberal IPE are international monetary and international trade regimes.

Liberals follow economists in arguing that international monetary systems may attain at most two of three desirable objectives. These are (1) stable, fixed exchange rates; (2) free convertibility of currencies; and (3) national monetary autonomy to permit Keynesian macroeconomic stabilization. The first two can be attained only through international cooperation, so systems like the gold standard of the nineteenth century (until 1914) and the Bretton Woods system of 1945–71, which many argue secured these first two objectives at the expense of the third, are viewed by liberals as exemplars of stable international monetary cooperation, at the sacrifice of some degree of national autonomy. The flexible exchange rate system that has pertained since the demise of Bretton Woods has abandoned the first objective in the attempt to secure the other two. During the world wars and their aftermath and the Great Depression, the first and third objectives were generally obtained at the sacrifice of free convertibility. During these periods governments licensed and regulated most foreign exchange transactions, as communist countries have generally done. Licensing foreign exchange also gives governments significant power to regulate international trade.

Hegemonic stability theory argues that the nineteenth-century gold standard worked because Britain, as the hegemon, made it work. It disintegrated along with British hegemony with the outbreak of World War I. Between the world wars the lack of a hegemon doomed the attempt to revive the prewar gold standard. A new open and cooperative international monetary regime, the Bretton Woods system, was only possible after the decisive US rise to hegemony during World War II. It collapsed as US hegemony faltered during the Vietnam War debacle, which ostensibly undermined US capacity to defend the value of the dollar. Liberals argue over whether the contemporary flexible exchange rate system is well or poorly managed according to their views of the success of cooperation among the world's major monetary powers.

My corporatist approach to international monetary issues is very different, as we shall see in the coming chapters. Although I agree with the broad characterization of international monetary regimes outlined above, I disagree with most liberals (and realists who take an interest in monetary policy) about the powers that created, sustained, and opposed these systems. Contrary to hegemonic stability theory, it is not principally the power of hegemonic states that creates an international monetary system, but big banks that share common interests. Governments may pass some of the enabling legislation, but they do so typically at the behest of the biggest banks. They cannot force banks to support a system opposed to their interests.

Furthermore, within each monetary system there is not one unified idea of the public good. Private interests contend vigorously, even during the supposedly "stable" hegemonic eras, leading to numerous periodic financial panics and crashes, especially during the less-regulated gold standard system, as we shall see in Chapter 8. The gold standard left considerable room for credit expansion and contraction independent of the supply of gold, but it did privilege the big bear banks and the large merchant and bond holder interests they aligned with. There were other financial interests, let alone broader societal interests, that were vulnerable or handicapped under the gold standard. On the other hand, the contemporary flexible exchange rate system is heavily biased in favor of financial trading interests and the financial instability that profits them most, as we explore in Chapter 14. No particular international financial system is in any sense a universal public good. Every system privileges some interests and hobbles others.

Despite liberals' faith that free trade is a public good beneficial to all, free trade has been unusual in the international system and trade policies are among the most hotly contested political issues throughout modern history. Realists are generally less enamored of free trade. They often recognize that a nation's wealth and certainly its national autonomy may benefit from protectionism. In fact, in many ways, realism is the logical IR perspective of protectionist interests, which I call business nationalists, whereas liberalism is the IR view most congenial to business internationalists or free traders. I contend that both realism and liberalism will exist in any country polarized by trade issues, at least, because each school of thought represents the concerns of a substantial bloc of powerful interests. Free trade does not predominate in a system merely according to the successful cooperation of states, but also because internationalist business interests cooperate globally to influence states to lower tariffs and other barriers to trade.

On the other hand, free trade, in the way economists typically conceive of it, is a misnomer. It does not actually signify trade free of restrictions or regulations. The liberal and economistic conception of free trade considers only government obstacles to trade, not private ones, such as monopolies, cartels, and other applications of credit power and pricing power. Forms of cartels masquerading under various pseudonyms include financial consortia, shipping conferences, railroad pools, patent-sharing agreements, and orderly marketing agreements. I know of no comprehensive history of cartels, but the anecdotal evidence I have seen from numerous sources is that much if not most of world trade and investment has been conducted at cartel prices. Today at least half of world trade is intra-firm trade, and so occurs at administrative rather than market prices (Robins 2006: 35). Most of the rest is subject to cartel pricing or at least long-term contracted prices. Very little of modern trade is free in the sense of occurring within free markets. Most trade is subject to agreements reflecting private power whether or not it is also free of governmental regulation.

The first significant drive toward universal free trade occurred during the nineteenth century. Hegemonic stability theorists consider it a consequence of British hegemony. Chapter 8 explores this. The British drive to open global trade for its own merchants did also open it for others as well, though not perfectly freely since many restrictions, public and private, remained. The British victory in the long series of wars with France, 1793–1815, also caused the disintegration of the Spanish and Portuguese colonial empires in the Americas, which had previously been closed for most legal outside trade by strict mercantilist restrictions favoring the colonial power. During the early decades of the nineteenth century the British East India Company's near monopoly of the India and China trade was broken. Strong resistance to freer trade by

China and Japan was overcome by war and armed threats. During the last decades of the century, large areas of Africa were opened to commerce, often by force. Following the Anglo-French trade treaty of 1860, tariffs among many European countries were significantly lowered.

These free trade trends began to be reversed during the last decades of the nineteenth century as the major powers tried to cope with a long period of price deflation and several severe depressions. Hegemonic stability theorists attribute this reversal to the relative decline of British power. As this brief outline of its history shows, much of the process of "freeing" trade involved violence. Clearly there were substantial interests around the world that did not appreciate how much better off they would be with freer trade! There is thus, at least on the surface, some reason to associate freer trade with the actions of a hegemonic power. However, although the progress of freer trade outside of Europe and North America often required significant violence, lending credence to the IR realist view, progress among industrializing nations depended largely upon cooperation and negotiations, as expected by liberals.

The second great era of globalization, including liberalization of trade, began at the end of World War II and is still underway today. Similarly, hegemonic stability theorists point to the predominance of the United States after World War II as the primary cause. Part IV explores this in more detail. Conversely, the period including the two world wars and the Great Depression is often seen as a period of world economic turmoil, national self-assertion, and, of course, war, during which cooperation broke down since Britain was too weak to remain a hegemon and the US (or any other power) was not yet strong enough to assume the hegemonic role.

There is a rough truth in this, although the picture becomes clearer when we realize that within each nation similar broad nationalist and internationalist interest blocs contended, especially during the interwar period. World War II, somewhat like the Peloponnesian War thousands of years earlier, was not a contest among unified, autonomous powers, but largely a civil war between nationalism and internationalism. The Soviet Union, though economically nationalist, was unwillingly cast into the internationalist camp by the Nazi invasion of 1941. The Cold War continued the unfinished struggle against the economic nationalism of the Soviet bloc. Japan and Germany were quickly "rehabilitated" to become allies of US internationalism after the war because they already included powerful internationalist business interests eager to support the new postwar world order. Hegemony, in the corporatist view, is not just hegemony of a single nation, but the hegemony of a bloc of interests well represented in all nations, though not, as in liberalism, in any way universally representative.

All wars are financed

Realists neglect a critical dimension of the international system: international finance. Since the Italian invention of war funding by long-term bonds and annuities during the thirteenth century, nearly all major wars involving Europeans have been financed by private bankers. Since banks big enough to finance wars are very large and operate internationally, they become an important part of the international system. Bankers choose which wars and which nations to finance. They are seldom successfully coerced into lending. Aspiring great powers therefore must have some regard for their creditworthiness and cultivate their relationships with bankers. Often a power loses a war when it can no longer borrow. Unpaid armies are dangerous. They tend to revolt, desert, or defect. Bankers are not in the business of losing money, so they try to be judicious about the wars they finance. Backing a winner can be profitable. Backing a loser can lead to losses or even bankruptcy. By the nineteenth century, if not before, international bankers also constituted a potent peace interest, refusing to finance potential wars that might depress bond values, contributing to the relative peacefulness of the century from 1815 to 1914. Throughout the remainder of this book there are examples of the important consequences of the private financing of wars.

More than any other factor, the development of financial markets, especially long-term bond markets, enabled Europeans to explore and dominate the globe. Throughout most of history ships require among the most massive commitment of concentrated capital. Navies are so expensive that few powers can afford them. Long-distance merchant voyages may be profitable, but financing the ships and their cargo on a risky long-distance trip requires immense capital resources. Virtually all the voyages of exploration during the early modern period were privately financed. Once new lands were discovered, their conquest and exploitation were also privately financed for the most part. The rich new trade routes also tempted pirates and privately financed privateers with the promise of plunder. Tiny countries and even city-states like Venice, Genoa, Portugal, Netherlands, and England were able to establish large trading fleets and defeat the navies and later the armies of large empires, including the Ottoman Turks, Indian Mughals, and Chinese emperors, while competing successfully with much larger but not as well financed European powers like Spain, Habsburg Austria, and France. Realism does not understand the secret of the success of small trading powers. The secret was leveraged financing.

Consider a simple example of leverage. How did a small city-state like Venice dominate the sea trade with the massive empire of the Ottoman Turks? The Turks were sometimes trading partners and sometimes enemies, particularly when one of the other Italian rivals of Venice was favored by the Ottoman sultan. If a sultan was able to borrow significant funds at all, it was as an ally of one of the Italian cities, but to finance a war he might not be able to count on them. If he relies only on his own tax revenue, even if it is ten times greater than the tax revenue of Venice, he cannot finance a fleet as big as theirs. First of all, a large empire needs a large army just to hold it together, so that takes a big part of its funds. Second, Venice and similar city-states with their own bond markets can leverage their tax revenue through massive borrowing in a war emergency. Suppose Venice has a maximum annual tax revenue of

100,000 ducats and normal annual expenditures of 60,000 ducats. If the government issues bonds paying 5 percent interest, it could borrow up to 800,000 ducats using the 40,000 surplus ducats to pay the interest on the bonds. Thus it would have up to 800,000 ducats immediately to pay the extraordinary expenses of war, rather than a mere 40,000 ducats per year of surplus tax funds. Such a massive capital fund can equip a large fleet and army, hopefully win the war, and then recover at least part of the capital outlay from plunder, ransom of captives, tribute, and surplus revenues from newly won territories, including selling offices, tax farming, and trading rights. Bond markets are also highly flexible. They enable capital to be lent to trading ventures during peace time and then, when war comes and trade falls off, capital can redirected to the armed forces. The rich greatly prefer financing necessary state activities by marketable debt that pays them interest on their capital rather than by confiscatory taxes.

Since bond markets provide such an efficient way to finance overseas trade and war, why did only a few European countries and a few of their colonies, such as North America, make extensive use of them? Large financial markets are few, often fewer than the number of great powers, and not necessarily coincident with them. It is not military power that creates financial markets, but financial markets do create military power through leveraged financing. Financial markets can only operate where legal contracts are enforceable and arbitrary exercise of power is rare. They depend on secure rule of law. Where wealthy people can be coerced by force of arms, financial wealth is hidden or flees. Even stable monarchies, if rule of law is not secure, that is, tyrannies in Aristotle's terms, do not attract bankers, since the tyrant or his government may default with impunity. They are above the law.

This is why through history, at least until the later nineteenth century when secure property rights and the gold standard helped discipline and secure financial contracts in a broader set of countries, large financial markets have been confined to a handful of places, usually with merchant-dominated republican governments or constitutional monarchies. At first, Italian city-state republics dominated global finance, later joined by a few independent German city-states, such as Frankfurt and Hamburg, and especially independent city-states of the Netherlands (Homer & Sylla 2005: 134). Wealthy Jews, prohibited from owning land by the laws of most Christian states and, unlike Catholics, not barred by their religion from lending at interest, were prominent in many early banking centers. When the Jews of Spain were expelled in 1492, many moved to Portugal, where they helped finance the first world trading empire. When Spain took over Portugal in 1580, many Jews fled again to the Netherlands. They included those with banking acumen who helped establish Amsterdam as the world capital of finance (Neal 1990: 7, 10–11). Many Protestant bankers also fled to London, Amsterdam, and Switzerland from French-controlled territories after 1685 because of religious persecution. Amsterdam remained one of the top two financial centers until 1795, when it was conquered by the French revolutionaries and many financiers fled to London, already thriving as a financial center since the Glorious Revolution of 1688 enhanced the power of parliament and put a Dutch merchant king on the English throne. New York, the financial capital of the New World, started as a Dutch merchant colony then shared the commercial spirit of London. One of the first post-independence governors of New York was Alexander Hamilton, founder of the first two large American joint-stock banks and the first Secretary of the Treasury. Hong Kong, long the financial capital of Asia, was founded by British merchants. Its currency was still issued exclusively by private banks throughout the twentieth century. Financial markets thrive where merchants and financiers are confident they can maintain a pro-business government without the possibility of a profligate or exploitative tyrant.

International relations theorists have debated what forms of government are more effective at war and more conducive to peace. A common answer, especially among liberals, is that democratic governments are more inclined to peaceful relations, especially with like-minded democracies they tend to trust. Liberals also expect that tyrannical or autocratic governments are more war-prone and perhaps, being more ruthless and secretive, more effective at war. This view was popularized by Kant, though he talked of republics, the virtuous form of popular rule in the classical view, not democracies, as peace-loving. Modern scholars tend to conflate these two, as mentioned in previous chapters. Yet throughout history many of the most successful naval powers, trading powers, and imperialists have been republics or democracies, including classical Athens, early Rome, Venice, Genoa, the Netherlands, England, and the United States. The virtue of these governments is their capacity to mobilize private wealth in the service of collective projects, including war.

Statism and nationalism

Realists tend to be great believers in nationalism. It is the glue that unites great powers to make them effective and coherent actors on the world stage. The heyday of nationalism was probably the later nineteenth century through World War II, as we explore in Chapters 9 and 10. Yet the ideology of nationalism, which made ethnic nations synonymous with juridical states, is less persuasive when subjected to sober analysis. The unification of Germany and Italy during the 1860s excited great ambitions to unite other nations, but these efforts have all failed. Pan-Turkish, pan-Arab, and other "great" nationalisms foundered during the twentieth century. On the other hand, "petty" nationalism, dividing larger existing states into their constituent ethnic nations, seemed to have had more success, especially at the end of World War I with the breakup of the Russian, Ottoman, and Austro-Hungarian empires and the end of the Cold War with the breakup of the Soviet Union, Yugoslavia, and Czechoslovakia. Yet on balance, arbitrary juridical statism has been much more successful and enduring than ethno-cultural nationalism. Neither realism nor liberalism has thought deeply about why the international system is populated by rather stable juridical states, legal entities with enduring boundaries that are almost all arbitrary lines drawn by European leaders during the last couple of centuries.

Realism, so fixated on state power and territorial autonomy, should expect that with the great ebb and flow of power since 1815, boundaries might have changed more than they have. A few nations, such as Germany and Poland, have witnessed profound boundary changes. But the vast majority of the world's states, no matter how strong or weak, no matter how arbitrarily their initial boundaries were drawn, have endured within those boundaries since their creation. One of the exceptions that proves the rule is the breakup of the Soviet Union, which occurred not along ethno-cultural lines, but along the arbitrary boundaries between various Soviet republics drawn by Stalin in the early 1920s deliberately to avoid ethnic boundaries precisely in order to frustrate nationalist autonomy while appearing to be friendly to national aspirations. Conflicts have occurred, some of them certainly fueled by nationalist appeals, but juridical nations endure unchanged far more effectively than realist theory should lead one to expect.

Liberalism has no body of theory about why we have just the states we do, but it does supply reasons why numerous states endure within arbitrary boundaries despite their lack of power or ethno-cultural unity. Liberals for centuries have argued that international law protects the integrity of boundaries once legally – no matter how arbitrarily – constituted. Norms such as national sovereignty and non-aggression, while occasionally violated, do prevail most of the time for most of the world. As I write, the arbitrary accession of the Crimea to the Ukraine by Khrushchev in 1954 is being challenged by Russia, with the rest of the world rallying to the principle of border inviolability. Liberals do appear to explain better than realists the stability of the state system. It is not merely a function of power relations. Chapter 11 advances a corporatist explanation for the durability of nations and their occasional disintegration or amalgamation, involving the interests of private trade and finance, including the need to affix responsibility for the assignment of public debts to stable juridical tax territories, which states are, at least.

Corporatist international systems

Neither liberalism nor realism has a fully satisfying explanation of the systemic patterns of war and peace. Liberals over-predict peace, and thus are often surprised by the outbreak of war. Liberals too often explain wars as an accidental failure of diplomacy or a consequence of mad or irrational leaders, seeing no systemic causes of war in the modern era. Realists, even more egregiously, over-predict war. They expect wars even when their likelihood is greatly diminishing. War is diminishing since 1945 for reasons more congenial to liberals than to realists, but neither have an adequate understanding of the specific nature of international systems, and therefore of the prospects for war within various systems.

Corporatism classifies international systems not according to the number of states or their relative power, as in Waltz, but draws on elements of Organski and the liberal tradition to describe how the types or characteristics of nations comprising any international system do matter. Corporatism, like liberalism, also contends that private non-state actors have power, though corporatism evokes conflicting business interests typically neglected by liberalism. Realism tends toward quantitative classification of states, whereas liberalism and especially corporatism insist on qualitative analysis. What matters is not just the amount of power a state has, but its specific interests of its government and private powers relative to those of other states. Like liberalism, corporatism understands that the interest of states is not just a matter of security, but of economy too. But whereas liberalism generally sees economic interests driving states toward cooperation, corporatism recognizes economic interests as a key element of both cooperation and conflict, both among and within states. Allied economic interests promote cooperation. Rival economic interests promote conflict. Understanding the prospects for peace within any international system requires knowing the roots of both cooperation and conflict, and not focusing one-sidedly on one or the other, as both realism and liberalism do.

The chapters that follow classify and characterize several distinctive historical international systems. Chapter 7 evaluates the mercantilist system of early modern Europe. Its characteristics helped give birth to the realist theory of international relations. As a first approximation, realism does describe some of the typical features of the mercantile era. However, because realism abstracts too much from business and the internal contradictions within states, it misses the causes of the tumultuous demise of the mercantilist system. Realists tend to view the two centuries before and the century after 1815 in a similar light. For them both involve multipolar systems in which the balance of power was a decisive dynamic aspect, explaining alliance patterns and the incidence of war and peace. In fact, these two eras were vastly different. Chapter 8 shows why the century after 1815 was much more peaceful (at least in Europe) and why more of the world was open for business. Liberalism, in theory and practice, flourished during that era. Chapter 9 argues why this liberal era, often called the first globalization, came to a crashing end with World War I. Imperialism, which led to international polarization and then the Great War, defeated liberalism before it, like mercantilism, disintegrated in turn under its own contradictions.

Finally, Part IV is devoted to the foundations of the modern era of business internationalism, which, except for the security aspects of the Cold War, looks like another flourishing of liberalism, the second globalization. The Cold War divides the post-1945 period into two different international systems. Liberals feel vindicated and confident this system is working as they expect an international system should, especially since the end of the Cold War, but even prior to that, at least in the portion known to liberals as the Free World, a sort of Kantian "zone of peace" seemed to be taking hold. However, the idealism of liberals gets the better of them when they conflate the decline of war with the absence of conflict. Deep, polarizing conflicts remain, but by their nature they are more likely to unfold through business and political struggle rather than through war. During the heyday of Keynesian-liberal economic optimism, it seemed that economic conditions globally were entering a period of "great moderation." Yet, as I conclude in Chapter 14, this is not to be. The chronic economic instability of the first liberal globalization is still with us during the second.

Part III

From mercantilism to imperialism

7 The power of mercantilism

> The ordinary means therefore to increase our wealth and treasure is by Forraign [sic] Trade, wherein we must ever observe this rule; to sell more to strangers yearly than we consume of theirs in value. ... That part of our stock which is not returned to us in wares must necessarily be brought home in treasure.
>
> Thomas Mun, 1630 (Buck 1974[1942]: 13)

> We cannot carry on trade without war, nor war without trade.
>
> Jan P. Coen, 1619, first governor-general of the Dutch East Indies (Robins 2006: 40)

> War made the state, and the state made war.
>
> Charles Tilly (1975: 42)

Mercantilism is a policy common among western European powers from the sixteenth through the eighteenth centuries that promoted a positive balance of trade by restricting imports, favoring nationally owned shipping, and encouraging exports. Foreigners would pay for this positive balance of trade by exporting their precious metals, that is, gold and silver coins or bullion, thus balancing net payment by exporting durable specie rather than consumable goods. Draining coinable metals from foreign sources was believed to weaken them and strengthen the successful mercantile power. The key instruments of mercantilism were government regulations and private corporations chartered as monopolies by law. The force required to sustain trading monopolies led to frequent wars among the mercantile powers, as Coen suggests.

A difficulty for mercantilism is that what might work for one country is not possible within an international system of similar powers. If some countries run a trade surplus, others must run a deficit. It is not possible for all major countries to be in surplus at the same time. Therefore mercantilism creates a highly contentious international system in which each major trading state is striving to expand its trade surplus and drain specie from the others. If they are equally good at it, they will all fail. Some must lose in order that others may win. International relations realism developed during the mercantile era.

This is no surprise. Mercantilist theory has much in common with realism, including the ideas that the international system is a contest between rival powers within which relative power matters and that economic goals must be subordinated to – or at least consonant with – military power. The accelerated power struggle among mercantilist powers rapidly developed the capabilities for war, trade, taxes, and credit.

On the other hand, liberalism follows economics in rejecting mercantilism as a war-prone and inefficient economic system. It provides little incentive for international cooperation. Therefore global "public goods" like free trade and stable international monetary relations are poorly provided. Most political economists since David Hume and Adam Smith and nearly all economists have lambasted the inefficiencies of mercantilism's many protectionist and monopolistic aspects. Among these are not only tariffs and export subsidies or rebates, but also outright prohibitions of some imports and exports, often including bans on the export of specie and items of military value. Mercantilism included strict rules regulating and sometimes prohibiting foreign ships trading in or through national territorial waters, which in England were called the Navigation Acts. Such legal restrictions were further reinforced during wartime by widespread recourse to privateering. Enemy and often even neutral ships anywhere on the high seas might be captured and sold by privateers, operating as a business venture and often selling shares of their privateering to investors, just as with a merchant voyage. Liberals and economists often argue that free trade would have been a better policy than mercantilism without recognizing that mercantilism was highly profitable for those who organized it, whether or not the general public benefitted, and since the seas were not safe, free trade by vulnerable small merchant companies would have been too dangerous anyway.

Merchants under mercantilism bound themselves together into great chartered companies and sought monopoly rights by law in order to reduce the risks of competition and to concentrate enough naval power to deter or punish any interference with their trading ventures. Until the world's seas were made relatively safe for all powers by the hegemony of the British Royal Navy after 1815, most long-distance trades were either done by great armed companies or by armed smugglers who doubled as privateers or pirates. There was little room on the dangerous oceans for small-scale competitive trade. The great trading companies also established fortified bases called factories along their trade routes as places to rest, wait out storms, repair ships, store goods, and trade with local people. The first of these were a string of Portuguese factories established during the fifteenth century down the west coast of Africa and on offshore islands. During the first part of the sixteenth centuries, Portuguese factories reached Brazil, India, China, Japan, and the spice islands of what is now Indonesia. The Spanish established an empire in the Caribbean, Mexico, and Peru, seeking gold and finding much silver. By the end of the sixteenth century, Portugal had been taken over by Spain, and the Netherlands, in revolt from Spain, was rapidly displacing the Portuguese in Asia and raiding the Spanish in the New World. During the seventeenth century the

Netherlands won its independence from Spain and became the most successful mercantile power, though increasingly challenged by rival English and French mercantile companies. Although monarchs were often among the shareholders in the great mercantile companies, the conquest of world trade was almost entirely organized by private companies employing their own capital and arms.

Corporatism's view of mercantilism is closer to realism insofar as it appreciates the power of mercantilism. However, whereas realism, as the quote from Tilly implies, focuses on the power of states alone. Corporatism understands that mercantilism also greatly enhanced and concentrated private power. Until the middle of the seventeenth century, the public navies of states (alternatively, consider these the private navies of monarchs) were small in comparison with the armed private fleets of the great mercantile companies. National navies typically stayed in home waters, leaving the wide oceans of the world for private capital to exploit. Although most of the policies of mercantilism were reversed during the laissez-faire and free trade era of the nineteenth century, the concentration of private power, especially in the form of great banks, endured. The long-term legacy of mercantilism was not just the victory of Britain as ultimately the most successful of the mercantile powers, but also concentration of financial and mercantile power and the consequent enhancement of private credit and pricing power.

Modern financial and business institutions emerged during the mercantilist era. Giant armed trading corporations pooled the capital of great merchants and other investors, not just for a specific voyage, but for an enduring joint-stock enterprise. The stock of these corporations and others soon led to the creation of stock markets and, along with them, financial derivatives that facilitated leveraged long and short strategies. Several of the leading mercantile powers experienced a financial revolution leading to huge declines in interest rates for both government and private borrowers. These lower rates were partly attributable to the development of large joint-stock banks and the markets they facilitated for both short-term bills of exchange and long-term bonds. The first such bank outside of Italy was the Exchange Bank of Amsterdam, founded in 1609. The Bank of England, founded in 1694, imitated the success of the Amsterdam bank, but was also awarded by law a monopoly right to issue circulating bank notes, in other words, paper money. A liquid market for international bills of exchange, mostly merchant issued, was perfected in Antwerp during the sixteenth century, which was largely superseded by Amsterdam during the following century. These bill markets facilitated the easy transfer of wealth and credit across borders. They were also vital to financing both international trade and the operations of fleets and armies.

Tax farming

Most histories of public finance focus on quantitative analysis, about how increasing revenues were extracted by the state from society, as in the pioneering work of Tilly (1975), quoted above. More interesting for understanding polarized private power dynamically is how the forms of revenue affect the balance of power between debtors and creditors, and between bears and bulls. Tax farming was a common means of raising state revenue throughout much of the world from ancient times through the early modern era. It lasted even later in some places such as the Ottoman Empire and India. Tax farming takes a great variety of forms. Perhaps the most common is a contract for some period of years between the state or ruler and the private tax farmer, usually a rich merchant or financier with ample liquid resources. The tax farmer promises to provide the ruler with a lump sum at the beginning or, more commonly, a fixed stream of payments over the life of the contract, like an annuity. In this chapter I focus on this second form, which was common in France, for example. When the contract involves annuity payments, rulers typically offer the tax farm because they need to borrow short-term from the tax farmer, often to finance a war. The tax farm serves as collateral for the lenders, who use the taxes they collect as the security for the loan. Thus the tax farmer is a creditor whose security is a monopoly right to collect a certain tax or the tax from a specified region. Essentially rulers mortgage a portion of their taxing authority as collateral for short-term loans.

Tax farming sets up incentives somewhat opposite to those of long-term bond financing, which is of great consequence to the dynamic history of mercantilism. I am perhaps the first to write about this clearly and directly. Since the typical tax farmer receives a fixed payment regardless of the value of the tax collected, the tax farmer's position is bullish. If the economy is growing so that the tax takes increases or if inflation causes price-related tax income to increase, the tax farmer reaps the benefit. On the other hand, the government's position is bearish since it receives payment from the tax farmer fixed in money terms. Inflating prices or debasing the currency will therefore reduce the value of the government's income. If most of a ruler's regular income is from tax farms, then that ruler is somewhat constrained from using another typical ruler's expedient – debasing coined money – since this would cause a loss of real income from the tax farms. In effect, tax farming secures the interests of the financier-farmers in two ways: providing collateral for short-term sovereign loans and insurance against the ruler devaluing debts through inflation or debasement of the currency. Tax farming is a hedge for private financiers against the arbitrary power of rulers.

Most historians discuss such themes as "the absolutist state" or "absolute monarchy" without considering how much of their presumed power most "absolute" rulers mortgaged to tax farmers. Such historians are Platonists who habitually treat the absolute state or ruler as an idealized entity with power unlimited by law. They make the mistake of considering legal limits as the only impediments to power. Law is not the source of power; control over arms, wealth, and property are. Many monarchs first rose to power by being the largest landlords and greatest warlords in a region. When the income from their own domains was insufficient to maintain or expand their power, they tried to harness the fickle wealth of merchants and money-lenders.

Taxing them with tolls was one way, but was too often evaded or insufficient. A more effective way to tap into the private resources of the wealthy is to induce them to lend voluntarily by offering favorable terms, including collateral in the form of tax farms or other attractive monopoly privileges. Monarchs such as Louis XIV may have overawed contemporaries and historians with claims such as his famous quip, "*L'état, c'est moi,*" (the state is me), but few monarchs ever enjoyed power without allies, especially allies among the moneyed rich to provide them with liquid resources for war. Bond holders who have bought debt voluntarily have aligned their fortunes with those of the state. It will be useful if more historians study monarchs as not just statesmen and warlords, but also consider their balance sheet as landlords and business investors. A dynastic state is like a large armed corporation; as Clausewitz said, "Politics ... may be considered as a kind of commerce on a larger scale."

It is the tyranny of oligarchic private wealth that finances monarchical tyranny, which in turn rewards its oligarchic creditors with private monopolies to further enhance their wealth. Private and public power are not constant adversaries as so often portrayed in the modern conservative idiom that contrasts private market freedom with public regulatory abuse. More accurately, if we must speak in broad abstractions, democratic freedom struggles against the overweening power of both concentrated private wealth and its allies in government who wield public power. Both the American and French revolutions were revolutions against mercantile tyranny, against both monarchical abuse and private privilege.

The financial revolution

The financial revolution that swept the Netherlands during the seventeenth century and England during the eighteenth century both perfected mercantilism and nourished the seeds of its demise. A similar financial revolution attempted in France aborted, which contributed to France's social revolution of 1789 and its defeat by Britain in the series of wars that punctuated the period 1689–1815. The main element of the financial revolution was replacing tax farming and the short-term borrowing secured by it with long-term negotiable debt in the form of bonds and perpetual annuities. Taxes were collected by state agencies instead of tax farmers and pledged to pay the interest on specific bond or annuity issues. Somewhat coincident with this was the rise of huge armed private corporations chartered by rival mercantilist powers to fight each other for trade monopolies, involving in some cases tax farming as well, in various parts of the world. The negotiable stock of these corporations and the ballooning long-term government debt formed the basis for new public financial markets, especially in Amsterdam and London, with Paris playing catch up. These financial markets became the battlefields of emerging bear and bull interests that animated a lively business cycle punctuated by numerous booms, bubbles, and crashes. Nearly all the instrumentalities and strategies of modern finance had fully emerged by this time, including financial derivatives. Credit power allied with pricing power to create powerful engines for the growth and centralization of wealth.

One of the most visible impacts of the financial revolution was the precipitous decline of interest rates. This, more than any technological invention, gave the European mercantile powers global dominance over the much larger and richer empires of Asia that could not leverage their private wealth so easily for war and private trade. As I mentioned in previous chapters, it was Italian city-states that invented and first benefitted from similar financial revolutions, which enabled them to dominate trade and finance throughout much of Europe during the Renaissance, but their resources were eventually depleted in frequent wars with much larger adversaries and by the defaults of some of their foreign sovereign borrowers also engaged in costly wars. The mercantile powers of northeastern Europe succeeded rather better at the game after they applied and extended Italian methods of finance to global empires largely administered by private corporations.

The decline in interest rates led to a rapid increase in the scale of war possible in Western Europe, creating something of a vicious circle. As debt became cheaper, fleets and armies were easier to finance, which simply increased the scale of warfare and piled debt upon debt. Even winning wars proved exorbitantly expensive. Venice was the first to develop a system of long-term negotiable debt-financed wars during the thirteenth century. As other Italian city-states, especially Genoa, Pisa, and Florence, followed suit, Venice piled up what contemporaries referred to as "mountains" of debt. Rival Italian bankers also financed wars of other powers, such as the Hundred Years' War between England and France. Spain and Portugal relied on Italian bankers too. Later bankers and merchants from German free cities like Frankfurt and various Hanseatic towns joined in this business, along with Flemish and Dutch financiers of Antwerp and Amsterdam. Many of these Renaissance-era bankers were eventually bankrupted by various defaults of sovereign debtors. Interestingly, the only sovereign debtors who defaulted were monarchs. City-states and countries rules by councils or parliaments, where wealthy merchants were always well represented, never defaulted on public debt during the mercantile period. This is one of the reasons why fully developed financial markets displaced tax farming only in polities where merchants ruled.

Financing sovereign debt using long-term bonds and annuities also changed the strategic balance of bears and bulls. In any particular tactical positions involving specific assets, investors may alternatively take bearish or bullish positions according to their interests at the moment in that particular asset, but large investors also may have a strategic bias given the nature of their overall portfolios. The proliferation of long-term government debt during the financial revolution reversed the typical pattern from tax farming. Now governments emerged as huge net bond debtors owing fixed coupon payments to bond and annuity owners just like what the tax farmers used to owe to them. Governments thus traded places with the tax farmers, even less ambiguously becoming a powerful bullish interest in favor of economic growth, inflation, and lower long-term interest rates, without the short-term creditor interest of the typical tax farmer. Government interest in higher revenue creates a bullish interest since tax revenues were increasing under the direct control of governments rather than tax farmers, and these were often increased by economic growth and sometimes by inflation (as in the case of *ad valorem* tariffs). Governments also have a bullish interest in bonds, since rising bond prices mean falling interest rates, thus lowering the cost of refunding the public debt.

The financial revolution also divides private financial interests between broker-dealers and bond owners. Broker-dealers include brokers whose main business is trading securities on behalf of third parties; stock jobbers, who are market makers trading securities on their own account as well as for clients; and investment banks, which the British more aptly call merchant banks, reflecting the historical origins of much of their capital and their short-term trading mentality. The term "investment banks" is a misnomer because through history most such institutions, like brokers, make their profits largely on the fee income from IPOs and from trading assets in secondary markets, rather than by investing their own capital long term. Broker-dealers profit largely from fees for arranging deals or trades for others and from trading on their own account using their market power and inside information. Broker-dealers may be either bears or bulls or both at any moment, according to their current position and strategy, but in general their interest is in deal flow and therefore excitement and volatility, no matter which direction things move. Whereas large owners of capital need to take a long position in *something*, broker-dealers can be more flexible and footloose. Today nearly all big banks are primarily acting as trading or "merchant" banks, decreasing their historical emphasis on deposit banking involving holding loans as assets, which none-theless remains the predominant myth of banking presented in economics textbooks.

Nearly all the large private corporations of the mercantile era, whether ostensibly mercantile enterprises like the British East India Company or banks like the Bank of England, held a significant part of their capital in the form of long-term government debt. Thus like all bond holders, they had a bearish creditor's interest in that debt capital yielding as high an income as possible. Though they could, in some short-term financial operations, benefit from a bullish inflation of bond prices if they intended to sell their inflated bonds and thus realize their enhanced value, this was only useful when there was some even more attractive asset yielding even higher income to which they could switch their capital while bond prices were thus elevated. During a broad bubble, when all asset prices are inflated in relation to the income they generate, bond holders and other creditors lending at fixed rates, such as mortgage holders, will typically turn bearish to drive down prices in at least some asset classes (best if these are not those that they currently own) in order to buy those declining assets and restore their capital earnings. When yields are judged too low in all classes of assets, as happens when broad asset price bubbles peak, creditors have the strongest bearish impulse to restore asset yields by driving down asset prices, whether those assets are bonds yielding interest, stocks yielding dividends, land yielding rent, or productive physical capital yielding profits. Thus the headquarters of nearly every major bear movement in history is the large bondholding banks. This is the origin of every slump, crash, financial crisis, and panic.

Blowing bubbles, cornering stock

Broker-dealers exercising market power strategically emerge from the earliest years of financial capitalism. They are already a major factor in Amsterdam's seventeenth century financial markets, as documented in Joseph de la Vega, *The Confusion of Confusions* (Held 2006). The Dutch already had terms then for what we now call bears and bulls. By the 1690s, with the influx of Huguenot refugees from France and Dutch financiers who arrived in the wake of the new Dutch king of England, London developed Dutch-style financial markets. Gradually these moved into the burgeoning coffee houses and eventually into more permanent facilities. These brand-new financial markets almost immediately and from then on began to exhibit the typical boom-and-bust cycle of financial markets everywhere.

A fascinating paper by Anne Murphy (2009) based on analysis of the ledger books of one London stock broker of the 1690s, Charles Blunt, shows in detail how what contemporaries called "stock jobbers and projectors" could profit from stock manipulations using options. Stock options were already, at the inception of the English stock market, almost as common as stocks themselves, according to the available broker records. Of the top 40 investors recorded in these ledgers, all but one bought both stocks and options. Stock options were much like the modern versions, though apparently all of them then used what is now called the "American" maturity option, meaning that they could be exercised any time until the maturity date. The maturity date could be any date mutually agreed between issuer and purchaser, but apparently six months in the future was most common. Both put and call options existed, although calls were then called "refusals." The most common options were "at-the-money," that is, the strike price at which they could be exercised in the future was the market price at the time of issue. Others, more expensive, were "in-the-money," which means their strike price was above the current market price for puts or below for calls. Options "out-of-the-money" are the opposite. One of the fascinating things about this particular broker is his identity. Charles Blunt was the cousin of one of the chief architects of the great South Sea Bubble and crash of 1720. Evidence from his ledgers show that his more infamous cousin, John Blunt, was already honing his skills at strategic manipulation of markets a quarter century earlier, but on a much smaller scale.

The ledger books of Charles Blunt show early detailed evidence of what would become a common tactic in asset markets throughout the coming centuries: cornering a stock. Unfortunately, the author who provides the evidence does not herself apparently recognize the strategy behind it. In fact, she finds it "seemingly far-fetched" that stock manipulation, which she cites numerous contemporaries bewailing, was actually occurring since, apparently, she believes that efficient markets are less far-fetched than market power. She is, like so many trained in textbook finance theory, primarily concerned with demonstrating the supposed efficiency of markets and thus misses, even with hindsight, the strategies of those with power to manipulate them, saying, "The varied uses to which options were put were little appreciated by contemporary commentators who focused instead on the flaws in the market" (Murphy 2009). Yet she supplies the fascinating evidence that those "varied uses" and the "flaws" were both well understood and exploited at the time; better than in modern textbook finance theory! The ledgers provide enough evidence to see the cornering strategy unfolding, but not all the details of its execution, since the surviving ledgers cover only a limited time period and do not preclude the possibility that the investors involved were also placing other trades with other brokers, which seems likely. Nonetheless, the case is extremely interesting for the possibilities it does show.

John Blunt and two fellow "projectors," as Adam Smith would call them, hatched a project to create a joint-stock company, Estcourt's Lead Mine, in February 1693, the same month Parliament passed a law allowing mine owners to profit from all mineral resources on their land without interference from the Crown. This was a relatively small venture with an initial capital of £5,000 apparently divided into 500 shares at £10 each. During 1693 it was mostly trading tamely between £8 and £12 a share. Meanwhile John Blunt and his associates accumulated call options on a minimum of 282 shares of the stock at strike prices between £10 and £20, using his cousin as intermediary to numerous investors who each sold small quantities of calls at around £2 each, in some cases simultaneously covering these calls with purchases of the same number of shares of the stock itself. In other cases, small investors sold Blunt apparently uncovered or "naked" calls on stock they did not own. Thus Blunt built up a large pool of suckers, though Murphy, like these suckers, apparently does not notice what is coming next. In the case of the suckers of that day, this ignorance is understandable, because they may not have known that a small circle of insiders was accumulating so many calls. Charles Blunt knew, but his customers likely did not. Yet Murphy, with the benefit of hindsight, is wrong to argue that it is "seemingly far-fetched" that stock manipulation using market power was underway. That is exactly what her evidence shows. This is the typical sort of blindness to private power that the myth of the market encourages.

The stock began rising in late 1693, part of a bubble that affected many other stocks as well. During the last week of January 1694 it jumped from £35 to £100. Other brokers were apparently executing trades that reached as high as £150 on these shares. If during this time Blunt and associates exercised their calls, buying stock at the strike prices of £10 to £20 and then immediately selling it at £100 or more, they would have made a tidy trading profit many times the initial capitalization of their company, which would easily make up for the fact that, as stock jobbers, they evidently knew nothing about running a lead mine. This is the very *least* that the available evidence suggests.

An even more complete sucker play, most likely given the hindsight that the broad market movement at this time was a boom *and crash* (Robins 2006: 29), was that Blunt and company, after they accumulated the calls at low strike prices, began to buy more shares of the stock itself through other brokers to create whispers about their buying interest in the coffee houses of Exchange Alley. At the same time, Blunt or other friends may have begun to spread rumors about the great potential of this lead mine. After all, England was in the middle of the Nine Years' War with France, so lead was in great demand for musket and cannon balls. Is it not "natural" that the stock price should spike up in such circumstances? Blunt's own purchases would also help drive it up. Furthermore, any naked issuers of his or others' calls would rush to buy the stock to cover their positions as they saw its price shooting up and heard rumors it was likely to go higher. As the price approached £100, and the insiders began exercising their calls, any remaining naked issuers of calls would be desperate to buy in order to be able to cover these calls on them, and yet by then there would be few free shares left to buy. This is the corner.

Now the only problem of a good corner is to find a way to sell as many shares as possible – by then Blunt and company owned the majority – before the price falls too much to cut into your enormous paper profits. This can be done near the peak of the bubble by buying out-of-the-money put options at whatever strike prices sellers are willing to offer, the higher the better, but even, say £50 might be sufficient. This counts on the gullibility of outsiders who do not know how much of the recent increase in the stock price represents real value and how much of it is "wind" (from the contemporary Dutch term for speculation, the "wind trade") puffed up by a short-lived bubble. Thus any puts were likely brokered by outsiders, not Blunt's cousin, so that his customers see only a high-flying stock and not a manipulated bubble. As Blunt and company start to sell the stock, some shares may sell near the peak price, but with so many to sell, the price will likely come tumbling down rapidly. As it falls below £50, Blunt can start exercising put options at £50 and thus lock in a highly profitable price spread over the cost he paid for the shares when he exercised the calls. The issuers of the puts become suckers too.

Stock manipulations like this occur throughout the history of markets. They are not exceptions; they are the rule. However, if you expect perfect markets, if you expect that current market prices reflect all available information, even that of insiders, in other words, if you believe textbook finance theory, then you will contribute to the pool of unwary sucker capital waiting for the next projector to take your money. Projectors do not always succeed. They can fail if someone with equivalent market power discerns what is happening and locks up many call options and shares before they can. This is called front running. As projectors inflate a bubble any wise opponents might take each step just before they do, making it more costly for them to buy and forcing prices down before they can sell. Typically it is large brokers who might have enough information to discern a pattern of trades portending a strategic operation, which is why projectors typically spread their trades among multiple brokers and why Blunt trusted his cousin with the core trades that set up his position. Manipulations can be very profitable, but only if the projector has reliable market power and the advantages of deception.

Three bubbles influence the destiny of nations

Economists typically treat bubbles as unfortunate accidents of history, intemperate moments of collective madness during which normally efficient markets generate statistically unusual error terms. This view was articulated in the widely cited popular nineteenth century book by MacKay (2013) and more recently by Kindleberger and Aliber (2011). Many public commentators treated the recent worldwide financial crisis as a similar sort of random madness. Corporatism, by contrast, understands bubbles as battles in financial markets between rival bear and bull interests who have staked large positions on the outcome of their respective market bets. Rather than being odd and extra-ordinary moments of error, bubbles are the strategic battles of the capitalist age. Like battles in war, there are self-conscious and identifiable "generals" on each side, sometimes discerned by historians, who are inflating or deflating a bubble strategically for private gain. Like decisive battles in war, they often have extraordinary effects on the redistribution of power, public and private. Yet compared with the highly visible public spectacles of war, their machinations are necessarily concealed at the time and too often ignored by historians subsequently. Very few dig deep enough or find sufficient remaining evidence to uncover what actually transpired.

Although boom-and-crash cycles had been occurring for centuries, the first famous international financial crisis involved the very similar twin bubbles inflated in France and Britain in quick succession during 1719–20. Though the strategic purpose behind both bubbles was very similar, the results diverged markedly. While the Mississippi Bubble soured France on corporate banks and financial markets for a century, Britain's South Sea Bubble, though it ruined many investors and plunged the economy into a recession, was a great success for reducing the cost of British debt and expanding the power of the Bank of England. The divergent outcome of these twin bubbles may be a core reason why France suffered, by the end of the century, debt default, a revolution, and defeat in war, whereas the largest British corporations increased their power and Britain came out on top in the competition among mercantilist powers.

One of the most interesting recent studies of the mercantile era is *The Rise of Financial Capitalism* by Larry Neal (1990). It is as fascinating for what it leaves out as for what it includes. Neal is strongly influenced by the Platonism of neoclassical perfect market ideology, so he cannot easily see what he often shows, despite himself. He narrates how modern international financial markets emerged and new financial products and methods were developed and applied. It is a tale of teleological ascent toward the efficient markets of today. Like all market aficionados, Neal overlooks the growing power and strategic action of financial capitalists in favor of the Platonic singularity, "the market." If I were to rewrite his book, I would change the title to *The Rise of Financial Capitalists*, to focus more on the strategic intent of private investors. Yet Neal does show interesting data showing how the two bubbles were linked by the flow of investor capital into and out of both bubbles from abroad, especially Amsterdam and Hamburg. They were demonstrably international financial crises fueled by hot money, much like those in recent decades.

Both bubbles were designed by their projectors for similar purposes. Useful details are found in Wennerlind (2011). England and France had accumulated huge sovereign debts fighting each other during the quarter century following 1689. Much of that debt was illiquid and at high interest rates, often over 10 percent. The leaders of both countries were in a race to reduce the cost of this accumulated debt and restore their credit for the next round of fighting. John Law, a Scottish gambler, stock jobber, and drifter, was the projector behind the French scheme. John Blunt and George Caswall developed a similar scheme in Britain. Both projects were designed to reduce government debt service burden by what is now called a debt-equity swap while creating huge new corporations, modeled on a hybrid of the Bank of England and the various East India companies, that would buy up most of the government debt as its principal capital stock and make new low-interest loans to the government while also, by reducing the cost of the existing government debt, improve the government's credit with the public and thus its ability to raise new public loans at lower rates. The new corporations would in turn be granted new monopoly trading privileges by law that would hopefully enhance the value of their stock. The exact details of both bubbles are still somewhat shrouded in mystery, in part because many of the historians who have examined the primary documents do not themselves understand the financial tactics involved.

The British scheme was conceived first but took longer to develop as the political prerequisites for executing it took some time to put in place. A serious financial crisis rocked Britain during 1709–10 as the war with France and Spain dragged on. The Whig-dominated government was overthrown, replaced by a new Tory government more interested in peace. The first corporate casualty of the crisis was the new Whig-dominated rival to the original East India Company. Soon after the Whigs came to power in the wake of the Glorious Revolution of 1688, the Whig-dominated Parliament bridled at the power of the Tory-dominated monopoly corporations such as the Royal Africa and East India companies, not the least because they were a means of financing monarchs largely beyond the control of Parliament, but also because of their rampant corruption of the political process. The Whigs thus sponsored corporations of their own to compete against these, the Bank of England and a new East India Company. For some years England had two and even a smaller company chartered in Scotland (Robins 2006: 50–52). However, the financial crisis hit the East India companies hard, and induced them to merge in 1709, thus curbing one Whig challenge to existing royally chartered monopolies.

During the same crisis Blunt and Caswall conceived an ambitious scheme to refinance Britain's sovereign debt and at the same time create a rival to the remaining pinnacle of private Whig power, the Bank of England. The two apparently founded the scheme on the success of their much smaller Sword Blade Company in building its own value by buying up devalued government debts. Sword Blade, like many companies chartered in this period, was ostensibly chartered for another purpose, making swords, but like other companies in the hands of projectors and stock jobbers, acted more as a vehicle for leveraging other people's money on behalf of their financial manipulations. They gained Robert Hartley, newly appointed head of the Board of Treasury, as their key ally in government. Queen Anne had appointed Hartley to replace Francis Godolphin since he and his Whig allies in the Bank of England had tried to withhold credit from her war effort unless she guaranteed continued support for Whig ministers. Hartley understood that the plan Blunt and Caswall proposed could break the Bank of England's dominant role as financier to the Crown and thus undermine the last bastion of Whig power.

Blunt and Caswall proposed to create a new huge joint-stock company, the biggest in Britain, the South Sea Company, to purchase the entire unsecured sovereign debt, most of it in the form of heavily discounted bills of various government departments. The Bank of England had performed similar operations in 1697 and 1709, thus greatly expanding its own capital and influence. South Sea would purchase the debt by selling its stock to the public. The stock would be more attractive because South Sea was also to be guaranteed a monopoly on all trade with Latin America, including slaves, expected to flourish soon since one of the government's war aims was to force Spain to grant trading rights with its colonies in the Americas. Hartley presented the plan to Parliament in 1711 and secured its enactment against objections from Whig opponents. Though the peace settlement at the Treaty of Utrecht in 1713 did grant limited British trading rights with Spanish America, largely selling slaves bought from the Royal Africa Company, another Tory concern, to buy sugar and rum, it was insufficient for the ambitions of the huge new company, chartered four times larger than the short-lived new East India Company the Whigs had created in 1698, which had been merged into the old one in 1709. South Sea did sell nearly all it stock within a year and buy up the heavily discounted government debt, which was a profitable deal since the Tory peace plan would cause the value of this debt to rise. The Queen knighted Hartley as a reward.

Yet the stock of the South Sea Company languished since the trading rights granted by treaty were resisted in practice by recalcitrant Spanish officials, predated by pirates, and less profitable than expected because of increasing competition in the slave trade. The company turned increasingly to smuggling rather than legal trade. Queen Anne had Hartley arrested but then was herself soon deposed and replaced by a dynasty of German Hanoverian monarchs, starting with George I. The Spanish retaliated for South Sea smuggling by seizing the company's assets and ending its legal trade in 1718, prompting a new war with Britain, but fortunately not involving France, still struggling under burden of its debt from the last war. British victories on the sea enabled the South Sea Company to resume highly profitable smuggling operations, and thus set the stage for an even more ambitious scheme and the bubble of 1720.

Chartered companies had shown their value in buying up short-term and unsecured government debt. That still left significant government debts mostly in the form of long-term annuities that paid high interest and were largely illiquid. In other words, it was difficult for their original owners to resell them if they needed cash or if they felt the risk owning government debt was excessive. The government was also locked into high interest payments, since many of the annuities endured for decades, some until 1807. The government had no right to redeem them. Most had been secured against specific tariff and excise taxes, making it impossible for the government to use the sequestered tax revenues as collateral for new debt. Meanwhile the Whigs had returned to power and would dominate for decades to come. They were interested in reducing the government debt burden to allow for a new round of trade finance and mercantile wars, but this would only be possible if the massive annuity debt could somehow be liquidated.

The projectors of the South Sea Company came to the rescue with a new scheme to induce annuity holders to exchange their government debt contracts for new shares of South Sea stock. While the East India Company and the Bank of England refused to sell their portion of the sovereign debt to South Sea, that left over £30 million up for grabs in private hands. Buying most of it with new capital would make South Sea vastly bigger than the other two large corporations. The trick would be to convince annuity owners to give up the high interest but illiquid annuities, paying 8 to 12 percent interest, for highly liquid South Sea stock paying a dividend somewhat less than this, but promising significant capital gains if a bubble in its value could be conjured. It was time for Blunt to unveil on a far larger scale his bullish talent for blowing bubbles that he first practiced with the lead mine in 1693.

The net result is clear, though the private details of this operation are less clear because few are revealed by the available sources. The par value of South Sea stock was £100. During its first nine years it had typically traded in the range of £80 to £120. During 1720 it reached over £800 per share before collapsing back to near its normal range. During the ascent of the bubble, South Sea projectors eagerly bulled the stock by every available means, including inflated stories of its successes and highly attractive terms of sale. As in nearly every bubble, purchasers of stock are encouraged to buy more than they could afford if they paid the full price both by the company lending cash to potential buyers, including many political supporters in Parliament, and allowing buyers to pay in installments, with as little as 10 or 20 percent of the price due initially. These initial buyers could then quickly resell into a highly excited rising market, thereby profiting enormously with little of their own capital at risk if they had leveraged their purchases, as many did. Call options were probably used as well, as in the case of Blunt's lead mine corner. The net result was a huge success for refinancing, since the vast majority of the illiquid annuities were traded for South Sea stock.

The many private winners and losers are hard to specify now, but it is clear that anyone foolish enough to buy into the rising bubble and hold their stock lost heavily when it collapsed. Others, including apparently much of the hot money coming from savvy foreign speculators, were experienced enough to recognize a bubble for what it was and liquidated before it burst. Some may have bought put options on the stock to facilitate liquidation as it fell. Certainly some of the insiders who promoted the bubble knew it was mostly wind and must have sold before it collapsed. The biggest losers were likely many excited but inexperienced investors who rushed in to profit from the rising stock. Many of them bought stock with borrowed money and were bankrupted when the bubble collapsed, which contributed to the financial crisis that followed.

There is also evidence that the Bank of England, always suspicious of this rival company, organized the bears on a selling spree of South Sea stock that probably included short selling. They may also have raised their discount rate on bills issued by known projectors of the stock to rein in their credit and thus staunch the bubble. There is no doubt that the Bank of England ended up as one of the big winners, since in the aftermath the South Sea Company, suffering under the defaults of many of those to whom it had lent funds to buy its own stock, was forced to sell much of its government debt to the Bank of England, which roughly doubled in size as a result and secured its own monopoly by law against further challenges by the Bubble Act passed by Parliament in the aftermath of the crisis. Many parliamentarians were among those who were burned in the scheme. The South Sea Company itself survived, unlike the companies created by John Law in the more calamitous Mississippi Bubble scheme in France.

John Law's scheme was quite similar. It fact, it seems that the two plans advanced in rivalry with each other, since the one to best succeed would also secure the debt-raising and thus war-fighting ability of their state and therefore secure the lucrative gratitude of their king. Indeed Law did depend more than Blunt and other South Sea projectors on the generous trust of the monarch, Louis XV. The only significant addition in Law's scheme to the South Sea blueprint was that his newly created corporate bank, Banque Générale, would also be a bank of issue, like the Bank of England, issuing paper bank notes in profusion to help finance customer purchases of both its own stock and that of Law's centerpiece, the new Mississippi Company. Law's trading company suffered from the additional disadvantage that its area of monopoly trade, France's Louisiana territory, was a scarcely developed wilderness, so his scheme relied on even more fantastic hype than that of the South Sea Company, which at least had the promise of trade with the well-developed territories of Spanish America. Many of the privileges that bulled Law's companies, including a tax farm that placed most of France's taxes into Law's hands, were subject to the whim of a powerful monarch less restrained than George I by countervailing institutions like Parliament. What was given could easily be taken away again as the bubble became untenable and was attacked by jealous rivals. Otherwise the details are similar, including the installment buying of stock. However, Law and his companies, unlike the British projectors, were bankrupted and ruined when the bubble collapsed.

The drastic failure of Law's scheme contrasts with the relative success of the South Sea Bubble. Although the South Sea Company's wilder ambitions failed and the Bank of England gained at its expense, at least Britain still had a highly successful bank of issue and several powerful trading companies. Furthermore, the debt scheme worked. British debt costs fell dramatically from that point on, making it much cheaper for the British to leverage their private wealth to finance the repeated defeat of France in the wars to come, with the exception of the War of American Independence. France, by contrast, was soured on banks and bank notes for nearly a century to come, falling farther behind Britain and Netherlands in its ability to leverage private wealth cheaply. Instead, France fell under the thrall of a cartel of 40 tax farmers who extracted a high price in taxes for their loans to the king. The French Revolution of 1789 was a direct result of King Louis XVI calling an assembly of the estates to vote new taxes to secure debt refinancing. The commoners were heavily taxed even though the king's share of per capita revenue was not so high compared with that of the governments of England and the Netherlands. The difference in France was that much of the tax paid by the public was diverted to the purses of the tax farmers, 28 of whom paid the price with their heads when the revolution overthrew not only the king, but also his hated tax farmers (Brewer 1988).

Finally, the third bubble mentioned in the title of this section helped give rise to another revolution, the American. It was another victory of the Bank of England against bullish speculators using as their vehicle the other great mercantile company, the East India Company. The East India Company had limped along during most of the seventeenth century under the shadow of the much larger and more powerful Dutch company. After 1688, the Netherlands and England were allied, but the Dutch company began to suffer from competition by newer French companies, especially along the southeast coast of India. Meanwhile the British company prospered, especially from its base in Calcutta on the northeast coast. By the early part of the eighteenth century, the united British company began to overtake the Dutch (Robins 2006: 55). Then it scored an enormous success when it was attacked by an impetuous local ruler. After the company's army defeated him, the nominal ruler of northern India, the Mughal emperor, granted the company a tax farm for the entire Bengal province of about 20 million people, as populous as France and several times larger than Britain. The new ruler of the province was a puppet of the British company since he depended on it for his revenue and on its army for his defense. The company evolved from being primarily a trading company to being effectively the ruler of Bengal, gaining an expected net tax income of several million pounds per year on top of its trading revenue. From this base, the company began to expand its control over more and more of India.

East India Company stock had been trading fairly steadily for decades in the range of £150–200, except for a brief spike to £420 during the South Sea Bubble, and paying reliable dividends in the range of 6 to 8 percent. From a wartime low in 1757 after the initial disaster in Calcutta, the stock nearly doubled to £276 in 1769 after some years of heavy trading and contentious annual board meetings as rival investor groups struggled to gain control of the now more lucrative revenue stream from plunder and the massive tax farm. Dividend payments were raised, which also helped bull the stock price. But there was danger on the horizon. The company had traded the steady profits of a trading company for the uncertain fortunes of a foreign military enterprise. It became embroiled in decades of war against Indian rivals often financed and equipped by the French. The costs of war and falling tax revenue that followed from the greedy hoarding of food, which exacerbated a famine, quickly depleted the supposed windfall of the tax farm. The stock bubble was based on exaggerated expectations of wealth from extracting the surplus of India's richest province. It burst in 1769 and began a slide from which it did not recover until the 1820s. Gradually the falling fortunes of Britain's greatest bull unleashed broader bear sentiment, again apparently orchestrated by the Bank of England, reaching a nadir in 1772.

The British Parliament stepped in to save the East India Company in the interest of numerous investors, but also to regulate it a little more closely, not the least because the company was in a position to drag Britain into wars started for its own profit. That effort included the Tea Act of 1773, which attempted to extend the East India Company's monopoly into North America, where its sales had dwindled to almost nothing because of colonialist boycotts in protest of British tax policies. Colonial merchants had replaced East India Company tea with their own smuggled product. Meanwhile the company's London warehouses were filling with huge unsold stocks of tea, so it prepared to take advantage of the Tea Act by shipping 2,000 chests of tea to Boston, Charleston, New York, and Philadelphia. Colonial activists boarded the East India Company ships in Boston and threw the tea overboard, prompting the British to reinforce their garrison in Boston. The colonials reacted by arming their militias. The American Revolution broke out two years later over this growing tension. Modern American conservatives style themselves as the "Tea Party" in honor of these Boston patriots, but without realizing the irony that their revolt was as much against monopolistic corporate power as it was against governmental taxation.

Bubbles and other forms of financial crises need to be examined for what they are: decisive battles between contending investor schemes. As in these three cases, they may have dramatic effects on the balance of both private and public power and on the future direction of political economy. Economists have unfortunately diverted attention from them by trivializing them as irrational manias and unpredictable errors. They are strategic events of the greatest importance. They deserve far closer and more informed scrutiny than they have hitherto received, at least as much as the far better documented decisive battles of war.

Economists' critique of mercantilism

One of the key reasons Adam Smith is honored above all other political economists is his vigorous support of free markets in opposition to mercantilism, epitomized in the debacle of the East India Company a few years before Smith wrote his famous *Wealth of Nations*. It is often ignored that Keynes, the most celebrated economist of the twentieth century, explained why mercantilism could benefit a country, contrary to the inherited "wisdom" of nearly every economist before and since. Keynes saw what other economists cannot because he is one of the few to consider mercantilism outside the static analysis of equilibrium markets. However, even Keynes missed key features of mercantilism because he is too focused on the economists' concern about its effect on national welfare. He neglects its importance for national and private power. Mercantilism is not just a policy for accumulating wealth within a national territory, but more importantly, for concentrating that wealth in the hands of the great merchants, financiers, and the central government. It is a strategic policy, not just an economic one. Because all economists, even Keynes, neglect private power, they ignore the significant and permanent success of mercantilism in concentrating private power.

Most economists also fail to notice that while Smith criticizes many of the elements of mercantilism, he disputes mainly a naïve form of mercantilism that assumes that the object of mercantilism is to accumulate precious metals. In fact, that was not the true object of mercantilism, but just a peacetime consequence of mercantilism working successfully. Smith discerns the true object of mercantilism without attributing it to mercantilists per se. That object was maintaining a positive balance of foreign trade in order to finance foreign wars. By the Thirty Years' War (1618–48), "Military success usually depended on the success of merchant bankers in moving funds to purchase and sustain mercenaries" (Neal 1990: 12) and then refinancing the accumulating expenses using private corporate monopolies. Wars ended or were lost when financing ran out. The most successful mercantile powers developed the most effective private financial systems.

Mercantilism is principally a policy for centralizing power and financing foreign wars. Economists and others have miscast it as strengthening the state against private interests. Instead, it involves simultaneously centralizing public and private power against foreign and domestic rivals. Social theory, especially since Hegel, has drawn a hard line between the public and private spheres, between power of the state and the interests of the society, exemplified by the market. State and market are both Platonic ideal types that do not represent actual lines of conflict. No monarch ever centralized power without allies in the private sector whose power was also elevated along with his. It would be more useful to view dynasties as business ventures asserting certain monopoly rights within a designated territory, not unlike the great private trading companies that emerged during the seventeenth century. Monarchs and private companies equally required financing and used many of the same methods to acquire it. The large dynastic wars that prevailed in early modern Europe for centuries largely disappeared after 1815 because they had become too risky in relation to the expected profit. Even if monarchs wanted to pursue war, the private financiers they depended on grew increasingly dubious while becoming more powerful and better organized themselves. Many of the institutions of private power erected during the mercantilist era endured more successfully than the dynasties they had financed, particularly as they switched more toward financing private commerce and industry.

Several competing powers pursuing mercantilism within the same international system creates what economists call a zero-sum game. That is, victory for one is a loss for another. All countries cannot run a positive balance of trade at the same time. Those who succeed best secure the resources to finance their foreign wars more effectively. Success in war also increases the value of the private monopolies cooperating with the state, thereby making it less difficult to finance the next war. Victory creates a virtuous circle; defeat a vicious circle. Among private merchants and financiers the most bullishly aggressive gained or lost the most depending on their specific bets and timing, but more conservative bears gradually centralized their power around the largest banks and came to dominate the international financial system during the nineteenth century.

Mercantilism's demise amidst revolution and war

Realists believe that states motivated by a unifying national interest animate patterns of international relations. Generally they are wrong. But there are some periods of history when societies are more unified and therefore act more coherently in international politics. The mercantilist era was one such period. Others, treated in future chapters, include imperialism and communism. These share some features with mercantilism. Most importantly, governments cannot be unified when business is fundamentally divided. Polarized business creates a two-party state. A "one-party" state can thrive only when private interests are also unified or at least dominated by great hegemonic corporations. Mercantilism was a sustained but flawed effort to unify the major private interests of early modern societies. It failed for two reasons: success in one state presumed that other major states would be non-mercantilist or at least fail at mercantilism in effect, a zero-sum game; and internal contradictions emerged between rival interest blocs, between monopolistic trading companies and their free trade rivals, including ultimately the great financial corporations like the Bank of England and private banks like those of the Rothschild family. But, ironically, free trade was barely possible until Britain came out on top in the series of mercantile wars and secured the seas for all traders. Imperialism and communism failed for similar reasons, as we shall see in following chapters. The internal contradictions that split mercantilism are highlighted below.

Theorists like Hume and Rousseau believed that the war-prone international system generated by European mercantilism would tend toward a balance of power. Their insights are the foundation of the modern realist theory of international relations. But they overlooked a crucial transnational business actor that tended to subvert such balancing: finance. International financiers had no interest in lending to losers. Finance tended to lend to and concentrate in the country that most consistently won within a system of mercantilist states. International relations theorists call this tendency to ally with the winner bandwagoning. It is the opposite of balancing.

The American (referring to all the Americas, not just the United States) and French revolutions helped create an international civil war in the world political economy that bears comparison with the similar circumstances of the two world wars, which likewise occurred in the midst of aborted attempts to unify societies by unifying the private sector around nationalist interests. They are part of a common phenomenon. The second species of revolution was the industrial revolution, which disrupted mercantilist political economy in much the same way that twentieth century business internationalism subverted both imperialism and communism. These two revolutions transformed every aspect of international relations, undermining the balance of power, limited war, and national unity. Nations bifurcated into rival interest blocs. In a pattern as old as Thucydides's portrayal of the Peloponnesian War, international wars are most destructive and all-enveloping when they are simultaneously civil wars rending most nations. The ultimate British victory in the war against Napoleon drew its divisive energy from Britain's pioneering role in the industrial revolution. The British war effort depended on the armies of its continental European allies, but also, less obviously, on massive voluntary financial contributions of continental investors in British bonds, in effect voting for British victory from within the French empire with their private capital (Neal 1990). It was this financial outflow that crippled Napoleon and allowed the British to pay ever larger subsidies to the other great powers to keep resuming the fight against him, even after repeated decisive defeats, until victory was finally theirs. Polarization between Britain and France exacerbated the contradictions of mercantilism within both.

The French Revolution did favor the development of native capitalism, but its wars and the insecurity of the propertied elite drove much liquid wealth to Britain as a more secure haven. Furthermore, despite Napoleon's conquest of most of the continent, in the absence of a technology such as railroads, trade still flowed much cheaper by sea, which was dominated by Britain because of its string of victories in the mercantilist era. So the bread-and-butter of international finance – trade credits and insurance – remained centered in London. Napoleon's protectionist Continental System failed because it drove all the feudal landed wealth of Europe into alliance with Britain. For feudal interests, Britain was an ally for multiple reasons: (1) British financiers lent them money to finance their grain exports and fight their wars against the Revolution in the interest of preserving their feudal property; (2) London capital markets provided a safe haven for their liquid wealth, giving continental investors (including feudal landlords) a monetary stake in ultimate British victory; and (3) British factories offered them a cheaper source for manufactures than local producers, giving them an incentive to smuggle rather than cooperate with the French-imposed prohibitions on imports from Britain. Thus the irony that while capitalist industrialists in Britain were antagonistic to feudal remnants in their own country, they could profitably ally with feudal and slave-owner interests abroad. On the other hand, nascent capitalist interests abroad tended to be their adversaries as they moved to protect their home markets from British competition.

8   The hegemony of free trade

> British loans and investments in foreign lands first attained substantial volume
> in that same era – the first half of the nineteenth century – in which British
> industry and commerce found their growth by supplying the rest of the world.
> Like those who carried on industry and trade for their own profit, those who
> had capital to invest ... Their affairs, they argued, were best run, judged both
> by their own interest and by the national interest, without government inter-
> ference. To this *laissez faire* argument official opinion subscribed. Such a view
> was natural in the country which did not impose legal reserve requirements for
> banks, which permitted gold to enter or pass out without control, which left to
> private individuals the direction of the Bank of England, and which allowed
> the Stock Exchange, as a private institution, to manage itself.
>
> Herbert Feis (1930: 83)

The era of "British" hegemony, comprising most of the nineteenth century,
confounds both liberalism and realism. Liberalism, especially insofar as it has
adopted hegemonic stability theory, sees British power as essential to liberalizing
the world trading system and stabilizing the world currency system using a
gold standard managed by the Bank of England. Yet as Feis correctly notes,
the Bank of England, though like all privately owned corporations, publically
chartered, was controlled by private interests, specifically the greatest of the
London merchants and merchant bankers. The success of its operations is less
a feature of British state power than of the enormous credit and market
power of the merchant and financial interests it collectively represented. British
naval hegemony throughout this period was not trivial for the liberalization of
world trade outside of Europe, since it may have deterred the sort of private
chartered trading companies that flourished under mercantilism from again
carving out significant areas of the globe for their own exclusive monopolies.
The Royal Navy in some small ways helped British business open large areas
of the underdeveloped world to foreign trade, but naval hegemony was not
necessary for this since many lesser powers, including the USA, accomplished
parallel penetrations in various parts of the world. Yet it was not primarily
the power of the British state that opened the nineteenth century to trade, but
the power of the private interests represented by British *and allied foreign*

business interests against resistance both at home and abroad. This period is often called the "first globalization" by liberals, who consider recent decades as the second, but I consider this the second globalization and count the mercantilist era as the first. This liberal second globalization was not engineered by British subjects alone, but an international alliance of business interests. Thus I refer to this as the era of free trade hegemony, abandoning the more narrow term, "British hegemony."

Realists and most liberals have the story backwards. It is not primary British military hegemony that made British business success possible, but British business success that enabled the British victory over Napoleon and also financed British naval hegemony. British business success threatened some foreign competitors but also gained British interests powerful allies eager for access to British goods, markets, and financing. In polarized political economy, most initiatives threaten some and provide opportunities for others. The resulting alignments of friends and foes transcend national boundaries and thus should not be conflated with specific territorial states. For example, there was little specifically "British" about the German-Jewish Rothschild banking family, the single most powerful financial group throughout this period, although one of the five Rothschild brothers did set up a powerful branch of the family bank in London and was eventually knighted by Queen Victoria while representing Rothschild interests on the board of the Bank of England. The Rothschild and other similarly cosmopolitan banking interests were a large part of the power behind the "British" hegemony.

Liberals also overestimate the role of laws, rules, and norms in governing the international system. Whereas they are correct that distinctive practices characterize this era, the key question is why. Both before and after this liberal period, powerful private trading groups carved out spheres of influence for monopoly domination. The free trade era, on the other hand, occurred concurrently with the first industrial revolution. Whereas the principal interest of the great trading corporations of the mercantile era had been importing the exotic products of foreign lands, the industrial revolution stimulated the export interest of thousands of firms producing products very competitively by mechanical means. The British East India Company had come under criticism during the 1772 crisis for neglecting the promotion of British industrial exports, paying for imports with silver exports instead. Critics of mercantilism like Adam Smith argued that removing the chartered privileges of monopolies would better serve the growth of trade, allowing each merchant and manufacturer to strive for their own best interest. The free trade drive of these rising industrial interests came to be called "Manchester liberalism," since that English city was the center of the thriving clothing and textile business at the center of the first industrial revolution. Manchester's liberalism contrasted with the great merchant and banking houses that had dominated the monopolistic mercantile period from London.

Finance too was evolving, with the increasing separation of financial and mercantile activities. Whereas merchant banking had predominately involved the short-term discounting of bills of exchange financing primarily trade, the long series of mercantile wars had created an enormous accumulation of long-term government debt in the form of negotiable bonds and annuities. Short-term bill markets can easily accommodate fluctuations in prices and interest rates. They suffer general crisis only when war interrupts trade or the creditworthiness of major issuers comes into question, often because bills are diverted from financing trade to funding unstable speculative operations, such as we examined in the previous chapter. Long-term debt securities, on the other hand, are more sensitive to gradual diminution during periods of inflation and war, such as during the last decades of the eighteenth century. Bond holder interests, including not only rich investors, but also banks issuing securities and those with large portfolios of government debt, like the Bank of England, begin to form a powerful bearish constituency for price stability, if not deflation. While historical price indices are not particularly accurate, the period of free trade hegemony and the gold standard seems to have been the period of greatest deflation in modern European history. Prices both before and after were more unstable and inflationary. It was the golden age for bond holders.

This enormous accumulation of government debts by 1815 also created among this bond holder community a powerful peace interest. Nothing would depress the value of this vast bond wealth more quickly than a resumption of war among the European great powers. Periods of peace during the mercantile era often resulted from the exhausted credit of the major powers, but by its end, with more and more of the total debt converted to long-term bonds, the peace interest of the bond holders became more powerful than ever and the accumulated debt harder to pay down. Realists generally see a continuity of multipolar balance of power from at least the seventeenth century through 1945, but they typically overlook the distinctiveness of the period from 1815 to 1914, during which international conflict and rivalry remained common, but war became much more rare.

Metallic monetary systems and the role of private banks

Monetary systems based on gold or silver prevailed for most countries for most of the period from 1819 to 1914. Economists have caused confusion about how these operated by conflating two disparate categories into a single abstract concept called the "money supply." The supply and demand for the monetary base metal, whether gold or silver, did help determine the value of money and thus also influenced the general price level. However, contrary to textbook economics, the supply and demand for these metals was not determined in free markets. It had much to do with private power and strategy. The details are known to some historians, but the impact of this knowledge has never been reflected in political economy. Furthermore, the supply and demand for the metallic standard of value was never the sole nor typically the primary determinant of the price level, contrary to the commonplace textbook explanation based on the quantity theory of money. Even without varying the quantity of the monetary base metal, credit could flexibly expand and contract and therefore influence both the general price level and also the specific prices of assets subject to bullish demand, as in the case of asset bubbles. Credit is much broader than what economists define as "money" in their concept of the money supply.

In particular, the credit supply is influenced by the state of the bill market. Bills of exchange are not defined as money by economists, though, more perceptively, business people often refer to the bill market as the "money market." Likewise, economic textbooks seldom make clear that the most quoted short-term interest rates are typically not loan rates, such as one would actually pay as interest, but are instead the yields on typical bills, that is, the annualized percentage increase in value between the discounted market price of a bill today and the face value the bill promises to pay at maturity.

A major reason why economists do not want to call bills of exchange "money" is that if they did it would draw attention to private power, since the bill market has never been controlled (though it can be influenced) by governments. It is not necessary to consider bills as money, as long as one is willing to give up the concept of "money supply" as anything important and instead focus on the credit supply, which certainly does include bills. However, if the bill market is ignored, then it is impossible to understand the business cycle or any of the rich dimensions of private power and strategy.

Most people believe that governments in some way control the supply of money, thus it is hard for them to understand the freedom possible in the bill market. Through most of modern history in most commercially developed countries, in principle almost anyone can issue a bill and nobody is legally limited in the number or paper value of the bills they can issue. The only limit is the practical limit of one's perceived creditworthiness. Perceptions of creditworthiness necessarily involve private power and strategy, as we shall see. A bill is a short-term bond, typically a zero coupon bond, that is, paying no interest. As with any bond, it is a promise by the issuer to pay the specified face value on the bill's maturity date, which is any date in the future designated by the issuer, but typically a few months to a year. Its current market value is some discount below the face value depending on the typical discount rate in the current bill market plus perhaps some additional discount if the issuer's perceived creditworthiness is below that of the best issuers. Some bills, for example, mine, might not be acceptable to any discounter, so they would have no market value. However, the judgment of whether to accept any particular bill and at what discount rate is always within the power of each discounter. It is an element of private credit power.

Though in theory anyone can issue bills, in practice only the bills of banks, governments, and creditworthy large businesses, including big merchants, are routinely accepted as means of payment. Business people routinely accept bills as means of payment since they expect them to be negotiable, in other words, they can sell them to others to realize cash. Typically merchants receiving a bill will deposit it in their bank for credit to their account. The value deposited depends on their bank's assessment of the appropriate discount rate for that issuer. The bank's judgment of the value of the bill may differ from that of the merchant who first accepted it. The bank may have more or different information about either the specific creditworthiness of that issuer or the likely future condition of the economy by the time the bill matures. That is, the bank may be more bearish or bullish than the merchant who sells the bill to the bank, according to its information and strategy.

Economists define a special role for what they call "the central bank," which is by assumption under the control of the government and thus implementing the government's Platonically ideal "monetary policy." There are at least two errors in this conceptualization. First of all, there is no necessity that a country has only one central bank. Hong Kong, for example, for most of its history, had two: the Hong Kong and Shanghai Banking Corporation (HSBC) and the Chartered Bank of India, both privately owned and led. This example also contradicts a second myth about "the" central bank, it need not be government owned or even government controlled. Through most of history, most of what economists call "central banks" were private corporations, like the Bank of England, the Banque de France, and the Bank of the United States, three of the most important during the era under consideration, although the latter was destroyed by President Jackson and his supporters early in this period.

Although these "central banks," like all private corporations, were chartered by law and thus subject to certain rules established by governments, they were owned by private stockholders and controlled by private boards elected by those stockholders. None of these were government employees or appointees. Later central banking systems, like the US Federal Reserve system established in 1913, included elements of both public and private power in their governance. In fact, any bank can exercise the functions and powers of a "central bank" within the bill market. Until the twentieth century at the earliest, central banking has never been a governmental power. Even today, the only practical requirement for acting as a central bank is having a size large enough to wield effective market power. Thus what makes a bank a "central bank" is not any specific legal mandate, but merely sufficient size.

A large bank can act effectively in the bill market by virtue of two things: the impact of its credit judgments on the market as a whole and the inside information it gains as a large bank handling the credit of a large number of borrowers. For example, a large private corporate bank like the Bank of England handles such a large volume of bill discounts from so many different issuers that on any typical day it would have a statistically significant sample of the total quantity of bills outstanding. This gives such a large bank means to estimate whether there are any bill issuers who are excessively bullish in issuing credit relative to what the bank knows about the issuer's business and capital. Many private banks also make loans to private businesses that may also issue bills. Loans are not usually given without examining the credit-worthiness of the potential borrower, providing the bank with further inside information. Any bank, not just a central bank, has several options when offered bills by customers. Bankers can discount the bill at any particular discount rate they think appropriate given what they know about the issuer or they can refuse to accept the bill. During a general financial crisis, many bills are refused, potentially bankrupting those holding them if they lack sufficient liquid reserves to cover their required payments without them. This power to say no to a bill holder or issuer is the only constraint that limits the quantity of credit issued. This is why I say it is only big bearish banks, not government, that has the power and interest to curtail private credit, but their means of doing so can reverse expectations suddenly and shockingly when bills that had always been acceptable are suddenly rejected. This is the moment when a financial crisis begins.

Economists assume credit markets are the ultimate free markets, so they are unable to grasp the significance of archival evidence of what big banks are actually able to do, if they are aware of this evidence at all. The policy of the biggest banks to accept or reject potential debtors, and the discount rates they are willing to apply to those they do accept, are extraordinarily influential among other creditors. If one of the top banks refuses to lend, others, often the most bullish, may still dare to lend, but at their peril. If they do lend to a creditor rejected by leading banks, typically they require a much higher discount, so the cost of credit is much higher for the borrower. Furthermore, it is common that if a big bank passes on a loan and others accept it, the big bank may communicate overtly through the public media and covertly through private channels why they think the borrower is a bad credit risk. Thus credit is not allocated by free markets, but by the strategic judgment of the rival banks. Bullish financiers may find their own credit threatened if they extend too much credit to customers considered dubious by the biggest banks.

If the numerous issuers do not create too many bills, prices may remain fairly stable, but there is no guarantee this will happen. When bills are issued in bullish excess, some prices must rise, but which prices rise depend on which specific goods or assets are in greatest demand. Rising prices do not necessarily jeopardize the gold or silver value of the currency. This is guaranteed not by laws of government, but by the sufficiency of specie reserves held by the big banks. How much is enough is never an exact science. This depends on the state of the business cycle and the concerns of various interests, including the shareholders and managers of the big banks themselves. Any particular bank that is running low on specie is usually able to borrow more from a bank that has extra if its solvency is not in question. However, if confidence in paper credit as means of payment collapses and many people scramble to acquire assets of more substantial value, such as gold, there are never enough to go around. It is like a game of musical chairs. Many businesses will be unable to meet contractual payments and will fail.

It is crucial to understand the bill market, because so few people are aware of its importance, but another form of circulating credit is bank notes, which are more familiar to people as paper money. Until the twentieth century, most bank notes were issued only by private banks, with a few exceptions like the "greenbacks" issued by the US Treasury during the Civil War. Original issues of paper notes, for example by the Bank of England shortly after its founding in 1694, were typically in the form of loans to the government, though notes issued by American banks during the nineteenth century were often loans to individuals or businesses. Most people are not aware that notes are a form of credit, but they are indeed accounted as such by the issuing banks.

Although the terms "note" and "bill" are sometimes used interchangeably, in this book I use them consistently with the most common banking practice. Notes differ from bills in that notes are not intended to trade at a discount and do not have a maturity date, thus they do not have the implicit interest rate that bills have based on the difference between their discount and their face value due in the future. Notes are also payable on demand, that is, the issuing bank pledges to redeem them at any time, not just on the maturity date, for silver or gold coins equivalent to their face value, though this connection of notes to the value of metallic money ended during the twentieth century.

Bills and notes are somewhat different in behavior, but almost equally liquid most of the time, especially high quality bills like those of governments or big businesses. The smallest purchases are made with metal coins of intrinsic value, also called commodity money. Slightly larger purchases and payments are transacted using bank notes, sometimes called bank money or, if government issued, fiat money. However, for centuries most large business and government transactions have used some form of credit instrument, including especially bills of exchange. Nathaniel Rothschild said during the 1890 financial crisis that the failure of Barings Brothers bank threatens "a catastrophe [which] would put an end to the commercial habit of transacting all business of the world by bills in London" (Ferguson 1999: 342). At that time, such a severe cataclysm was averted. Nevertheless, when bills lose value rapidly, it causes a financial crisis or panic. When notes are suddenly discounted below their face value, this causes a currency crisis and likely also a foreign exchange crisis.

It was extremely important for the balance between bears and bulls during the nineteenth century that in key countries, such as Britain, the private corporation that economists treat as the "central bank" also had a legal monopoly on issuing bank notes. All banks could, of course, also issue and discount bills. In some other countries, including France until 1848 and the USA, many banks could legally issue both notes and bills. In the USA this multiplicity was even retained under the Federal Reserve Banks, with its 12 independent regional banks sometimes acting at cross purposes. Banking laws in various countries usually regulate note issuance to some degree, but not bills. When, as in Britain, only one bank of (note) issue existed, then that bank had a particular interest in defending the value and negotiability of its notes. Avoiding excessive note issuance, or, in the words of economists, "regulating the money supply," was in the profit interest of issuing banks since outstanding notes were a significant portion of their liabilities. It they are trading at a discount it is equivalent to bills issued by the "central bank" trading at a deeper discount than the best commercial bills, in other words, it would represent diminishing credit-worthiness and perhaps even jeopardize their solvency to the great distress of all the commercial interests that depend on currency having a reliable value, not the least of these being the owners of long-term bonds.

All banks of issue, whether having a monopoly in one country or not, defend the value of their notes and therefore their own solvency by having liquid reserves of high quality assets and by having credit relationships with other institutions that will hopefully support them in their hour of need, during a crisis. During the nineteenth century, high quality assets were not just gold and silver, but also high quality commercial bills and government bonds. These could be easily sold or used as collateral for a short-term loan whenever pay-ments were needed in a hurry. High quality commercial bills were known as "real bills," meaning they represented the real value of capital circulating in mercantile transactions, including those of government agencies, as opposed to less real bills that might be issued in excess by bullish speculators to buy into an asset bubble that could collapse to the detriment of the value of the bills. Banks also have assets in the form of loans outstanding, but these are difficult to liquidate and thus do not constitute an emergency reserve, unless as collateral for a loan from another bank.

Banks of issue concerned with the value of their circulating paper notes were the most important force defending the gold standard and thus maintaining the free convertibility of their notes to trade without discount. International con-fidence in the value of bank notes depends on the perceived creditworthiness of that bank, including its reserves. When anyone doubts the face value of a bank's notes, they may demand gold or silver coins instead. If foreigners do so, they may drain specie from that country and from that bank's reserves. This is called a foreign payments or foreign exchange crisis.

Banks of issue have several powers to defend their creditworthiness and restore their reserves to an acceptable level. They may increase the discount rate or refuse to discount the private bills of some of their more bullish customers. This means that the bank will accumulate fewer risky bills on its books and those it does buy will cost less, increasing confidence in the bank's solvency, but their "tighter monetary policy," that is, more stringent discounting policy, may also have a bearish effect on the whole economy, bursting asset bubbles, raising the cost of short-term borrowing, and thus of trade, since all trade is financed. Thus a foreign exchange crisis often leads to a domestic tightening of credit, not because this is government policy, but because it restores the creditworthiness of big banks of issue. They restore their credit by being bearish.

Alternatively, banks of issue may restore their specie reserves by directly borrowing gold or silver. During the nineteenth century, the biggest financiers in the business of making loans of specie were the Rothschilds. The Rothschild banks were the typical international lenders of last resort in the nineteenth century, much like the International Monetary Fund (IMF) since World War II. Just as with the IMF today, Rothschild specie loans to "central banks" faced with an outflow of bullion were typically conditional on the borrower restoring their credit through steps like those outlined above. Therefore, the bimetallic and later the gold standard were not regulated by governments or even ultimately by so-called "central banks" like the Bank of England or the Banque de France. Behind these stood the biggest bearish private banks, of which the Rothschild banks were the most prominent and typically among the leading players in every crisis (Ferguson 1998, 1999).

Near the beginning of this section I mentioned that the value of metallic money depended on the supply and demand for gold or silver, according to the monetary standard. Issuing notes dominated in a currency based on a metallic standard, although it does increase the "money supply," contrary to most textbooks, it does not affect the supply of specie and therefore does not affect the convertibility of money as long as the metallic standard is maintained. Of course, excessive issuance of paper money, as in the case of John Law and the Mississippi Bubble and Bank of England notes during the Napoleonic Wars, will eventually call into question the relative value of that paper and the solvency of the bank that issues it, causing a rush to trade the notes for metal and thus precipitating a devaluation of the paper currency if not the bankruptcy of the issuing bank. As long as the standard is maintained, however, it is only the supply and demand of specie relative to the supply and demand for all other goods that determines the relative value of money. When gold or silver is relatively scarce, money based on either will become more valuable relative to other goods, resulting in price deflation. When specie is relatively plentiful, inflation results. Excessive issues of credit can cause inflation too, but the precise price effects depend on how the credit is spent. If the excess credit were spent mainly to buy gold and silver, raising their relative value, the result could even be price deflation. Textbook economics ignores this. Under a metallic standard, there is no necessity that an increase in the quantity of credit will decrease the value of the currency.

On the other hand, specie is an unusual commodity. The demand for it is partly driven by consumer desire for decorative items such as jewelry and silverware. But there are also two special uses not typical of other commodities: coins and monetary reserves. During the nineteenth century nearly all coins had a face value close to the value of the metal they contained. The quantity of coins in circulation for small transactions must be renewed from time to time as coins are lost or worn out as the volume of transactions increases. Coins and bullion are also used as monetary reserves in banks, especially banks that issue notes. However, specie reserves are never sufficient to cover the outstanding paper liabilities. Bank notes in principle are convertible into coin of actual metallic value. If too many customers demand coin from a bank at the same time and the bank runs low on reserves, this is called a run on the bank. Normally it does not happen because people prefer the convenience of bank notes to heavy coins, but when it does the bank must either borrow coins from other banks or suspend convertibility of its paper notes. If the latter is not legal, a bank might have to declare bankruptcy instead. If it does suspend convertibility of its notes into coin, typically the notes will then trade at a discount to their face value, much like a bill whose issuer's credit becomes suspect. The same issue exists today, though now no paper notes are convertible to specie at fixed rates, but if their value becomes questionable, they will typically fall in value relative to the currencies of other countries and the government may suspend their free convertibility into other foreign currencies and regulate foreign transactions using exchange controls.

The supply of gold and silver has never been a perfectly free market since large mining, trading, and banking interests that produce the supply of specie may have market power. This was certainly true during the nineteenth century when the Rothschild family not only controlled the most powerful network of banks, but also a significant part of the specie supply chain, including mining, refining, and lending the specie to other banks, including so-called central banks like the Bank of England and the Banque de France (Ferguson 1998, 1999). Economists argue that central banks have a crucial role in managing financial crises as the lender of last resort to other banks in danger of failing, as in 2008. However, during the specie standard systems of the nineteenth century, when central banks faced a run on their bullion reserves, it was primarily the Rothschild network of banks that lent them the bullion to prevent devaluation of the currency or suspension of convertibility. Often the Rothschilds would require some policy changes as conditions for their loans, much as would the International Monetary Fund (IMF) making similar crisis loans today. Like the IMF, Rothschild advice was often bearish, requiring measures to tighten credit. Their choice to lend or not and under what conditions is an aspect of private credit power.

During the century from 1819, when Britain restored the gold convertibility of pound notes to 1914, when the outbreak of World War I suspended the free convertibility of nearly all currencies, there were both strong and weak currencies. Strong currencies are those that seldom suspend specie convertibility and do not devalue relative to other currencies. Strong and weak in financial terms has little relationship to military strength or weakness. IR realism believes military power is paramount, but actually currency strength is weakened by excessive war fighting. It is not even much related to national economies that are large or fast growing. Russia, for example, was fast growing, particularly late in the century, but had a weak currency. Currencies are strong when a country's businesses are not excessively bullish in issuing credit and when strong bearish banks exist to restrain bulls as necessary. Strong banks mean banks with good credit and liquid reserves. If bearish interests are too weak, excessively inflationary credit issuance is common. Whereas neoclassical economists believe it is in the interest of governments to promote price stability, typically governments are prone to deficit spending since taxes are unpopular and government spending is not. Thus governments often borrow bullishly if they can. As major debtors, they benefit from inflation insofar as it reduces the value of their debts. Therefore, the least inflation-prone countries are not those with strong governments, but those with big private banks with sufficient information about creditors to know which are over-extended and thus which bills to discount or deny. As mentioned previously, large banks are often bearish as large bond holders. Bearish banks are what make currencies strong, because they tend to restrain credit in their own interest.

Through most of the middle of the nineteenth century, Britain was the only major country on the gold standard. Other major countries were either on the silver or bimetallic standard, which was effectively also a silver standard since silver tended to become less precious relative to gold throughout the century, losing roughly half its relative value. The British pound was the strongest currency not only because it maintained the more bearish gold standard, but also because London was the commercial and financial capital of the world, with by far the largest bill and bond markets, and because England avoided expensive wars during this period. A portion of its large debt from the centuries of mercantile wars ending in 1815 was gradually paid down during the century, while other countries' debt increased significantly during periods of tension and war, weakening confidence in the value of their currencies. Generally, France, Netherlands, Belgium, Germany, Switzerland, and the Scandinavian countries had fairly strong currencies, whereas those of Russia, Austria, Italy, Spain, the Ottoman Empire, and most other small countries were weaker. The US currency was among the stronger of the bimetallic currencies, benefitting from little debt until the Civil War weakened it. It was restored to strength by the end of the 1870s when the US was induced to adopt the gold standard as a condition for Rothschild-syndicated loans (Ferguson 1999: 270, 348–49).

The leading role of the Rothschild banks in establishing the gold standard is highlighted by the fact that the second most profitable year for the family's banks before World War I was 1873, the year several major European countries, including France and Germany, adopted the gold standard. The following year the total Rothschild banking capital reached a peak not exceeded until 1889 (Ferguson 1999: 507–8). Establishing the gold standard was so profitable for the Rothschilds because they supplied much of the gold newly required as reserves. They also were the lead bank syndicating most of the loans to "central banks" to provide those reserves. The deflationary pressure of the bearish gold standard led to an immediate worldwide depression, followed by two more at roughly ten year intervals. Adoption of the gold standard was one of the principal reasons for the chronic deflation that occurred worldwide for most of the third of a century ending during the mid-1890s.

There is a close correspondence between strong currencies and exporting capital, which during the nineteenth century indicated active bond and bill markets widely used by foreigners to raise credit. By the latter part of the century, the major capital exporters in order of importance were Britain, France, Germany, USA, Netherlands, and Belgium. All these had strong currencies. Major powers that were significant capital importers include Russia, Austria (Austria-Hungary after 1867), Italy, and the Ottoman Empire, all with relatively weak currencies. As we shall see in the next section, all powers were restrained in making war by the vicissitudes of private finance, but the restraints were most telling on these capital importers who could neither finance nor supply war without support from major foreign private banks. Since warfare depended more on sophisticated machinery as the century proceeded, including railroads and armored ships, the expense of war escalated along with the debt required to sustain it. All war is financed.

Transformation of the balance of power

Britain's victory in the global civil war against Napoleon's Continental System and dramatic industrial revolution set the stage for nearly a century of British international hegemony in much the same way as the US victory in World War II set stage for the twin hegemony of the United States and business internationalism. Little noticed by realists, this fundamentally changed the functioning of what they likewise label the balance of power system. Before the French Revolution the balance of power, to the extent it functioned, was regulated by frequent limited wars, the largest of which pitted an aspiring mercantilist hegemon against an alliance of rival powers that ultimately frustrate it, in classic balance of power fashion.

During the nineteenth century British hegemony, a Concert of Europe tried to maintain the balance of power largely through diplomacy, with few wars, and no major ones. International merchant bankers, such as the Rothschild and Baring brothers, reinforced the diplomacy of states by denying credit to several would-be war-mongers, except in a few exceptional cases that prove the rule. The effectiveness of "British" diplomacy in maintaining the peace through most of the century was facilitated by an international alignment of private interests that profited from the trading patterns that free trade financial, commercial, and industrial hegemony established. The global hegemony of free traders was challenged, including within Britain itself, but protectionists, aka business nationalists, fought a rearguard action until the series of severe depressions of the later nineteenth century helped centralize and unify business in several of the major powers around a policy of protectionism at home combined with international expansion of the national sphere of economic dominance abroad, as detailed in Chapter 9. Four elements had changed to bring about what is often called the Concert of Europe: fear of the revolutionary consequences of war, application of the principle of compensation to prevent disproportionate gain by one power, and, as already mentioned, the power of banks and bondholders to prevent debt devaluation or default by denying credit needed for war. The fourth element that contributed to the Concert of Europe is examined in the next section: the development of multilateral principles of freer trade.

The French Revolution and the wars that followed for the first time put the fear of war in the old aristocracy of Europe. Until then, the ostensible purpose of the aristocratic class since its inception during medieval times had been to lead a nation's armies in war. "Aristocracy" means rule by the good, specifically, those ostensibly good as war leaders. Aristocrats had always existed as a distinct class freed from mundane labor in order to have the time to educate themselves in the arts of war. They required wealth sufficient to equip themselves as mounted warriors, at least. While their unique pretension to excellence in war had been eroded gradually during the early modern era, war had remained the preferred sports of kings and the aristocratic class as a whole.

The French Revolution shattered this in two ways. Armies led by aristocrats were repeatedly and often decisively defeated by armies led by young generals of talent but typically without aristocratic pedigree. Furthermore, the consequences of defeat were not the mere loss of a border province and the ransom of any captured leaders. The period before 1792 witnessed frequent but limited wars. Wars were limited not so much by their cost, which was often crippling enough to end them, but by their consequences for the ruling elite. During the preceding centuries war had not been as decisive as it became. The balance of power functioned to preserve not peace, but at least the continued existence of the major powers. Yet during more than two decades of revolutionary war after 1792, almost every capital city of continental Europe, from Madrid to Moscow, fell to invaders. Almost every ancient nation of Europe was overthrown and humbled by defeat and occupation. Defeat often meant replacing a dynasty, at least, if not disenfranchising the entire aristocratic class in favor of a free peasantry. The Concert of Europe endeavored to avoid such devastating revolutionary wars to preserve Europe's ruling class.

The principle of compensation was a diplomatic means of adjusting the balance of power without the risks of war and revolution. It was applied during the last decades of the eighteenth century when Russia, Prussia, and Austria, though jealous of each other's power, made a series of three agreements to divide among themselves the entire territory of Poland, which was large but weak. At the Congress of Vienna in 1815, this principle was applied in redrawing the map of Europe. The various victors were each compensated with enlarged territories that preserved enough of a balance to alarm none of them. The principle was violated during the brief but decisive wars that unified Germany and Italy, weakening both France and Austria. These unifications, however, were supported by some of the great financial powers of Europe in the interest of greater economic efficiency. The principle of compensation was again restored in a series of conferences from 1878 through 1908 that adjusted Europe's boundaries, primarily to adapt to the fading power of the Ottoman Empire, reflected not only in military weakness, but also financial weakness, which involved an international consortium of major foreign banks administering Ottoman finances.

The power of large private financiers had an enormous impact on the course of wars during the century before World War I. There were numerous instances when potential wars were averted and actual wars truncated by the refusal of the largest banks to float the bonds necessary to fund the belligerents to the full extent they desired. Major cases include the Belgian crisis of 1830, the War of Italian Unification of 1859–60, and the Russo-Turkish War of

1875–78. In other cases, one side was able to borrow abroad, but the other was not, typically resulting in a quick defeat for the side with inferior credit. A case in point was the Seven Weeks War of 1866. In a few instances, both sides borrowed abroad. In these cases, the scale of war could be larger and the duration longer, but victory inevitably went to the side with the best credit. The most important cases are the Crimean War of 1853–56, the American Civil War of 1861–65, the Franco-Prussian War of 1870–71, and the Russo-Japanese War of 1904–5. Ferguson (1999: 94) summarizes the importance of private financing for mid-century wars:

> The wars of the 1850s and 1860s were fought by states which were, by and large, strapped for cash; this more than anything else explains the importance of the role played by bankers in the period – and the substantial profits they could make. Tax bases remained narrow. Indeed, it might be argued that they were especially restricted in this period, as more and more states followed the British example of trade liberalization – Austria cutting tariffs and signing a trade agreement with the Prussian-led Zollverein in 1853, France signing a free trade treaty with Britain in 1860 – for in the short term the effect of tariff reductions was to reduce revenue until increased trade volumes filled the gap.

Multilateralism in trade

The biggest difference between trade during the mercantile era and after 1815 is that trade was increasingly governed by multilateral principles rather than the monopolistic power of specific national mercantile companies. Multilateralism is the core of liberal trade theory. Multilateralism may also be called non-discrimination. The principle is that all merchants in all countries should be able to trade freely with all other nations, with the same laws and regulations applying to all. Non-discrimination is embodied in trade treaties using the Most-Favored Nation (MFN) clause. Whenever any two nations sign a trade treaty granting each other MFN status, any reductions in trade barriers, such as tariffs, included in that or subsequent treaties, is automatically extended to all other countries that have MFN status with the signatories. Therefore each bilateral move toward lower tariffs had a broader multilateral impact, especially the Anglo-French Trade Treaty of 1860.

The first step toward multilateral trade was the opening of the former colonies of Spain and Portugal to freer trader during the last years of the Napoleonic Wars, accompanied by a wave of independence movements that created new nations all over Latin America. During mercantilism, as mentioned in the previous chapter, the trade of these territories had been dominated by companies of the colonial power, aside from smuggling and a few minor exceptions. Opening them benefitted British trade and finance, in particular, but other merchants and financiers of other countries participated as well.

Even the private trading monopolies of the victorious British were curtailed. The British Parliament revoked the monopoly privileges of the British East India Company in the India trade in 1813 and in the China trade in 1833. Subsequently, the company remained as the main governing power in India until a massive revolt in 1857 required British government intervention and the subsequent takeover of the company's remaining governing powers. The formerly mighty Dutch East India Company had already been liquidated after the French Revolutionary armies conquered the Netherlands in 1795.

Freer trade within Europe itself proceeded gradually until the mid-century. The first big step was the repeal of the Corn Laws by British liberals in 1842. These laws had imposed heavy tariffs on food imports into Britain. Their removal lowered food prices, which enabled the newly rising industrialists to lower wages and thus increase their competitiveness. The Zollverein, mentioned above, was a customs union that eliminated most tariffs among the numerous petty German states during the 1830s. Its internal liberalization had a broader European impact as this German customs union then entered into trade agreements with other European states, such as the one with Austria, mentioned above. These various steps culminated in the Anglo-French Trade Treaty of 1860, which had a Europe-wide impact because of MFN agreements of those two with other European countries.

Just as all war is financed, all trade is also financed. Seldom is trade carried out on a cash or barter basis. Consequently, trade and indeed capital flows occurred so freely during the nineteenth century not only because of lower trade-specific barriers, but because of the success and stability of global trade financing, anchored in the London bill market. Textbooks and courses in international economics today almost invariably divide the topic into two disparate branches: trade and finance. But in actual fact these two are very closely linked. Free trade depends on a reliable international payments system, typically organized by private banks.

Contradictions of the second globalization

The major contradiction of the free trade era, the second globalization, was that the combination of freer trade and a bearish gold standard to secure the payments system led to persistent deflation that undermined the balance between debtors and creditors. The transition to free trade itself is bearish. The reduced costs of trade and the increased specialization of production in the lowest cost countries tends to lower prices, a net welfare gain celebrated by economists, but also harms debtors by making their debts more expensive relative to their incomes. If freer trade is accompanied by bullish credit expansion, this deflationary tendency may be counteracted, but during the later nineteenth century a series of depressions occurred when creditors tightened credit after a bout of expansiveness. The broad trend went from mildly inflationary during the first half of the century to chronically deflationary during roughly 1860–95, with some variation in timing among individual countries.

Rapid technological development also contributed to falling prices. The railroad and the steamship greatly lowered transportation costs. The telegraph increased the speed of communications, including especially of business data, tending toward greater global integration of markets, allowing buyers to seek the lowest cost alternatives. The second industrial revolution, involving especially steel, chemicals, and the new transportation technologies, reduced the cost of many products. All these are broadly positive developments, but the lowering of prices contributed to the deflation. In every crisis, as prices fell and the burden of debt did not, many companies were bankrupted, even the large new corporations like railroad companies. Business, led by finance, reacted to the crisis by organizing and concentrating to an unprecedented degree. The movement toward private organization began to limit the free market flexibility of classical liberalism, leading to the era of imperialism considered in the next chapter. The liberal era was a great success for lowering costs, advancing technology, and even securing a greater degree of peace, but it never managed to tame the extremes of the business cycle.

9 Imperialism and international polarization

> Imperialism is a specific historical stage of capitalism. ... The supplanting of free competition by monopoly is the fundamental economic feature, the quintessence of imperialism. Monopoly manifests itself in five principal forms: (1) cartels, syndicates and trusts – the concentration of production has reached a degree which gives rise to these monopolistic associations of capitalists; (2) the monopolistic position of the big banks – three, four or five giant banks manipulate the whole economic life of America, France, and Germany; (3) seizure of the sources of *raw material* by the trusts and the financial oligarchy (finance capital is monopoly industrial capital merged with bank capital); (4) the (economic) partition of the world by the international cartels has *begun*. There are already over *one hundred* such international cartels which command the *entire* world market and divide it "amicably" among themselves – until war *re*divides it. The export of capital ... is closely linked with the economic and territorial-political partition of the world; (5) the territorial partition of the world (colonies) *is completed*.
>
> V.I. Lenin (1964[1916]: 105–6)

Liberals agree that World War I decisively ended the first globalization, the era of British hegemony. The liberal world order of laissez-faire and peace-seeking diplomacy that seemed to dominate the century since 1815 came crashing down in the crucible of war. To liberals, the tragic excuses for such an irrational war seemed incidental if not accidental. Realists, of course, were not surprised that the war they long expected in Europe had finally arrived. What else could result within a Europe of suspicious powers racing to gain advantage in arms and grasping for advantage in every diplomatic dispute? Only a relatively stable balance of power deterred war as long as it did. Corporatism, by contrast, understands that liberalism was in decline for decades before the war broke out as its business basis eroded. Instead, an imperialist business and political strategy evolved as a solution to a series of sharp depressions during the last quarter of the nineteenth century. It tended to strengthen national business unity at the expense of international cooperation. Europe gradually polarized into two hostile great power blocs. War was not inevitable, however. If it could have been deterred until the 1916 election in Germany, there is a reasonable chance that a fundamental realignment within Germany and Austria-Hungary might have transformed European diplomacy and avoided the war altogether. It is in part to avoid such a potential realignment that the war party pushed the crisis of 1914 over the brink into a world war that nobody expected could drag on so long with such socially devastating effect.

Probably the two most famous and widely read arguments in the history of international relations theory are those of British liberal Norman Angell (2012) and Russian Marxist V.I. Lenin within a few years of each other around the outbreak of World War I. Angell argued in multiple editions just before the war that a Great Power war was virtually impossible and in any case illogical and uneconomic. He advanced detailed economic and business arguments why any such war would bankrupt all the major powers. Even the "victors" would lose since they could not possibly extract concessions from the losers that could even begin to pay for the titanic cost of the conflict. Lenin, writing midway through the war, argued after the fact that the war was an inevitable consequence of the rivalries generated by imperialism, "the highest stage of capitalism." Lenin copied much of his argument from a less famous book by fellow Bolshevik Nikolai Bukharin, who in turn borrowed from Marxist political economist Rudolf Hilferding, who described imperialism in 1910 in *Finance Capital* (Hilferding 2006). Ironically, both Bukharin and Hilferding were murdered within a couple years of each other: Hilferding by order of Hitler and Bukharin by order of Stalin. There is a considerable measure of truth in both the arguments of Angell and of Hilferding and his Bolshevik adherents.

My corporatist argument is that imperialism was the dominant strategy during the decades before World War I and that it was a consequence of business alignments in much the way that Hilferding described. Yet Angell was right that a war among the great powers must be financially devastating and would be illogical for many if not most business interests. There were indeed progressive elements of both business and labor that had a viable interest in avoiding war and a potentially profitable way of doing so. They might have been able to come to power by election in 1916 as they did two years later in the German revolution of 1918. Had they done so, war and the Bolshevik Revolution of 1917 might have been avoided. Imperialism had indeed aligned many of the forces set in motion in 1914, but had war been delayed for just two more years, other forces were in motion that might have prevented it altogether. The imperialist alignment of business was not without contradictions. These opened a wide gulf between business nationalists and internationalists by the end of World War I. The prospects for a decisive realignment were already appearing in 1914 when they were circumvented by the machinations of the most reactionary interests in several powers: the old aristocracy of great landlords in alliance with business nationalists. Lenin was wrong in believing that imperialism was the highest stage of capitalism. Imperialism would soon be undermined by the rise of business inter-nationalists and the emergence of a chronic interwar conflict between them and nationalists within most of the great powers and in the international system as a whole.

The rise of finance capital

Rudolf Hilferding coined the term "finance capital" to refer to the unification of banking, industrial, and commercial capital during the late nineteenth century that created many huge corporations (many of which still exist) and even larger cartels, trusts, combines, and conglomerates. The series of international sharp depressions during the last third of the nineteenth century prompted a profound transformation of the global political economy. Average prices dropped by at least one third, probably the greatest price deflation in history. Long-term debtors faced a particular squeeze since demand fell during each depression, as well as prices, yet long-term debt burdens did not since the face value of bonds and mortgages are fixed in money terms. While economics textbooks frequently argue that cartel cooperation is difficult to maintain, they ignore the historical fact that many successful cartels were enforced by banks that helped suppress competition among their debtors in order to secure their ability to raise their prices and profits, and thus service their debt without default or bankruptcy. Cartels in many countries (less in Britain and Japan) pushed for higher tariff protection to prevent their cartel prices from being undermined by foreign competition. The mid-century trend toward freer trade was reversed. Cartels were often the first step in the creation, usually by banks, of ever larger corporations through mergers of former competitors. The largest banks thus assembled conglomerates, more or less loosely coordinated, extending across many branches of industry, finance, and commerce.

Most political economists make the mistake of thinking that trade protectionism is only a policy of the weak, those vulnerable to competition. Chapter 7 shows that during mercantilism powerful monopolies, the great trading companies, protected their high prices using tariffs combined with export drawbacks (rebates) and other protectionist measures. This sort of protectionism by the powerful reemerged during the imperialist era. Economists pay little attention to trade systems of this type because they are not possible except in conditions of enormous and concentrated private power. During the first three quarters of the nineteenth century, business was not so centrally organized as during either mercantilism or imperialism. The great private trading companies lost their monopolies early in the century. Powerful banks still existed, but they concentrated on short-term trade finance and sovereign lending. Except for the massive spurt of railroad lending in the middle third of the century, they did not issue much long-term debt to industry and thus had little power to organize it. The second globalization was the era of "Manchester Liberalism" with trade relatively free of both trading and industrial monopolies and with tariffs declining. However, during the last third of the century the second industrial revolution took off. The new heavy industries required much larger scale of production than was typical of the older industries, such as textiles, that led the first industrial revolution. Therefore banks took a growing interest in industrial finance and thereby gained the power to regulate their debtors, especially as a series of depressions hit at roughly ten-year intervals. As banks formed cartels to raise prices during each depression, they needed higher tariffs to protect the high cartel prices from being undermined from abroad.

Hilferding gives the details of this massive concentration of private power. There is still, a hundred years later, no more comprehensive account of it. Details have been filled in, but the outline is the same. Hilferding is most valuable because he sees every related element of this new business system and why these elements emerged in the context of a long period of price deflation and multiple sharp depressions. Hilferding calls the new business system "finance capital," the title of his book, but in the final part of his book he also shows how finance capital gives rise to imperialism, thus the entire business and international system is aptly called "imperialism."

Realist critics of imperialist theory often say imperialism is nothing new. After all, it is in the nature of a state system to generate war and imperialism. But most realists gloss over the fact, already discussed in the previous chapter, that with the incidence of great power war does vary dramatically. Until 1815, the great powers of Europe fought so many wars, most of them protracted and many of them global. The century 1815–1914 was much more peaceful. The wars that occurred were generally short and limited and there were none involving a coalition of powers on each side. Britain, the greatest industrial and naval power of the era, fought only one war in Europe, the Crimean War, to protect the Ottoman Empire from Russian advances. Europe seemed to have tamed war, yet it was revived again with even more devastating power. Realism has no adequate explanation for the ebb and flow of war.

Liberalism's best explanation for the advent of imperialism is the decline of British hegemony. According to the hegemonic stability theory, as long as Britain was the dominant power, it could enforce a system of global "public goods" that supposedly benefitted everyone, including free trade, stable, and convertible currency, and peace through a diplomatically managed balance of power. A balance of power arranged by diplomacy is significantly different from one enforced by frequent wars. Once other powers industrialized rapidly, Britain could no longer bear the burden of hegemonic leadership or lacked the power to maintain its hegemony in the face of fast rising challengers like Germany, Russia, and the USA.

Both liberalism and realism explain the dynamic for change at the level of the international system, as Waltz required. Hilferding's argument is different. The impetus for change comes from within each of several powers. He intended finance capital to describe all the great industrial powers, but his model was Germany. His account also applies well to the USA and, to a lesser extent, France. The phenomena he describes occurred in other major powers, but not in every detail. Britain and Japan, for example, did develop some very large business groups that look like finance capital elsewhere, but because of their international competitiveness and lower debt, they did not need tariff protection to thrive. These two imperial powers kept their trade freer than the other powers until the war. Austria-Hungary, Italy, Japan, and Russia were great powers, but lacked the strong internationally competitive banking systems of the others and were thus heavily dependent on foreign capital for their financing, like developing countries. Yet since it is especially German policy that drove the alignments that led to World War I, understanding its internal developments is key to understanding the causes of that war.

The organization and centralization of capital

Neither realism nor liberalism considers private power systematically, thus they do not notice the significance of the massive centralization of capital during the last decades of the nineteenth century and the beginning of the twentieth century. This development is well known and documented within business history, but, except for imperialism theory, its importance for international relations is largely lost. Some accounts, including many of those by Marxists, ascribe this centralization entirely to technological imperatives. The second industrial revolution, involving such heavy industries as steel, chemicals, shipbuilding, and railroads, did lead to larger firms because of the technological efficiency of large-scale production, but centralization went far beyond what was required merely by technological economies of scale. Thus, most large corporations did not have a single huge factory, but numerous factories each of an efficient size of production. Furthermore, as Hilferding indicated, capital was combined into larger conglomerates that spanned many industries. There is no purely technological reason for combinations on such a grand scale. The main driving force for conglomeration of capital into huge firms, cartels, and conglomerates was the debilitating effect of heavy indebtedness in the context of the chronic deflation of the later nineteenth century.

There is a long tradition in economics arguing that cooperation among firms, for example, in cartels, is difficult and unstable because competitive firms have an incentive to cheat or defect from any such cooperation and therefore gain unilateral advantage vis-à-vis their competition. This is called the collective action problem. Like most ideas in economics, it completely ignores the realities of private power, especially credit power. In fact, throughout history many if not most cartels and other combinations of firms have been orchestrated by finance in order to suppress competition among their debtors, raise prices, and thus avoid debt default. Thus cooperation among firms does not depend on themselves alone, but is enforced by external credit power.

One of the first large-scale examples of this was the formation of railroad pools in the USA and other countries, particularly during the depressions of the latter part of the nineteenth century. Railroad pools are so named because funds earned from shipping along competing roads are pooled in a common account by a major bank, and then reallocated to the various railroad companies not according to their contribution to the revenue, but according to some formula, often devised by the bank or banking syndicate that financed the railroads. Because each railroad no longer controls its individual revenue, a pool is a secure way to enforce a cartel. It is also security for the debt of each railroad, since funds in the pool can be applied first to service the debt of the railroad before any surplus is released back to it. Since the pool is operated in the interests of the creditor banks, individual railroads dare not defect from it or they may find themselves cut off from future financing or even bankrupt. "Finance capital" is not just a slogan invented by Hilferding, it reflects the real leadership role played by major creditors in organizing capitalism.

Banks and other major financial companies have an incentive to force cooperation, especially during deflationary depressions because deflation places a serious burden on their debtors. Most debts, whether in the form of direct loans or bonds, have a principal value that is fixed in monetary terms. During a depression, business slows down, leading to falling revenue. Even worse, if prices are also falling, as was typical in this period, many firms are facing declines in both the prices of their output and the quantity of their sales. While revenue declines, often severely, during deflationary depressions, debt burdens do not. The firms that carry the heaviest debt load typically suffer the most. Many face bankruptcy. Banks will suffer too if bonds and loans default. Financing for large-scale projects like major railroads is typically not handled by a single bank alone, but by a syndicate of banks each taking an agreed share of the loan or bond issue. Through such syndicates, banks are already organized, typically in a hierarchical fashion, around one or a few of the largest banks who are the lead bank on most major financial operations. Therefore it is not so difficult for these large banking syndicates to cooperate together to avoid bankruptcies among their most important debtors by creating pools, other forms of cartels, or even merging the formerly independent companies. The point is to restrict output and raise prices. Higher prices mean higher profits and therefore allow debt servicing to resume, staving off bankruptcy. Individual firms have no real choice but to cooperate. The most indebted bulls are typically the most vulnerable to reorganization during a downturn. These are, in every era, the fastest growing and most capital-intensive industries. Such firms are most in need of debt to fund growth. When depression hits, they must be consolidated, forced to cooperate, or suffer bankruptcy.

This basic outline is a story that repeats hundreds if not thousands of times throughout business history, but especially during the later nineteenth century. This was the period of the most spectacular centralization of business precisely because it was also a period of both fast growth and deflation. The business cycle was most vigorous during this period, elevating new bulls during boom times and bankrupting many of them at the next crisis. The physical capital created during boom times, for example, new railroads, typically did not disappear during the succeeding crash, but was often redistributed to new corporate owners.

Interestingly, private financiers hit on this solution to depressions long before economics "discovered" and then mostly forgot it. Irving Fisher was one of the most famous American economists during the first half of the twentieth century. He is still cited in many textbooks, especially for his work on interest rate theory. More neglected, however, except by critics of modern textbook "Keynesianism," are his arguments made during the depths of the Great Depression, when he departed from the neoclassical equilibrium of his earlier years and propounded his debt-deflation theory of depressions (Fisher 1933). Fisher's explanation is much like mine here: depressions become severe because of the pressure of excessive debt in the context of deflation. The major difference between Fisher and me is that he sees excessive debt and deflation as "diseases" rather than the product of competing strategic behavior among bears and bulls. In any case, Fisher's solution differs from that of Keynes. He argues the main issue is deflation and the main cure is raising prices. It was partly because of the influence of Fisher and like-minded economists that US President Franklin Roosevelt framed his first New Deal as a generalized cartel scheme organized by National Recovery Administration to reverse deflation and stabilize or raise prices and wages. Nazi Germany also implemented a similar system of state-organized cartels, as discussed in the next chapter. What became public policy during the 1930s was already private policy during the depressions of the later nineteenth century.

Other forms of business organization proliferated during this deflationary period. Whereas a cartel could reverse price deflation in an industry and restore profitability, it did so at a cost in productive efficiency. Many of the businesses that formed cartels already had excess productive capacity because of slack demand during a downturn. The cartels themselves raised prices by further cutting output. The net result was massive excess capacity. Many factories and other productive facilities were idle much of the time and consequently many workers unemployed. Since large industrial facilities were built at great cost, often with borrowed money, leaving so much productive capacity idle was a huge waste of social resources and a large overhead expense for companies. In a competitive economy, some of the least efficient producers would have gone bankrupt, eliminating their productive capacity from the industry and allowing the remaining producers to take up their market share, but in a cartelized economy, even the inefficient producers may be saved from bankruptcy and thus all firms operate with significant excess capacity, sometimes long into the next boom. Financiers noticing these inefficiencies sought ways other than free competition and bankruptcy to eliminate the weaker productive units. The solution was a massive wave of business mergers. Leading bankers talked about the virtues of organized capitalism or rationalization of production, code words for merger mania, the building of giant trusts. This process not only increased the power and efficiency of the new mega-corporations, it was also extremely profitable for the big financial interests that orchestrated it.

Consider a national industry, say steel or electrical machinery, where there are many producers facing falling prices, shrinking demand, and excess capacity during the depressions, say 1893. The first solution, already outlined above, is to create an industry-wide cartel to further cut output, but thereby raise profits and restore solvency. This leaves the industry with enormous excess capacity. Now a leading bank, such as J.P. Morgan & Company in the

USA or Deutsche Bank in Germany, creates a new company to take over most of the existing companies. The new company starts with no assets but prints, for example, $1 billion in new stock certificates. (US Steel, created by J.P. Morgan in 1901, was the world's first billion dollar corporation.) Then the bank calls the presidents of the leading firms in the industry and their largest stockholders to a meeting, proposing to exchange stock in the new corporation for their existing company stock at what is usually a fairly attractive rate of exchange. All these insiders will then support the investment banks' plan at the next general meeting of each company's stockholders, so the takeover of the old competitors by the new giant corporation can be finalized. Any holdout companies can be isolated or threatened with a price war. Once most of the major companies have accepted the deal, the new company, whose management was selected by the organizing bank, now owns the stock and thus all the operating assets of the various companies that were merged into it.

When all the productive assets and all the debts are owned by the same company, rationalization of production becomes easier. The least efficient plant can be closed and liquidated and the most efficient ones run at closer to full capacity, increasing the efficiency of their utilization of fixed capital assets. The merged company may be a national monopoly, or close to it, eliminating the need for a cartel, like US Steel, RCA, American Sugar Refining, IBM, Du Pont, AT&T, White Star Lines, Western Union, or Standard Oil. Or, if several major banks are playing the same game at the same time, the result may be an oligopoly of several large firms in a national industry, as with General Electric and Westinghouse or the US copper mining industry. In either case, production can be rationalized, inefficient plants eliminated, and all economies of scale exploited.

What made these mergers so lucrative for the financial giants that assembled them is that the resulting mega-corporation was typically more valuable than the sum of the various less efficient companies assembled to create it. So the bank can, say, print its $1 billion in stock certificates, use perhaps $800 million to buy out all the underperforming component companies, and still have $200 million in stock left for the new corporation to sell to the public, eager to own a piece of this promising new behemoth. The profits could be immense. All the "robber barons" of this age got rich using this method. This is also known as "watering stock," though it is not necessarily fraudulent, because real economies can result from such combinations. Remember, these inefficiencies solved are not so much of a technical nature, for the most part, but are a consequence of excess capacity and the excessive debt accumulated to acquire it. They are a product of the business cycle. Such combinations typically give very ample returns to all insiders, who have the chance to buy first at the best prices and reward themselves with hefty fees. This process was so enormously attractive, it occurred in most major industries in every developed country during this period, but especially in heavy industries because larger indebtedness made these more vulnerable to takeover during every downturn. Debt vulnerability made it possible both by weakening the companies' ability to resist their creditors and by giving creditors an incentive to act. This is another way bears eat bulls.

Typical business histories stop at this level of organization, with the formation of hundreds of giant new companies worldwide. Sometimes they also discuss the cartels among those few that remained as potential competitors. Less noticed is that because all these mergers and cartels were orchestrated by a handful of large banks, who installed the new management teams and were typically represented on the boards of directors of the new mega-corporations, there was a level of more or less informal coordination among all the corporations assembled by the same bank, at least. In my own research into the business records of J.P. Morgan partners, the Rockefellers, and HSBC, I found that the banks coordinated the participation of the informal members of their group in various sorts of large projects. For example, when J.P. Morgan was contemplating financing the expansion of the Japanese-owned South Manchurian Railway in northeastern China during the 1920s, the proceeds of the intended loan were to be tied to purchases from other corporations put together by Morgan, including rails from US Steel, train engines from American Locomotive, and electrical equipment from General Electric. Similarly, when Morgan made a close tie with the largest Japanese combine, Mitsui, early in the twentieth century, the two groups also tied together several of their component companies, which included a broad and long-lasting patent-sharing and marketing agreement between Mitsui's Toshiba and Morgan's General Electric. The enormous combinations of big banks and the many mega-corporations they formed are the pinnacle of finance capital.

Unfortunately, though there is much evidence of such combines or conglomerates detailed business histories, there is little discussion of them in broader histories and virtually none in business, economics, or international political economy, with the exception of imperialism theory. The big four Japanese combines, called *zaibatsu* in Japanese, controlled up to a third of the Japanese economy by the 1930s, though they were formed during the later nineteenth century. The Mitsui zaibatsu alone controlled about 300 corporations, many of them the largest in their industry, including Mitsui Bussan, Japan's largest trading company, and Mitsui Bank, one of the top five. Japanese combines have been studied more than most of those in other countries, in part because the USA tried, unsuccessfully, to break them up after World War II. But similar groups, if not quite so tightly owned and controlled, existed in all the major countries, centered around the big banks.

Hilferding argues that the enormous centralization of capital into massive bank-centered groups also gave those at the helm of those combines great political power, and effectively unified capital into a single interest bloc. Even within such massive centralization, however, conflicts remained, particularly between less competitive nationalist firms and internationalists, by definition internationally competitive. During the protectionism surge of the late nineteenth century, these differences were papered over, but they reemerged with a vengeance in the new international environment after World War I, explored further in the next chapter. Imperialism resulted from what was at best a temporary and contingent unification of capital, not a permanent condition as assumed by Hilferding and his Bolshevik interpreters like Bukharin and Lenin.

Increasing protectionism

One problem with cartels and other business combinations as a solution to deflation was also highlighted by Hilferding. Raising prices for goods that are internationally tradable, such as steel or locomotives, will tend to induce a flood of new imports as producers in other countries take advantage of the higher prices. There are two solutions to this: (1) raising tariffs to protect the higher cartel price, or (2) forming international cartels to raise prices worldwide. The first solution was more typical of the later nineteenth century, whereas the second solution emerged more strongly during the twentieth century along with the rise of business internationalism.

Standard accounts in international political economy have long recognized that tariffs in several major powers did trend upwards during the later nineteenth and early twentieth centuries, but they ignore business history and so do not see the private power at work behind these developments. Instead, they blame the decline of British hegemony or the revenue needs of governments. The second explanation is, I believe, backwards. The naval arms race that began during the 1890s was possible because of increased revenue generated by tariff increases. The arms race came after the revenue was available, it did not drive tariff policy. Germany and the USA, two of the most vigorous participants in the new naval arms race, preceded their naval increases with tariff increases. Neither had been a significant naval power previously and there was no new threat inducing them to become one. Yet, within a couple of decades, they became the second and third largest naval powers in the world. In both countries, many of the same big business interests that supported the tariff also supported private navy leagues to promote naval power and then benefitted significantly from the resulting government spending.

German historian Eckart Kehr (1973, 1977) documents both the business politics behind German tariff increases and the naval buildup. He shows that tariff politics not only explains these, but also how Germany thereby isolated itself in international politics and stimulated the Franco-Russian alliance that ultimately confronted Germany in World War I. German heavy industry supported tariffs to protect its cartel prices from British competition, especially, and supported building the large navy that antagonized Britain. At the same time, the *Junkers*, Germany's politically powerful rural aristocracy, supported tariffs on grain to exclude cheap Russian grain newly competitive in German markets with the rapid development of railways. Throughout most of the nineteenth century Prussia and then united Germany could usually count on either Britain or Russia as an ally in every crisis. But when the *Junkers* and industrialists cooperated to raise both industrial and agricultural tariffs and thereby fund naval expansion as well, Germany alienated both British and Russian business interests to the detriment of their relations with the governments of both countries. These new adversaries were added to France, already fuming from Germany's territorial gains at its expense. Furthermore, whereas German banks had participated in loans for Russian development, especially railroads, in earlier periods, by the early 1890s they turned their back on Russian loans. French and Belgian bankers largely took their place. This growing financial alliance led within a few years to the military alliance of 1894, initiating the polarized alliance system that divided Europe into two rival armed camps by the eve of World War I. Tariff politics surrounded Germany with enemies.

US tariffs began increasing somewhat earlier than those of the major continental European powers. The Republican Party was consistently pro-tariff during the first century of its existence. It held national power for most of the period 1861–1913. A particularly large tariff increase was passed in 1890, called the McKinley tariff, after its chief architect in the House and later US President William McKinley. McKinley and his ally, Mark Hanna, greatly increased funding for the Republican Party by essentially "selling" tariff protection in return for campaign contributions. Their system was regularized to such an extent it became a mainstay of Republican Party funding for decades and helped them greatly outspend the Democratic Party in most national elections until the 1930s. The Democratic Party was strongest in the former Confederate states, which were also the main source of the major US exports: oil, cotton, and tobacco. Consequently, the Democratic Party during this period supported free trade. The Republicans were stronger in the manufacturing centers. US protectionism did not have such severe consequences for international relations as did German protectionism, but it did contribute to US business interest in bringing major Spanish-controlled sugar producing regions (Cuba, Puerto Rico, and the Philippines) inside the US tariff wall, a major motivation for the 1898 US war against Spain.

The Republicans also supported the gold standard, whereas the Democrats split on it between "gold Democrats" strongest in financial centers like New York, and "silver Democrats" dominant in the farm and silver mining states. From the depression of 1893 until 1912, populist silver Democrats dominated the party's national conventions, favoring a more bullish bimetallic monetary standard beneficial to debtor interests, including not only farmers, as many textbooks emphasize, but also some railroads and other debt-strapped corporations. Thus those financiers who favored free trade, who were gold Democrats, sometimes cast their lot with the Republicans because of their even stronger aversion to excessively bullish monetary policy.

The previous section mentioned that many national cartels were faced with an expensive burden of excess productive capacity. One way to use some of it was to export to world markets. Since for the most efficient producers the tariff-protected domestic cartel price was typically well above their cost of production, they could profitably export at lower world market prices. In fact, the high prices earned on domestic sales helped cover debt and other over-head costs, allowing companies to sell cheaply abroad at much lower prices and still exceed their marginal costs for that additional output. This sort of behavior is quite common when national cartels exist. It is called dumping in trade law. Since many of the major industrial countries were raising their tariffs during this period, dumping was easiest in developing countries without powerful rival industrial companies. Another way of achieving export sales was the common practice of tying sales to foreign loans. Governments wanted foreign loans to promote their own exports, but this was then typically not a matter of law. Since it was private banks making the loans, it was up to them to negotiate loan agreements tied to purchases from companies within their own combine. This tendency was particularly strong among German banks. Thus exports often followed foreign loan patterns.

Growing military polarization

The most memorable feature of the imperialist era was the increasing intensity of international conflicts, often directly related to specific business concessions. The most serious conflicts arose in Morocco, Mexico, and the Balkans. On the other hand, conflicts over financing sovereign loans and railroad projects within the Ottoman Empire and China were somewhat ameliorated by coop-eration among the leading banking syndicates from each financial power, illustrating that there were potential internationalist solutions to rivalries of national groups. However, cooperative solutions were harder to implement when national syndicates backed opposing sides in regional or civil conflicts, as in the first named cases.

To some degree, liberals are right. There was a sort of decline of international hegemony that contributed to imperialism and the outbreak of the war, but it was less a decline of hegemony of the British state and more the relative decline of a handful of cosmopolitan banks, especially the Rothschild banks, and the rise of rival national banking groups in countries like Germany and the USA. This allowed war finance to be nationally based rather than cosmopolitan, at least for the key aggressive power, Germany. Its relative robust national financial system enabled it to finance 90 percent of its enormous war effort by domestic borrowing and the rest from taxes. That sort of financial mobilization of national wealth was a relatively recent development.

World War I broke out over disputes in the Balkans, and involved the USA when conflicts in Mexico and financial-industrial interests aligned the USA with an Allied victory. Yet as soon as the war broke out, Anglo-American business internationalists organized to plan a postwar peace that would promote freer trade, economic reconstruction, and dialogue through a league of nations. This business internationalist vision had some success in establishing the League of Nations, the Washington Conference and subsequent agreements for deep cuts in arms spending, and cooperation in East Asia along the lines pioneered by the China Consortium (the formal name of the international banking syndicate there), but the economic devastation, dislocations of the war, and the threats posed by revived trade polarized business into rival nationalist and internationalist blocs in most major countries. Business internationalism was unable to prevail consistently within several major powers in the face of the nationalist, bullish, and protectionist opposition of business nationalism.

Whereas the free trade era had been characterized by polarization at home and greater international cooperation, the imperialist era leading up to World War I featured increased national unity within several major powers while international politics became more and more polarized. Yet there was still an undercurrent of liberal internationalism championed by the most competitive elements of business and finance in several countries. Business internationalists pushed for cooperation in overseas finance and development, notable examples being the China Consortium, the six-nation Ottoman Finance Board, and the Anglo-German Baghdad Railway consortium. They also promoted peaceful resolution of disputes and limits to war, such as negotiated at the Hague Convention. If war could have been avoided until 1916, when there was a good chance of electoral victory by the German Social Democratic Party, that might have prevented the war entirely by breaking *Junker* political power and realigning German foreign economic policy toward the development of Russia. War was not inevitable.

Marxism's strategic errors

Marxism developed remarkable strategic insights into world political economy during the half century from Marx's *Capital* to Lenin's *Imperialism*. It brought advanced perspectives on political economy and strategy into Europe's first mass parties to create a powerful political movement by the eve of World War I. However, Marxist strategists committed two fundamental and related errors that have plagued the Left's understanding of global political economy ever since. Lenin and other Bolshevik leaders condemned the "revisionist" socialists and social democrats for being insufficiently internationalist, doing too little to oppose the entry of their nations into World War I. But this is not the error I see. As of 1914, Marxist-inspired parties had no governmental power anywhere and would surely have been severely suppressed had they opposed the war more vigorously at the outset. Not knowing how long the war might last, they were right to bide their time and await a better opportunity to seize power during the aftermath of the war, which socialists did in several countries of central and eastern Europe.

Marxists instead made a deeper error, shared by their "bourgeois" economic critics: they failed to understand adequately credit power and the strategic capacity of capitalists to realign. The predominance of imperialism in the immediate prewar years helped conceal this error, since, as Hilferding correctly discerned, the imperialism tended to unify banking, commercial, and industrial capital into strong blocs that he called "finance capital." Since finance capital in turn had predominant influence in several states, it seemed unnecessary to differentiate its elements thereafter. Finance capital morphed into monopoly capital in Lenin's more widely known terminology and all became one undifferentiated catechism without much updating of the analysis during the century since.

Yet the leading capitalists had not dissolved all their disparate interests into this one undifferentiated mass: monopoly capital. They retained a degree of strategic independence and adaptability befitting captains of capital. They did not all mindlessly march over a cliff of catastrophe, despite appearances to the contrary during the horrendous blood-letting of two world wars and the intervening economic catastrophe of the Great Depression. The devastating failures of imperialism, not the least for financial interests, led to a substantial realignment of business internationalists in favor of global cooperation and against imperialism, in the sense Hilferding defined. Some precedents for this realignment already existed prewar in the international financial consortia that began to unite the finance capital of all the great powers in places like the Ottoman Empire and China. World War I had barely begun when Anglo-American business internationalists formed the League to Enforce the Peace to design a cooperative postwar order. The next chapter details this emergence of business internationalists and their struggles against business nationalists who had once been allies in a common imperialist project. Postwar socialists often aligned politically with business internationalists without fully understanding how this was changing the course of capitalism. They did not realize that the strategic initiative was slipping from their hands.

The second, more fatal flaw of Marxists since Marx himself is their failure to understand money and credit power. Marx believed that materialism required things to have value by virtue of the labor embodied to create them. Therefore *real* money must be silver and gold, which have real value because of the labor cost of producing them. Various forms of credit money must be less significant tokens of value that can temporarily stand in for real commodity money. Marx gained his view from a careful study of the history of political economy, where such views are indeed common, though not ubiquitous. But he rejected the more sophisticated understanding of money and credit of such contemporaries as John Stuart Mill and Walter Bagehot (2013[1878]). Marx passed on this deficit to his successors.

Consequently, when Marxist-inspired socialists did gain some measure of state power after World War I, rather than being too nationalistic in cahoots with imperialists, as Lenin charged, they were in fact too internationalistic for their own good, supporting the cooperative international monetary schemes of business internationalists, including the postwar restoration of the gold standard, the monetary system that recognized that money too, if it is a real measure of value, must exist only as a product of labor, as commodity money. Hilferding himself twice became finance minister of Germany. Socialists defended to their death, often literally, as in Nazi Germany, gold money when in fact the political advantage shifted to bullish business nationalists who best understood that the lifeblood of capitalism is credit, not gold.

Part IV

The rise of business internationalism

10 The business of World War II

Nineteenth century civilization has collapsed. ... [It] rested on four institutions ... the balance of power system ... the international gold standard ... the self-regulating market ... the liberal state. ... Of these institutions the gold standard proved crucial; its fall was the proximate cause of the catastrophe. By the time it failed most of the other institutions had been sacrificed in a vain effort to save it.

Karl Polanyi (1957: 3)

Like the series of depressions in the later part of the nineteenth century, the Great Depression provoked a severe realignment of nations and private interests around the globe. Economic nationalists already exercised power in Soviet Russia, but during the depression also gained power in Germany and Japan. In a sense, World War II emerged as the result of an economic nationalist revolt against the attempt of business internationalists to reshape the world order after World War I. Karl Polanyi understood this, though using somewhat different terminology. The victory of the Allied powers during World War II paved the way for a more consistent restructuring of the world economy (with the notable exception of the socialist bloc) along the lines planned by business internationalists at the onset of the war.

World War II originated from a revolt of nationalists in Germany and Japan against the internationalist aspects of the world order, including the constraints of the gold standard international payments system and various disarmament agreements, which, in addition to the obvious military impact, had dire economic consequences for some interests. Economic nationalism in the USA, France, Britain, and especially the Soviet Union made cooperation among them difficult as the world divided into rival currency and trading blocs during the 1930s. The economic and business basis for Anglo-American internationalist cooperation was not restored until their reciprocal trade agreement of 1938, too late to restrain a major Japanese invasion of China or the German expansion into Austria and Czechoslovakia. By 1939 though, Western vacillation had voided the chance for an Allied alliance with the Soviets, encouraging Germany to invade Poland, thus initiating the war in Europe. As in World War I, shortly after the outbreak of the war in Europe, Anglo-American internationalists began planning the institutions of the postwar world, assuming American entry into the war and a decisive Allied victory.

Polanyi understands the salient issues that led to the war, but he lacks a strategic understanding of the domestic forces on each side of these issues. Thus he writes in terms of the four "institutions" listed above in conflict with an amorphous collectivity he calls "society." As vague as he is, his account is better than most in recognizing the gold standard and the conditions of its restoration after World War I as a central issue. The true salience of the gold standard issue only becomes obvious when its powerful supporters and opponents are identified and recognized as the true protagonists in this drama. Remarkably, even such fundamental conflicts as this one largely escape focused attention because of the profound neglect of private power. The extraordinary polarizing impact of restoring the prewar gold standard and the bearish policies required to re-implement it remain obscure in most histories.

Some view World War II as another round in a fight against the ascendant ambitions of Germany, basically a repeat of World War I. However, in both economic cause and effect, the two world wars were quite different. World War I started because of rivalry among powers with roughly symmetrical imperialist war aims. Despite some differences in political regime type, both sides had remarkably similar configurations of private power and thus similar policies. The rival alliances did not champion fundamentally different designs for world order, but just a different balance of power within it. Business internationalism emerged during World War I, but, except in the issues of international monetary policy and the League of Nations, was rather unsuccessful in reshaping the postwar world order according to its radically different design.

The partial victory of business internationalism in restoring the gold standard clashed with the powerful nationalist aspirations within several great powers, creating postwar splits, greatly exacerbated by the Great Depression, which set the stage for multiple business nationalist revolts against the nascent internationalist order. The Great Depression was so severe in part because of this bifurcation. Internationalists championed an open world payments system, the gold standard, while nationalists in several countries countered with protectionist trade policies that undermined the functioning of the gold standard. The countries that prospered best during the 1930s were those that broke first and most decisively from these contradictory pressures: Nazi Germany, the Soviet Union, and, to a lesser extent, Japan. They prospered by restricting their links to the world economy and consistently pursuing bullish business nationalism. This also gave them a chance for a head start on rearmament compared with the USA, France, Britain, and China, recovering more slowly and inconsistently in the face of contradictory economic policies. Whereas World War I was a war among similar powers, World War II was more like a civil war within the world political economy between rival nationalist and internationalist interest blocs.

In theory, the bear–bull and nationalist–internationalist polarizations might have been independent and cross-cutting cleavages, but in practice through most of the interwar period internationalists were bears favoring creditor interests and nationalists were bulls favoring fast growth and debtor interests (Frieden 1988, 1991). Only from the mid-1930s did business internationalists develop a moderately bullish faction within several countries, including the USA, Britain, France, and Sweden, which began to reconstruct a limited degree of international economic cooperation that laid the basis for the design of a broader and more durable postwar internationalist order. However, the onset of the war interrupted progress toward greater economic openness and delayed implementation of a business internationalist world order until the war was won.

The bearish impulse and the Great Depression

The extreme difficulties of the interwar period are in part attributable to conflict between bearish creditor interests, typically represented by large banks, and bullish interests wishing to restore employment and growth. Heavy wartime borrowing and spending had created significant and uneven inflation among various countries. Bears, especially motivated by the vast bondholder debt created by the war, wanted to restore the value of national currencies to something close to their prewar levels. This would be of enormous benefit to the real wealth of bondholders and other creditors owning other fixed-value assets, such as mortgage loans. However, restoring currencies to prewar gold values required severe deflation in most countries. Some opted to restore prewar levels. Others did not.

Wars usually produce inflation, especially when the economies of belligerents are near full employment at the start. World War I was no exception. War mobilization simultaneously reduces productive capacity while increasing demand for new output. Millions of productive laborers, horses, and transportation equipment like trains are diverted from the civilian economy to support the war effort, significantly reducing potential output. At the same time, governments place vast orders for war supplies, including food, explosives, uniforms and tents, warships, aircraft, and weapons of all sorts. Typically it is politically difficult to drastically reduce civilian wages or increase taxes, so civilian buying power may also be left largely intact. Civilians may have a tendency for panic buying and hoarding, putting further upward pressure on existing supplies and productive capacity. Government purchases are typically financed by massive expansion of credit. All that fresh demand on top of restricted productive capacity creates strong upward pressure on prices. Higher prices, rather than wage cuts or large tax increases, ultimately ration goods in short supply, curtailing civilian purchases. Countries like France, Belgium, and much of Eastern Europe suffered additional losses of productive capacity because of enemy occupation of all or part of their territory, creating even greater shortages and inflation. The countries that suffered the greatest wartime destruction and exerted the largest war effort typically suffered the greatest inflation, though forms of debt financing also affect this. For example, Allied powers like Britain and France were able to relieve some of the excess demand pressure on their home economies by buying supplies abroad, mostly from the USA, and financing these purchases using bonds issued mainly in New York.

The Central Powers, on the other hand, were almost completely unable to borrow in New York. It would do them little good in any case, since it would be impossible to ship war supplies from the USA to Germany and Austria-Hungary through the Allied blockade. Thus during the period of US neutrality, 1914–17, US business interests were decisively aligned with an Allied victory both as the principal foreign suppliers of Allies and their principal foreign creditors. US owners of numerous Allied bonds invested in Allied victory and would suffer severe capital losses if the war dragged on too long or the Allies were defeated, inducing bond defaults. Although the proximate causes of the US entry into the war on the Allied side were unrestricted German submarine attacks and secret German diplomatic efforts to involve Mexico in a war with the USA, the enormous invested interest in Allied victory guaranteed strong business and investor support for US belligerency, especially among those internationalist businesses that exported to the Allies and financed them. The strong economic support given to the Allies even by a "neutral" USA also lessened the German military's reticence to resort to measures like unrestricted submarine warfare that might drag the USA into the conflict.

Massive Allied borrowing in New York transformed the world financial system. The USA quickly rose from fourth to first place as the world's leading creditor nation, a position it maintained until recently. New York surpassed London as the world's leading financial center. At the center of this movement was the investment bank, J.P. Morgan & Company, which was the lead bank syndicating nearly all of the Allied loans until the USA entered the war in 1917 and the US government began to extend government-to-government loans to most of the Allied countries. Morgan's central role in financing this massive trans-Atlantic movement of capital catapulted it into the leading role in global finance for the coming decades. Not only that, but the Morgan bank also increased its influence within USA because the Allied powers soon realized that their competing orders were driving up prices among US suppliers, so in 1915 they invited the Morgan firm to become the sole purchasing agent in the USA for the Allied powers, giving it enormous influence among all businesses eager for a share of these massive purchases, since it now fell to Morgan's newly created export department to determine which companies would get which orders and, if necessary, finance company expansion to supply the required goods.

Bullish nationalism of the Soviet Union

The most striking feature of the Soviet Union has been its socialism. The Soviet Union or Union of Soviet Socialist Republics (USSR) was the world's first enduring socialist state. Yet for purposes of international political economy, socialism as normally conceived is not the most interesting aspect of Soviet policy. More important is what its brand of socialism made possible: bullish business nationalism. The USSR was the first major power to break from the world order that was under construction at the end of World War I. Even without considering the prospect of the USSR sponsoring further socialist revolutions, which, despite its apparent efforts through the Communist International (Comintern), headquartered in Moscow, it was unable or unwilling to do, the USSR was a threat to the emerging internationalist world order and the specific peace settlement that the victorious Allied powers imposed.

The threat of the USSR to propagate socialist revolution certainly seemed a frightening specter to many pro-capitalists at the time, though in retrospect this was greatly exaggerated. It is more likely that the USSR, under Stalin's conservative "socialism in one country" doctrine and the ill-informed tactics of the Comintern weakened rather than strengthened worker movements abroad and helped pave the way for the defeat of the Left in Germany and elsewhere. If the Comintern had not been so virulently opposed to moderate social democrats, it is possible that broader leftist cooperation might have prevented the Nazi victory in Germany and therefore World War II as well. The Comintern itself apparently came to this belated conclusion when it shifted policy dramatically during 1934–35 to support "broad front" alliances against fascism, leading to Left coalition victories in elections in France and Spain during 1936.

On the other hand, there were real economic policy differences between communist and social democratic parties about how to respond to the Great Depression, so it is not clear that they could have cooperated earlier. Labor and social democratic parties throughout Europe tried to maintain the bearish monetary orthodoxy of international cooperation through the gold standard even as they resorted to expansionary fiscal policies to finance greater social spending. Even after Britain abandoned the gold standard in 1931, it took some time for Europe's socialist and social democratic parties to realize that monetary cooperation would not soon be restored. They supported the gold standard not just because it was monetary orthodoxy, but because creditors insisted on it as a condition for further borrowing. Foreign borrowing was necessary to sustain fiscal deficit spending typical of social democratic governments in a depression.

Meanwhile, the Soviet Union began a massive industrialization program relying in part on imported productive machinery and foreign technical assistance paid for by traditional Russian exports, including grain and oil. The grain surplus needed to feed the growing cities and finance machinery imports was squeezed out of a reluctant peasantry not by attractive prices, but by violent suppression and forced collectivization of agriculture. Foreign economists, beginning most famously with "Austrian school" founder Ludwig von Mises, criticized socialist planning for its non-market prices leading to static inefficiency. While this criticism is broadly true, though based on a false analogy to mythological free markets, it ignores the highly successful dynamic efficiency of the Soviet system in generating industrial growth, though at an enormous human cost. The rather artificial price and rationing system of the five year plans restrained consumption while forcing a high level of social savings to prioritize investment in new productive equipment and facilities.

A planned socialist system such as that of the Soviet Union cannot survive free trade competition with the capitalist world because Soviet domestic prices bore little relationship to world market prices. Thus the government needed to monopolize foreign trade and strictly control all of its long borders to prevent smugglers from undermining planning priorities by buying whatever goods were cheap according to Soviet prices and selling these abroad to import whatever was dear or lacking in the Soviet Union. The Soviet police state was not a superfluous sop to Stalin's paranoia, but an essential feature of socialist economic nationalism and its bullish growth strategy. Political democracy was incompatible with Soviet-style socialism since election-oriented parties might compete for public support by relaxing trade and police controls, therefore opening the door to massive smuggling and evasion of controls that would almost inevitably corrupt the political process with a flood of illicit wealth. This problem is revisited in Chapter 12 by the postwar experience of developing countries attempting to combine both democracy and stringent trade and exchange controls.

Bullish nationalism of Nazi Germany

The Nazi party in Germany was perplexing at the time and has confused historians and social scientists ever since. Its official name translates as German National Socialist Workers Party, which makes it sound very much like a left-wing party. Indeed its parliamentary votes during its ascent to power most often aligned it with the Communist Party. Its public propaganda vigorously attacked capitalism, especially cartels, big business combines, and all aspects of finance. It favored debt relief for *Junker* landlords, farmers, and many businesses faced with bankruptcy. Before it took power it usually supported strikes, unions, and higher social insurance for workers. Yet it attacked Marxism and economic determinism, the theoretical bases of the other two major socialist parties in Weimar Germany: the often ruling Social Democratic Party and the opposition Communist Party. Academics have usually followed the lead of these Marxist parties and rejected Nazi pretenses as a socialist party, assigning it instead to the far right.

The appeal of the Nazi Party to voters and activists most clearly positions it as one of the three major socialist parties in Weimar Germany. The objections to this are weak. The other two German socialist parties attacked the Nazis for raising funds from business, but actually every socialist party got some funding from individual business leaders, even the Communists. Nazi funding from big business was minor. Business as a whole mistrusted all three socialist parties, but, for self-protection, sought potential allies within them. The Nazis' broadest and most vigorous business support came from smaller businesses caught between the wage demands of powerful unions, the competitive pressures from the well organized and well financed big business, high taxes, and the financial pressures of creditors in the deflationary Great Depression (Turner 1985). The Nazis vaguely promised strong political initiatives to save workers, farmers, and nationally loyal business from the ravages of the Great Depression. They did indeed deliver on this promise as well. Germany under the Nazis became one of the first countries to recover from the Great Depression. Their economic policies in power were relentlessly bullish and business nationalist, not so different from the first couple of years of the New Deal in the United States.

The Nazis were also said to reveal their true anti-worker bias once they gained power, repressing workers, strikes, and democracy itself. In that respect too, Nazis differed little from Communists. By the time the Bolsheviks had renamed the Russian empire the Union of Soviet Socialist Republics, they had already banned strikes and eliminated both the power and the democratic representative character of the soviets – worker councils – that had been a key stepping stone on their road to power. The only major socialist party loyal to electoral democracy in Weimar Germany was the Social Democratic Party, which was vigorously condemned by the Communists as "social fascist" and by the Nazis for betraying the German nation during the revolution and defeat of Germany in 1918. Both Communists and Nazis viciously repressed dissent against their rule once in power, regardless of its social class origin.

The Nazi party did not differ from other socialist parties in its attitude toward using state power to solve economic problems. It did that too. In fact, in rejecting the alleged economic determinism of Marxism, Nazis were keen to put political power and the state above all else, including private business power, especially as manifest in credit and pricing power. Their use of state power to intervene in the economy was considerably greater than what Social Democratic governments had done previously. The Nazis certainly had no respect for the private property of anyone presumed to be an enemy of the German state. During their rise they often condemned financiers and war profiteers, vowing to confiscate the property of anyone whose gains they judged ill-gotten. Almost as soon as they gained power they began confiscating Jewish property and pushing Jews out of both public employment and private businesses. Their wartime plundering of all occupied nations was notorious. While the Nazis were certainly anti-Marxist, they were socialist in putting state above private interests.

The "national" in their party name was the key difference that distinguished Nazis from communists and social democrats, both of which they condemned as "internationalists." The Nazis aligned with the Communists on many domestic social policies, but virulently condemned them for putting the interests of the Soviet Union above the interests of German national power. Nazis supported rearmament and a strong German army, for example, whereas the Communist Party did not. Furthermore, Hitler obviously knew, not least from his early supporter, General Ludendorff, that Lenin had returned to Russia in 1917 with the support of the German army in order to undermine the Kerensky government and especially its war effort against Germany, which Lenin quickly did, over the strong objections of many other Bolshevik leaders who wanted to continue a revolutionary war against Germany. Thus Hitler undoubtedly viewed communists as fundamentally traitorous. He also condemned Social Democrats as traitors to Germany for their role in surrendering to the Allies in 1918 and for agreeing to high reparation payments to the Allied powers, which the Nazis vowed to cancel. The Nazis were what they said they were, a consistently *nationalist* socialist party, putting the interests of a strong nation above those of any form of international solidarity, including free trade, the gold standard, and peace itself. One suspects that if German socialists had launched a revolutionary war against the Allied powers in 1918, on the pattern of the French revolutionary war of 1793, Hitler and most other Nazis would have been fervent socialist revolutionaries.

The Nazis became such a destructive and genocidal force that it is difficult to put aside one's moral revulsion long enough to look realistically at their political appeal during their rise to power. By the 1932 elections, they had become the most popular party in Germany. The Communist Party was also gaining electoral strength. Both were ascending because of the utter failure of the other political parties to solve Germany's economic catastrophe. All the "bourgeois" parties of the center and right were committed to bearish monetary policies required by adherence to the gold standard, though they differed among themselves on the degree of desirable trade protectionism. The Social Democratic Party and its occasional allies among the Catholic centrist parties were willing to countenance fiscal bullishness in the form of deficit spending, but they undermined this by also supporting tight credit policies to maintain Germany's international credit standing and at the same time remit heavy reparations payments. With the partial exception of the Communists, the Nazis were the only significant political party that was consistently both business nationalist and bullish.

The Nazis were also consistently IR realists. They embraced all the premises of IR realism, including believing in the fundamentally conflictual nature of the international system, the subordination of domestic to foreign policy, the superiority of state power over liberal economic imperatives, and the necessary unity of the state, which they idealized in classic Platonic fashion. They were convinced social Darwinists. It is noteworthy that it was left-leaning British academic E.H. Carr (1964), who made his name as the premier English-language historian of the Soviet Union and also as a concerned observer of Nazi ambitions, who reintroduced IR realism most eloquently to an English-language audience at a time when IR liberalism in the form of international legal norms, collective security, and arms control were dominant in Anglo-American intellectual circles. Both Stalin and Hitler thought and acted as IR realists and distained liberal legalism, though Stalin tended toward cautious realism, whereas Hitler was more recklessly aggressive.

Bullish business nationalism succeeded brilliantly for the Nazis during the prewar years. If they had not disdained parliamentary democracy, they likely would have won re-election in 1936 based on their economic success alone.

During the seven years the Nazis ruled up to the outbreak of the war, the German economy grew at the phenomenal rate of almost 10 percent real growth per year. Industrial output grew even faster. Public spending doubled. Public debt increased rapidly, especially during the war years, but nearly all of the borrowing was domestic. Surprisingly, inflation remained quite low because of rigorously enforced foreign exchange and price controls. The pricing power of all private organizations, including both unions and business cartels, was ruthlessly broken, replaced by state regulation, yet private profits rose significantly. As in the Soviet Union, economic autarky increased (Ferguson 2002: 464–67). Similarly to the Soviet Union, the Nazis spurned foreign creditors and every rule of economic propriety, yet contrary to the "immutable laws" of economics, Germany prospered.

Whereas the Social Democratic Party had favored the income of workers, the unemployed, and state employees, the Nazis, like the Soviets, squeezed private consumption but spent massively on public investment, including both infrastructure and rearmament. The Social Democratic Party, in other words, favored social income, whereas the Nazis and Soviets favored social investment and bullish growth. The supply driven policies of these two produced full employment growth, whereas the demand-driven incomes policy of the social democrats, more consistent with textbook Keynesianism, led to social conflict, foreign payments crises, high interest rates, and consequently sluggish private investment with little compensating public investment. Many of the left parties of postwar Europe followed a pattern similar to that of the prewar German social democrats, most notably the British Labour Party until its decisive defeat after the "winter of discontent" at the end of the 1970s. Richard Overy (1996) argues that the Nazi economy was grossly unbalanced and could not have sustained such bullish growth much past 1939 without war. But that did not matter to the Nazis, because war was what they intended. For them the economy was always subordinate to the international struggle for power.

Bullish nationalism in Japan

Japan's political system was very different from that of Germany, let alone Soviet Russia, but by 1932 it too was dominated by violent bullish nationalists mobilized to action by the impact of the Great Depression on Japan. Japan had no equivalent of the Nazi party. The two major political parties were both committed to tight credit and a strong yen. Yet because of a severe earthquake that devastated Tokyo in 1923 and a financial crash in 1927, Japan was the last of the major powers to return to the gold standard. By the time it did in January 1930, the Great Depression was already underway. Within less than two years, Japan's major trade competitor, Britain, had itself abandoned gold and devalued the pound. Japan and Britain were the two largest world exporters of cotton textiles. Since high tariffs blocked most imports of such products into most of Europe and the USA, the British Empire, especially India, was one of the few remaining world markets open to Japanese exports.

After some months of facing increased British competition following the devaluation of the pound, Japan's military overthrew the party government, banned further elections, and likewise abandoned gold, letting the yen devalue massively. Britain reacted in turn by abandoning free trade with the new Imperial Preference System, effectively excluding Japanese products from the British Empire. Export-oriented Japan was forced toward autarky by prohibitive tariffs in much of the rest of the world.

The destruction of party government in Japan was a blow to the power of Japan's hitherto dominant business and political elite, concentrated in the five biggest private banks and the Big Four *zaibatsu* that included four of these that controlled about a third of total output and utterly dominated the competitive, export-oriented sectors of the Japanese economy since its rapid development after the Meiji Restoration of 1868. The Big Four included within their numerous companies nearly all the alliances with foreign firms that brought foreign technology and patents into Japan. They controlled nearly all trade-related services, including all the largest trading companies, shipping, marine insurance, and trade finance. They were thus a highly concentrated business internationalist elite with a bearish attachment to gold, both as traders and big bankers.

The Big Four had strong ties with the Japanese military too, but these were eroded during the interwar period as these business internationalists prioritized their alliance with foreign business partners to the detriment of Japanese military ambitions. The major issues that drove a wedge between Japan's military and the Big Four business internationalists are detailed in my PhD dissertation (Nolt 1994). Here I will summarize them briefly.

After World War I, a series of treaties set the parameters for postwar cooperation in East Asia. These treaties are often collectively referred to as the Washington Treaty System, since they were negotiated during 1921–22 in conjunction with the Washington Naval Disarmament Conference. They affirmed the territorial integrity of China and a multilateral open door approach to guarantee against any power pressuring China's weak government for unilateral economic spheres of influence to the detriment of other powers. A naval arms race was also averted by a moratorium on building battleships and fixing the ratio of capital ships in the five largest navies. Japan was awarded only 60 percent of the capital ship tonnage of the two dominant naval powers, USA and Britain. This was actually a higher relative strength than Japan could have achieved in an all-out naval arms race, since the USA was building many new battleships, nearly all scrapped by the treaty, at a rate twice that of Japan. All powers also promised not to further fortify their Pacific Ocean bases outside home territories. This treaty system replaced the Anglo-Japanese military alliance of 1902–22 with a more multilateral system consistent with international peace and collective security.

These government treaties were reinforced by the broad cooperation of the private business in Asia through the China Consortium. This banking cartel was first formed during the years before World War I by British, French,

American, and German banking groups. Each national banking group included all of that country's major banks interested in loans to China. Each was led by a bank that would represent the others in joint credit negotiations. The consortium operated on the principle that all railroad and sovereign loans to China would be jointly and equally shared by the four national groups, thereby presenting a strong common front to the Chinese government in loan negotiations and preventing segmentation of the Chinese railway system into spheres of influence based on specific national groups, as had occurred previously. Since the banking groups also had close business alliances with trading and shipping companies, engineering firms, and other businesses, they could jointly enforce broad international business cooperation in China, the private counterpart to the public "Open Door" Nine Power Treaty. The initial four national groups were joined in 1912 by two more from Japan and Russia, although in fact the banks of the "Russian" group were almost entirely controlled by foreign, especially French and Belgian, capitalists. Soon World War I and the Russian Revolution led to the ouster of the German and Russian groups, leaving only the American, British, French, and Japanese. After the war the consortium enforced a fairly effective credit embargo on successive Chinese governments until the mid-1930s since none were willing or able to resume interest payments on large consortium loans to China made in the years just before World War I.

Membership in the China Consortium opened vast opportunities to the Big Four *zaibatsu* that comprised the members of the Japanese group. The lead bank of the Japanese group, Mitsui Bank, was the bank at the center of the Mitsui *zaibatsu*, the largest of the Big Four. The Mitsui group as a whole had by far the largest share of Japanese business in China, including nearly all the large Japanese firms manufacturing cotton textiles there and much of China's foreign trade. Mitsui separately had strong ties with the other national groups, including especially the American group led by J.P. Morgan & Co. For decades Morgan syndicated nearly all Japanese loans issued on the New York market and tied several American companies under its influence with similar Mitsui companies. The most important of these Morgan-brokered alliances was between the largest electrical products firms in the two countries: General Electric and Toshiba. Bonds underwritten by Morgan also helped Japan's largest power company, Tokyo Electric Light, win a politically sensitive "war" within the electrical power industry of Japan around the time of the Great Depression.

The lucrative foreign ties of the Big Four infuriated nationalistic elements of the Japanese military and their business allies, mostly among what the Japanese called the *shinko zaibatsu*, meaning "new combines." Unlike the Big Four, the *shinko zaibatsu* did not have strong banks at the core. Furthermore, they had little foothold in the foreign trade sector or the export industries in which Japan had a strong comparative advantage, such as cotton and rayon textiles. They were concentrated in newer heavy industries, such as chemicals (including explosives), that were of great interest to the Japanese military, but unable to compete at world market prices. Therefore these newer businesses supported strong tariff protection and a protected empire that could exclude foreign business rivals, like the British and French empires. This idea came to be called the Japanese Co-Prosperity Sphere. It was in direct opposition to the Open Door commitment of the China Consortium and the Washington Treaty System and its Japanese sponsors, the Big Four, and their allies in government.

The Japanese military were also irritated by the budget and foreign policies of Japan's internationalists who supported cooperation with the Western powers. Morgan, as the fiscal agent of Japan's Finance Ministry in New York capital markets, repeatedly insisted on cuts to Japan's army and navy as part of the budget retrenchment required for Japan to establish prewar parity of its currency at two yen per dollar. Such fiscal austerity was the quid pro quo demanded by Morgan in return for continuing to back Japan's New York bond issues, including the loan that enabled Japan to restore the gold standard. The Washington Treaty system also forced the Japanese army to retreat from some of its conquests in East Asia and avoid creating any new exclusive national spheres of influence in China, antagonizing Japanese nationalists.

The bearish budget and credit policies required to restore Japan to the gold standard caused the 1927 financial crash that bankrupted some *shinko zaibatsu* and many smaller businesses, banks, and farmers. The internationalists gained enormously at the expense of their nationalist adversaries during this crisis. Many of the nationalist business leaders adversely affected by that crash and the depression a few years later contributed to the violent nationalist military secret societies, such as the Black Dragon Society, dedicated to overthrowing their internationalist enemies in Japan and creating an exclusive empire in East Asia, mostly in China. They organized the assassination of many of the leading Japanese internationalists, including former government ministers and even Baron Dan, the head of the Mitsui group and therefore the most powerful business leader in Japan and second only to the emperor in wealth. Nationalists in the military overthrew the government around the same time, eliminating party government and any semblance of democracy in Japan until after the war. Even before gaining full power in Tokyo, nationalist officers controlling Japan's Kwantung Army in northeastern China defied their own headquarters and direct orders from the emperor to begin the gradual conquest of China. As they gained control of more of the country, they turned over many of its resources to their business allies among the *shinko zaibatsu*, who gained business in China at the expense not only of the Chinese, but even trade-oriented Japanese rivals like the Mitsui group. The ascendency of business nationalism in Japan sidelined their internationalist rivals and led directly to war, first with China, then later with USA and its allies as well.

War aims of bullish business internationalism

Business internationalism emerged tentatively during World War I as a solution to the problems of international conflict that led to that war. It involved explicit rejection of business nationalism and the pattern of business alignment that produced imperialism. It was not against empires as such, but against empires that constituted protected and exclusive trading blocs. Business internationalists favor multilateral trade and financial systems, allowing the most competitive businesses to operate globally. They are not averse to cartels and financial consortia, as long as these are inclusive of the leading producers worldwide. Business internationalism emerged most strongly in Britain and the USA since these two had the most developed international financial systems and thus were best placed to exploit the opportunities of a more open world trading system. The most competitive companies of other countries were also attracted to the possibilities of business internationalism, if the world order could be reformed to make it feasible.

The major elements of an open competitive international environment are trade relatively free from tariffs and other government barriers and an international currency system, such as the gold standard, to stabilize international exchange prices and bond values. Business internationalists also favor peace through diplomacy and collective security in order to secure the benefits of trade, foreign investment, and stable prices. In other words, the liberal idea of international public goods corresponds broadly with the business internationalists' view of a favorable global business environment. Liberalism is the international relations theory most congenial to business internationalism. Business internationalists tended to be bearish well into the Great Depression, when some began to seek global means of promoting reflation and restoring the possibility of bullish credit expansion.

Business internationalism and IR liberalism were expressed institutionally in a plethora of new organizations founded during and after World War I. Funding data in the Rockefeller family archives show that many of these organizations were primarily financed by a small circle of internationalist business leaders, including the Rockefeller, Morgan, Carnegie, and Mellon interests in the USA. The central private foreign policy organizations for business internationalists have been the Council on Foreign Relations (CFR) in the USA and the Royal Institute of International Affairs (RIIA) in Britain. The same circles also founded many other organizations, including the League to Enforce the Peace, the Foreign Policy Association, the League of Nations Association, and dozens of other internationalist organizations (Nolt 1994; Maxfield & Nolt 1990). Business internationalists initially mobilized because of the shortcomings of the implementation of peace after World War I.

Many business internationalists turned more bullish during the 1930s as a result of the Great Depression. Whereas the first part of US President Franklin Roosevelt's (FDR) "New Deal" was protectionist in trade policy, by the mid-1930s, a significant realignment of major business interests promoted internationalism once again (Ferguson 1995b: 113–72). The first part of the New Deal was principally an effort to stop price deflation by promoting industrial cartels and labor unions to raise prices under the National Recovery Administration (NRA). USA also devalued the dollar from $20 to $35 per ounce of gold and suspended dollar–gold convertibility, which further discouraged imports on top of the record high Smoot-Hawley tariff of 1930. By raising import prices, the devaluation of the dollar contributed to both reversing deflation and protecting the higher prices of the cartels formed under the NRA. The US economy rebounded, but by 1935 the NRA was rejected as unconstitutional by the Supreme Court. Meanwhile, FDR had begun to court more internationalist business support during 1934 with two crucial innovations: the Reciprocal Trade Agreements Act (RTAA) and the Export-Import (Exim) Bank. The RTAA allowed the president to negotiate tariff cuts of up to 50 percent with foreign countries even without Congressional approval. Exim introduced the government into the business of subsidizing selected US foreign trade with low interest credit at a time when private trade financing had declined because of numerous bank failures and high real short-term interest rates. These policy tools enabled the US to begin to take the lead in reconstructing a multilateral international trade and monetary system. Many argue this is the beginning of the turn of the US toward accepting a leadership role in reconstructing a liberal world economy, the beginning of American hegemony.

The internationalist initiatives of the 1930s began to open the possibilities of a new world order, but they were more aspirational than successful in the difficult international context of the time. It would take the decisive victory in World War II and decades of peaceful development to implement them fully. But even these tentative first steps began to break down nationalist barriers and show the future promise of more extensive collaboration. After the failure of the London Conference of 1933, the first step in reconstructing a more stable and cooperative international monetary system occurred with the Tripartite Agreement of 1936, stabilizing currency relations between the USA, Britain, and France. Other remaining gold bloc countries, including Belgium, Switzerland, and the Netherlands, also cooperated with this agreement. This was the beginning of the reformation of the alliance that would soon confront the economic nationalism of the Nazis. A stronger foundation was laid in 1938, when the USA and Britain signed a reciprocal trade agreement, once again facilitating trade between the massive dollar and sterling blocs. Since most Latin American countries already based their currencies on the dollar and the British Empire and Commonwealth countries on the pound sterling, this was the most important achievement of the RTAA, even though it was effectively nullified the following year with the outbreak of World War II and the subsequent nationalization of all trade. It did at least set the USA and Britain on a cooperative economic path that contributed to their subsequent cooperation as wartime allies.

The bullish expansionary goals of the second New Deal were incorporated into Anglo-American war aims even before the US itself was involved in the war. At the outbreak of World War II in September 1939, the CFR formed the War and Peace Studies Committee to draft war aims and design institutions for the postwar world order. All the major institutions and policy initiatives of the postwar international system were designed by the end of 1940 in a series of more than 600 policy papers crafted through numerous policy discussions involving the foremost American business internationalists in cooperation with their counterparts at the RIIA. Business internationalists were determined to secure the peace after World War II, avoiding the weaknesses and failures of the previous peace. Their discussions even included designing the public relations campaign for the postwar effort to isolate and defeat expected business nationalist opposition to the program to avoid the sort of political failures that plagued internationalism after World War I. After the USA formally joined in the war, these CFR documents and many of the personnel who drafted them were incorporated into the Policy Planning Staff of the US Department of State to implement them, with minor modifications, as part of the official war aims.

After the end of World War II, a series of public conferences were held that drew the attention of historians ever since. Therefore most believe that the postwar international monetary system was designed at the Bretton Woods conference of 1944, along with the organization to implement it, the International Monetary Fund (IMF). Actually, that conference just put the finishing touches on a detailed system already designed during CFR–RIIA discussions in 1940, which most historians ignore, thereby losing sight of the central business role in its design. The same is true of the plans for the postwar unification of Europe, as discussed in Chapter 11. The multilateral trading system first implemented through various General Agreement on Trade and Tariffs (GATT) rounds and later completed as the World Trade Organization was originally designed as the International Trade Organization by the CFR. The American-financed economic reconstruction of Europe, credited to Secretary of State George Marshall as "the Marshall Plan," also had its roots in a War and Peace Studies Committee design. The International Bank for Reconstruction and Development (IBRD), designed to implement European reconstruction and protected industrialization of underdeveloped countries, precursor to what is today called the World Bank, was also designed in the same series of meetings during 1940, as discussed in Chapter 12. The only major aspect of the postwar system that was not well foreseen in 1940 CFR–RIIA discussions was the Cold War with the Soviet bloc. The World War II internationalist war aims were implemented only gradually after the war, but steadily, with no strategic setbacks, as occurred after World War I with the failure of the USA to join the League of Nations or ratify the Versailles Agreement, the resurgence of Anglo-French imperialism in Morocco and the Middle East, the increasing protectionism of major powers, the reparations debacle, and eventually the failure of the gold standard. The peace settlement after World War II was more consistently internationalist.

Vulnerability of nationalist powers

German and Japanese war aims in World War II were strongly shaped by the economic needs of their business nationalism. Whereas under a free trade regime, either country could have secured its resource needs through trade, as both have demonstrated so successfully since 1945, success as trading nations would mean growth and success for internationalist business and stagnation or even economic extinction for most nationalist interests. When nationalists believed that war offered them a better alternative, they took the gamble. Nationalist business interests in both countries funded the rise of radical nationalist political forces that would deliver not only protectionism, but also remilitarization and wars of conquest. Even during the war, however, internationalist business continued to resist, especially in Japan, and frustrated some of the more extreme plans of the nationalists. US business internationalists were confident enough in ultimate victory to begin planning how they would reshape the peace even before the USA actively joined the war.

This confidence was not misplaced. The very raw material weaknesses that drove Germany and Japan to war also proved to be their Achilles heel in a global war of attrition. Nationalist efforts to plunder the resources of conquered countries enriched some interests for a time, but ultimately merely debilitated their economies and spurred resistance without gaining much for the Axis war effort, always crucially hampered by scarcity of oil and other key materials (Milward 1977).

Oil was a crucial problem for the Axis. Italy, for example, was hobbled by a lack of oil from the moment it joined the war on the Axis' side in June 1940. It had to beg Germany for a share of its own scarce oil supplies. Its major fleet operations were always limited by fuel shortages. Japan was even worse off. It had almost no oil close by. It had to capture oil supplies during 1942 in Burma and the Dutch East Indies, using one of its few wartime paratroop drops to try, unsuccessfully, to capture the oil facilities intact. The oil of Indonesia was owned by Royal Dutch Shell and Standard Oil. The latter was at the time the largest single US foreign direct investment in Asia. Executives of Standard Oil had been anticipating a Japanese attack since the Munich Conference of 1938, and so had carefully rigged their facilities for demolition in order to destroy them before they fell into Japanese hands. Prewar the oil had been transported to Japan mostly in company-owned tankers. When these were withdrawn during 1941 as the Allies organized an oil embargo against Japan, even with a crash building program, Japan was never able to build enough tankers to transport the oil in sufficient quantity, even when it was captured and the facilities repaired, especially as losses from US submarines mounted. By 1944 it had to base its main fleet at Singapore rather than in Japan itself to be closer to the oil supplies, but the US landing in the Philippines threatened to cut off the supply route, so Japan sacrificed most of its remaining fleet at the Battle of Leyte Gulf in a vain effort to prevent the severing of its oil supplies. Its resort to kamikaze tactics at the same time was in part because shortage of aviation gasoline left it with inadequate supplies for sufficient large-scale pilot training. The simple training for suicide pilots required much less fuel.

Less well known is the Axis' shortage of other crucial supplies, such as rubber and certain non-ferrous metals in Europe and steel in Japan. The

Japanese army and navy were separate and equally powerful armed services both largely independent of the government and theoretically subordinate to the emperor, who was too remote from administration to act as a coordinating executive. Both services demanded larger shares of the scarce steel supplies. The army demanded a larger share in particular after 1937, when its large-scale invasion of China began, yet its operations were always hampered and limited by a shortage of munitions. After Japan abandoned the London and Washington Treaties limiting its naval arms in 1934, its navy launched a hugely ambitious rearmament program that was impossible to implement because of the shortage of steel. Thus, ironically, Japan's navy actually slipped further behind the US Navy rather than surging ahead. The US consistently built more ships throughout the 1930s. During the summer of 1940, Congress authorized a huge new building program that would by 1943, when it was complete, triple the size of the navy. Japan had not the slightest chance of defeating this force. Also in 1940, in reaction to the Japanese occupation of parts of French Indochina, the US further crippled the Japanese naval expansion plans by an embargo on exporting scrap steel to Japan. US had been the main source of scrap for Japan's electric furnace steel industry, which supplemented the output of its inadequate integrated steel plants that made steel from imported iron ore. There is a persistent myth that the isolationist USA was unprepared for the surprise attack by Japan in December 1941. In fact, decisive preparations had begun more than a year earlier, which is why Japan made the desperate but ultimately futile surprise attack in an effort to win quickly before it was too late.

Incomplete victory

The Allied victory in 1945 thoroughly defeated the German and Japanese regimes. The Allied powers tried to reorganize both countries not only to reform government, but also to restructure private power. In the case of Germany, consistent joint policy proved difficult since Germany was divided into four occupation zones. Nonetheless, some large combines, such as chemical giant I.G. Farben, were broken up. Within a few years three zones were reunited under a single West German government at Bonn, while the Soviet Union formed a very different communist regime in East Germany. The two German polities were somewhat constrained from the beginning both economically and militarily by being integrated into larger multinational blocs. American occupation of Japan attempted not only to institute democracy, but also to break up *zaibatsu* control of the economy. This was only partially successful. The family owners were somewhat removed from control of the huge combines, but the combines themselves quickly reassembled their constituent parts and most were reconstituted as *keiretsu*. Yet the balance of private power in both Japan and West Germany was reformed significantly because both were reintegrated into a more open global trading and payments system that enabled their export-oriented business internationalists to flourish.

The closed-in protectionist world of the 1930s gradually gave way to the second great era of liberal globalization.

However, there was a major exception to the more open trading system instituted according to the blueprint of the business internationalists: the Soviet bloc. Chapter 13 discusses the Cold War opposition between the Soviet bloc and the capitalist "free world." Compared with World War I, business internationalism was more strongly rooted after World War II, with the obvious and ultimately temporary exception of the Soviet bloc. Whereas until the end of World War II, the socialist world was largely confined to the Soviet Union itself, after the war China, North Korea, and much of Eastern Europe were incorporated into a socialist bloc. During the Cold War, Vietnam, Cuba, and a few other countries were added. The socialist countries maintained strong credit, trade, and foreign exchange controls that prevented free trading. These were reinforced by trade restrictions imposed by most capitalist countries on trade with the socialist bloc.

Furthermore, as we explore in the next two chapters, even within the capitalist world, the extreme wartime controls on trade, finance, and foreign exchange were lifted only gradually. The transition to relatively free trade and payments was slower than after World War I, but ultimately more effective, since there was no recurrence of the sort of severe economic downturn that followed a decade of uneven transition after World War I. Furthermore, the postwar progress of business internationalism was continuous, if not perfectly steady. There were no major setbacks or reversals. In fact, business internationalism made several huge leaps forward with the growing unification of Europe (Chapter 11), the industrialization of much of the developing world (Chapter 12), opening of China to world trade beginning during the 1980s, and the end of the Cold War and the demise of the Soviet Union in 1991 (Chapter 13). Postwar resistance to the plans of business internationalists was significant, but eventually largely overcome. Whereas the first great liberal globalization of the middle part of the nineteenth century produced deep deflation and a series of depressions that led to imperialism and World War I, the second liberal globalization has occurred within a somewhat more bullish political economy that permitted fairly sustained economic growth interrupted by relatively short downturns. Liberals typically do not count mercantilism as a period of globalization since they tend to equate globalization with liberalization, so I count the nineteenth century as the second globalization and the recent period as the third. Chapter 14 explores whether this third globalization will prove more sustainable than the first two.

11 European unification

The gradual unification of Europe during the decades since World War II is a world historic development. A large portion of the economically most advanced part of the world voluntarily surrendered significant elements of state sovereignty to a supranational European Union. This sort of development was long anticipated by liberals like Kant and long ridiculed by realists as an unworkable pipe dream. While the individual aspirations of Europeans sick from the nightmarish death and devastation of two world wars certainly played a role, it is unlikely that the unification of Europe could have been accomplished without the strong interest and pressure of internationalist business, not only within Europe itself, but also from the USA. Kant himself realized already during the eighteenth century that such a league of peace among nations would depend not only on the existence of law-abiding republican governments, but also what Kant called the "universal hospitality" of peoples that would develop only gradually as they came under closer mutual relations (Beck 1963: 102–5). But whereas Kant and other liberals emphasize the restraining effect of laws and norms, corporatism emphasizes that supranational integration such as the European Union can succeed only with the support of dominate elements of private power – business internationalists – acting in their own self-interest.

The business basis for the unification of Europe was already suggested by the formation of international cartels in Europe involving Britain, France, and Germany during the 1930s. Most notable of these was the iron, steel, and coal cartel (Johnson 1953). Ironically, the success of these cartels helped mollify some sectors of British and French business that might otherwise have been hostile to Nazi Germany earlier. They provided the business basis for appeasement. Once the war broke out, planning began among British, French, and American internationalists for a postwar settlement that would include economic unification of postwar Europe. Internationalists intended to avoid the reparations debacle that isolated Germany and weakened its economy after World War I. What became the "Marshall Plan" for US aid for European postwar reconstruction was already designed in 1940 by cooperation between business leaders in Britain's Royal Institute for International Affairs and the War and Peace Study Committee of the Council on Foreign Relations in New York. The plan was predicated on European economic integration that would include a revival of the prewar cartels. This plan was implemented after the war, beginning with a resuscitation of the iron, steel, and coal cartel known as the European Coal and Steel Community. During subsequent decades the deeper unification of Europe was pushed forward by business internationalists against weakening resistance from nationalists.

The "Marshall Plan" for European reconstruction after World War II involved massive US subsidies to European countries to purchase materials in the USA, especially productive machinery and building materials and equipment, to replace the vast quantities of durable capital, housing, and economic infrastructure destroyed or worn out during the war. It benefitted US business internationalists in a way similar to the industrialization of the developing world also sponsored by the USA during the same period, discussed in Chapter 12. Most obviously it stimulated demand for US exports at a time when Europeans may have otherwise been hobbled by insufficient export earnings to finance their needed imports. Related to this, it helped solve the worldwide "dollar shortage" that developed after the war as scores of countries needed dollars to import goods, especially productive capital goods, from the USA but lacked sufficient stocks of US dollars to pay for what was needed, especially since continuing postwar exchange controls and tariff protection of parts of the US economy made it difficult to earn sufficient dollars by exporting to the USA. All countries also needed a net inflow of dollars to accumulate reserve assets to support their currencies under the new Bretton Woods monetary system, which replaced gold with dollar assets as the major reserves backing the notes of most countries' central banks. Another benefit to US business internationalists is less often noticed: the Marshall Plan insisted on reducing the barriers to trade within Europe, which tended to benefit the largest and most competitive enterprises, including many US multinational corporations that established branch plants within Europe. The more Europe was integrated into a common market, the more easily a competitive enterprise located in any one country could compete successfully throughout Europe.

The integration of Europe was facilitated by the body of international trade law developed after World War II under the aegis of the successive rounds of the General Agreement on Trade and Tariffs (GATT), which eventually evolved into the World Trade Organization (WTO). At first glance, development of a European common market, formalized in the European Economic Community (EEC) of 1958, might seem to violate the spirit of the Most Favored Nation (MFN) principle, essential to GATT. MFN says that any trade privilege granted to any one trading partner is equally extended to every other with which that country also maintains MFN status. Since all GATT and subsequently WTO members by joining these organizations automatically grant MFN status to each other, it might seem that the free trade privileges the EEC members granted to each other and common external EEC tariff charged against non-EEC imports would violate the non-discriminatory thrust of MFN. However, GATT and later the WTO always included an exception allowing free trade agreements among any subset of member nations. Other nations have subsequently taken advantage of the same provision, most importantly the USA, Canada, and Mexico in the North American Free Trade Agreement (NAFTA). Some realists have interpreted the formation of free trade blocs as portending a redivision of the world into a new set of superpowers based on rival trade and currency blocs, but nothing like this has happened since business internationalists at the heart of the integration process favor not only freer trade within each bloc but also the greater economic integration of the various blocs.

The greater integration of both the European and the world economies has been spurred especially by the integration of financial business and markets on a global, not regional, scale. The accumulation of dollar assets in Europe and other countries under the Bretton Woods monetary system helped spur this integration. The huge explosion of offshore finance, most notably, the Eurodollar or, more accurately, the Eurobond market, has contributed to an integration of world finance on a scale similar to what occurred during the nineteenth century as London became the center of global finance. Thus to better understand the financial underpinnings of business internationalism today, we must examine the impact of the rise and demise of Bretton Woods and the less studied development of the Eurobond and other offshore financial business.

The Bretton Woods monetary system and its demise

The conventional wisdom about Bretton Woods is that it provided many of the same benefits as a gold standard or bimetallic monetary system but with a little more flexibility for bullish monetary expansion. This is true regarding its design, but not how it actually operated for the most of its quarter century. Historically, the gold standard and the bimetallic standard before it had provided very stable exchange rates among major currencies for about a century with only a few minor adjustments. Furthermore, during most of that period, nearly all the major currencies of the world were freely convertible into one another. The only major exception was during World War I and its immediate aftermath. There were also a few periods during the nineteenth century when some of the weaker currencies suspended free convertibility. The Bretton Woods system operated with limited convertibility of currencies for at least half of its existence and included significant revaluations and devaluations of currencies far more than during the specie standards prior to World War I. Although the dollar was linked to gold during Bretton Woods, inflation occurred consistently and increasingly among all major countries. Prices were less stable than during the gold standard, but deflation did not occur.

Bretton Woods was somewhat more congenial to economic nationalism than the gold standard had been, though this was not the main intent of its design. The exchange controls and revisions of exchange rates under Bretton Woods increased national economic autonomy, allowing countries to follow divergent national fiscal and monetary policies. The first few postwar years witnessed turmoil greater than after World War I. High inflation ravaged the currencies of Germany, Japan, Italy, and China, among others. Several currencies were sharply devalued after the war, including the British pound. Most European countries maintained foreign exchange controls throughout World War II until 1958. Japan did not end its controls until 1964. Most developing countries, as discussed in the next chapter, maintained stringent foreign exchange controls throughout the Bretton Woods era. Even after exchange controls were eliminated, most countries maintained significant capital controls throughout the Bretton Woods period, which stimulated the development the Eurobond market, discussed in the next section. Even considering only USA and Europe, Bretton Woods functioned stably as designed for less than a decade from 1958 to 1967. By the end of that period, the British pound was again devalued and the price of gold among private traders began to diverge from its official price. Within two years France devalued the franc, Germany revalued the mark, and France and other countries, expecting the dollar to devalue, began demanding gold in exchange for growing dollar reserves. President Nixon ended the convertibility of dollars into gold and devalued the dollar in 1971. By 1973 all major currencies were floating vis-à-vis each other. A fundamental problem of the Bretton Woods design was that major global reserve currencies, such as the dollar and, to a lesser extent, the British pound, were vulnerable to crises of confidence because of the need to run balance of payments deficits in order to supply the world with the necessary monetary reserves.

Although the Bretton Woods system was lauded by liberal IPE as a major cornerstone of postwar international cooperation, in retrospect it was not so successful. Nationalist regimes could still manipulate monetary and credit policies. Realists were not surprised and pointed to the failures of cooperation based on the continued autonomy of national states. Bretton Woods proved to be not a very strong vehicle for international cooperation or for the unification of Europe. In fact, although the demise of Bretton Woods initially worried many liberals that international cooperation was breaking down in much the way it had during the Great Depression four decades earlier, in fact the floating exchange rate system that replaced Bretton Woods, in the context of the liberalization and globalization of private finance, provided a firmer foundation for the eventual unification of Europe than Bretton Woods ever could.

Eurobonds and European monetary integration

European monetary integration was pushed forward less by cooperation among governments than by financial integration pushed by private financial interests. Realists are probably right. Left to their own devices, the independent nation-states of western and southern Europe might have never cooperated successfully to form a deeper European Union. But realists are wrong to believe that states are the only power in the international system. Private financial interests innovated to create new methods of financing that grew rapidly to become the driving force in European economic integration.

The most powerful new factor promoting European financial integration was the development of the Eurobond market, which essentially facilitated cross-border long-term capital investments. The market began slowly during the mid-1960s, pioneered by the London investment bank, S.G. Warburg, and Germany's Deutsche Bank (Ferguson 2010: 201–32). Eurobonds essentially created a supranational financial market within continued national limitations on capital mobility. The Eurobond market transcended currency controls of individual countries by issuing dollar-denominated bonds that would not be subject to the controls related to European national currencies. The precondition for this was the existence of substantial pools of US dollar funds within Europe, pools often restricted by currency regulations from crossing borders. Investing these funds directly in dollar-denominated bonds issued by American underwriters but sold largely by European banks provided an ingenuous way around national currency controls while developing pan-European capital markets. Dollar interest rates in Europe typically greatly exceeded those in the USA at the time, so Eurobonds also provided an attractive rate of return. As a result, the Eurobond market took off quickly so that by 1967 it outstripped the US market for foreign securities and was five times greater than European national bond markets. It continued to grow thereafter. Although the Eurobond market started out issuing primarily dollar-denominated bonds, it soon branched out into issuing in other currencies as well, including German marks and British pounds. Warburg even pioneered issuing dual currency bonds, payable either in pounds or marks.

Of course, as discussed in Chapter 4, the Eurobond "market" was actually not primarily a market at all, but a primary placement of bonds by a cartel or syndicate of banks. Like typical IPOs, primary issues of Eurobonds were handled by semi-permanent syndicates that suppressed if not eliminated competition among banks. The syndicate system involves a lead bank negotiating the terms of the bond issue with the debtor and then sharing the placement of the bonds with members of the syndicate according to agreed percentages. Primary "markets" involving IPOs are thus not actually the markets of textbook abstraction. Only gradually did a secondary market develop for Eurobonds. The public secondary market is a true market in the sense that it is open to all buyers and sellers at public prices. But new credit originates only on the primary "market"; the secondary market is a market for existing assets but not for credit. Ferguson (2010: 226–27) discusses the composition of some of these private financial syndicates.

Eurobond markets might have begun to diminish somewhat after the demise of the Bretton Woods system during the early 1970s. The emergence of a floating exchange rate system made it less attractive for borrowers in weak-currency countries to issue bonds denominated in strong currencies like the German mark because of the risk that the cost of the loan would increase as the weak currency devalued against the strong one. However, this risk was offset by the increased use of financial derivatives and thus prompted the subsequent explosion of derivatives trading, including especially currency swaps, which allow holders of income streams (for example, from the coupon payments of bonds) in different currencies to swap them in order to receive the income in the currency that they most require for payments due. Thus, instead of diminishing, Eurobond markets only continued to grow, reaching about 90 percent of all international bond issues, of which about 70 percent is now traded in London (Ferguson 2010: 232). London thus reemerged from the doldrums of the world wars to become once again one of the two greatest financial centers in the world, along with New York.

Europe's complex political unification

Europe's economic unification preceded its political integration and provided the basis and the business interest for it. The rapid growth of inter-European commerce has made it more and more cost efficient for the business internationalists who are competitive across national borders to seek common laws and rules to govern their business activities within each member state. Thus more and more political institutions were gradually added to the original postwar framework that was primarily concerned with a limited set of trade, price, and production rules within the coal and steel industries. The growing financial integration of Europe via the Eurobond market fostered this process and contributed to the eventual adoption of a common currency, the euro, for most of Europe. Two business interests have driven the unification of Europe: the internationalism of Europe's (and indeed USA's) most competitive businesses and the credit power of the financial interests behind the Eurobond integration of Europe's financial business.

However, in order to buy off the potential resistance of opponents to European integration, one of the most expensive and controversial of the European Union's programs is the Common Agricultural Program (CAP). It has fairly successfully neutralized potential agricultural resistance to the EU in many countries where agriculture is uncompetitive and therefore objectively nationalist by protecting agriculture using common European tariffs, non-tariff barriers to imports such as the ban on genetically modified crops, and EU price support policies. Rural districts and agricultural interests are a natural constituency for anti-EU conservative nationalism. Although the CAP satisfies some rural constituencies with high agricultural prices, others are frustrated by its expense and anticompetitive bias.

Europe's political unification was pushed forward by growing attention to non-tariff barriers to trade once the EEC had eliminated internal tariffs in favor of a common external European tariff. Political unification was needed both to set those common external tariffs at a pan-European level and to deal with the proliferation of non-tariff barriers to trade represented by national regulations in such areas as product quality and safety and environmental regulations where the regulations of one country were often tailored to the products of that country and discriminated against those of other European countries.

An interesting example of a non-tariff barrier was Europe's long-running "chocolate war" that was finally resolved by the European Commission in 2000. This "war" pitted France and Belgium, especially, against Britain and Scandinavian countries. The former insisted that anything sold as "chocolate" must be made from cocoa butter, according to their national regulations. Thus they excluded products from the latter that were labeled as chocolate but substituted cheaper vegetable fats for cocoa butter. The eventual resolution was a victory for the lower standard that did not require chocolate to include cocoa butter, as long as the actual ingredients were clearly labeled. This resolution reflects the general trend that European product safety and quality regulations have tended to be eased downward to the least common denominator among the various European countries. The effect is to both lower standards and reduce non-tariff barriers to trade.

While some realists, in particular, repeatedly predict the demise of European unification, in fact it had continued to advance, if only by fits and starts. Even the recent Eurobond crisis did not derail progress as many skeptics predicted. Although the boundaries of political and monetary union do not exactly coincide, this has not been a major obstacle to deepening of relations among European countries and further integration of European financial markets and powers. One of the most persuasive signs of the success of both the European Union and the overlapping eurozone is that both remain strongly attractive to potential new members and both continue to expand successfully. The European Union (EU) started in 1993 with only six members and has expanded today to 28, with several more applying to join. The euro currency was adopted initially by 11 countries in 1999 and has expanded to 27 today. The competitive strength and political influence of European internationalist business is the main reason why European unification cannot be reversed without enormous countervailing power.

Significance of the European Union for IR theory

The European Union is a watershed in international history and a major challenge for international relations theory, especially realism. Whereas liberals long held that international cooperation stimulates gradually closer and closer integration of nations, eventually leading to regional integration and perhaps even world government, realism believes nation-states are the fundamental units of the international system whose power cannot be transcended. Therefore

European unification is a major vindication of liberal theory, even though few liberals have clearly described the private business motives underlying it. Liberals remain too mired in the minutia of laws and administrative organs to see the private power at the core of unification.

Because realism considers nation-states as the fundamental constitutive element of international politics, it is unable to provide an adequate theory as to why these supposedly atomic units could choose voluntarily to surrender sovereignty to a larger union. Realism considers conquest the main means of amalgamation of nations, as in the unification of Germany and Italy through a series of wars during the nineteenth century. Yet voluntary integrations of nations into larger units are not so rare in history.

Among the first integrations of states in recorded history are the Delian and Peloponnesian Leagues described by Thucydides. The Delian League started as an alliance of Greek city-states fighting against Persia during the fifth century BCE. It was named for the original location of its treasury in a temple on the island of Delos. Even though it started as an alliance, because it had a common treasury it was already something of an international organization transcending the sovereignty of the individual city-states comprising it. As Athens was the pre-eminent city within the league, it gradually gained hegemony over it, eventually usurping the treasury and moving it to Athens. Yet even as the Delian League evolved into the Athenian empire, it was not created predominantly by conquest, but by the common interests of democratic parties in numerous states against the Persian threat to re-impose tyrannies. Likewise, the Peloponnesian League started as an alliance of regional states led by Sparta meeting as a deliberative council distinct from any of its individual members. The two leagues fought on opposite sides during the two long Peloponnesian Wars. During later centuries other such leagues emerged in Greece until it was conquered by Rome.

The Holy Roman Empire is another example of a kind of league of states from the ninth through the early nineteenth century. Critics have quipped that it was neither holy nor Roman nor an empire. In fact it was a fairly loose association of mostly German states, a few of the larger of which had the privilege of electing the emperor. During its last centuries, the influence of the Austrian Habsburg dynasty over several German states was great enough that the archduke of Austria was habitually elected emperor. Nevertheless, the empire was something less than a united state but more than an informal alliance. It occupies some sort of middle ground of international organization largely ignored by realist theory. Despite its somewhat amorphous character, the Holy Roman Empire deserves more attention if for no other reason than because it was the longest-lived confederation in history.

Europe also witnessed leagues similar to those of ancient Greece, including the Swiss Confederation and the Hanseatic League. The Swiss Confederation started as a league of independent cantons and only gradually evolved into a federal state. It shows the potential for such integration. The union of the seven Protestant provinces of the Netherlands into what became the modern state of the Netherlands is another similar example. The Hanseatic League was a loose association of mercantile city-states scattered around the North and Baltic Seas and along the navigable German rivers flowing into these. It was so geographically scattered, that may be one reason it never united into a single state like these other two examples. It did develop common rules for trading that helped promote the development of commerce in the northern waters of Europe until most of its member cities were absorbed into larger dynastic states.

Perhaps most importantly, 13 independent colonies allied together to fight for independence against Britain, but surrendered only a small portion of their sovereignty to the Continental Congress in Philadelphia. The various United States of America remained quite independent and formally sovereign at least until the US Constitution formed "a more perfect union" by about 1790. Even then, the formal sovereignty of the states comprising it was strongly disputed until the Civil War of 1861–65 decisively resolved the issue against the right of succession.

Some other cases of national integration, for example, the formation of Yugoslavia after World War I, were pushed by foreign business interests for much the same reasons as US business internationalists supported the integration of Europe. A united Yugoslavia provided a larger market for large foreign investors, but there was an additional reason in this case. The core of Yugoslavia was the Serbian state that had been the first of the Allied Powers engaged in World War I and had suffered defeat and occupation by the Central Powers. As a consequence of maintaining a large army in exile without controlling the country's tax revenue after being defeated, Serbia ended the war on the winning side, but with an inordinate foreign debt for such a small country. The easiest way to secure payment of this debt was to triple the population by adding to Serbia, and consequently burdening with Serbia's debt, the other South Slav "nations" that eventually split up again during World War II and during Europe's only significant war since, when Yugoslavia split up for good during the 1990s (Gibbs 2009: 55–62, 219–20). Romania was greatly enlarged after World War I as well, not simply to reward a loyal but defeated ally, but also to create a larger national state better able to pay its debts.

These and other cases seem to confound realism, though a realist perspective could be deduced to explain them because all of these were cases of weak states that originally banded together to resist more powerful external enemies. Although the thrust of their arguments is more typically liberal, several of the *Federalist Papers* make this sort of realist argument explicit in support of the American constitutional union. Pollard (1985) makes a similar realist argument to explain postwar European unification, arguing that it was greatly stimulated by the need to band together in the face of the powerful Soviet threat. However, this line of argument fails after the demise of the Soviet Union in 1991, unless realists can somehow argue that Europe faces a comparable security threat from the USA. What makes European unification so significant for international relations theory is that it largely occurs after the major external threat disappears. Furthermore, if the European Union is considered as a unit, it is the world's largest economy. It is not just an alliance of small powers, but includes four of the ten largest national economies in the world, including Germany, the world's largest exporter, and Britain, still the only rival to the USA in the depth and extent of its financial markets and private financial powers, although German competitors, dominant within the eurozone, are perhaps catching up. Yet, contrary to the fantasies of "currency war" realists like Rickards (2011), the Eurobond business shows how modern financial institutions tend to erode national boundaries rather than reinforcing them, integrating not only Europe, but the global economy.

12 The invention of economic development

> [The International Development Authority (IDA)] would guarantee capital invested in backward areas and at the same time establish certain conditions of investment and management ... the aim of the plan is to stimulate private investment ... If the world's economy is to run at high gear ... there will have to be a considerable shift in the production pattern of the world, as the primarily industries [agriculture and mining] decrease in relative importance ... Capitalists tend to invest in the older lines which they know and which are safe. This is exactly what is not wanted, and the IDA can help direct money into new channels ... The Authority should not limit itself to saying: "What resources are available in this country? Is it desirable to develop them?" but rather should ask itself: "What will these people want if their living standards rise? Can these needs be economically met by production in their own country?" ... The Authority must work within the present system of [trade] barriers.
>
> Council on Foreign Relations 1941, quoted in
> Maxfield and Nolt (1990: 55–56)

Surprisingly, industrialization of developing countries of the world was one of the war aims proposed during 1940 by the Council on Foreign Relations' (CFR) War and Peace Study Committee. Many of the "backward areas" targeted for economic development were then still colonial dependencies of the European powers. The plan supported by American internationalist business involved import substitution industrialization (ISI) of the newly developing countries, breaking the old colonial trading pattern of poorer countries exporting raw materials and importing industrial products. American business planned to profit in two ways: by jumping the ISI tariff barriers with local branch plants in each country and by selling the necessary machinery and equipment for industrialization. This was a major part of the postwar stimulus plan, in addition to the stimulation from the reconstruction of Europe and Japan. After the war ended, an addition impetus helped the plan become adopted: the Cold War rivalry with the Soviet Union and its allies. The US offered ISI as an attractive alternative for Third World nationalists to Soviet-style planned socialist industrialization. Each is a distinctive version of bullish nationalism.

ISI was originally designed as a temporary policy leading eventually to export-led industrialization (ELI), the current global economic development orthodoxy. However, graduation from ISI to ELI was delayed longer than originally expected because of the resistance of business nationalists in the developed world to opening their economies to industrial imports from the Third World. Once that was possible (by the 1970s), internationalist pressure for transition from ISI to ELI began in earnest. By the 1980s, with ELI succeeding throughout the world, even including China, economic development as a distinct field was redundant and began to fade away.

ISI accomplished several objectives simultaneously. Geopolitically it provided a way to separate newly independent countries from economic dependence on their former colonial rulers, while tying them closer to American business and keeping them out of the Soviet orbit. The anti-colonial ambition had been part of President Wilson's war aims during World War I as well. Several of his Fourteen Points comprising his public war aims involved keeping England and France from carving up the former Ottoman Empire by creating new colonial dependencies in the Middle East. US business internationalists, especially in the oil industry, were concerned about being shut out of the lucrative exploitation of Middle Eastern oil. Economically it was consistent with the broadly bullish internationalist war aims, expanding demand for US exports of productive machinery and equipment while allowing developing countries to pursue bullish business nationalism using policies not unlike those the Nazis employed so successfully. The only major differences between ISI and Nazi policies are that ISI would prioritize light rather than heavy industries and US and other foreign firms were encouraged to invest in ISI. Compared with Wilson's war aims, ISI was far more effective in realigning developing countries toward the USA politically and economically. It is one of the principal reasons, beyond merely the national power of the US itself, that the US became the leader of the Free World, to the great disappointment of declining colonial powers, especially France.

ISI origins

ISI had two origins. One was already mentioned. However, a few countries, notably Argentina, Brazil, Chile, Hungary, Romania, and Turkey, began ISI during the 1930s under the influence of Germany. Like most colonial dependencies as well, these independent countries had been exporting primarily minerals and agricultural products and importing consumer goods from the developed countries. When the Great Depression hit, their exports collapsed. The volume of trade decreased enormously and export prices fell as well. Prices of imported manufactured products did not drop as much since most developed countries were cartelizing their industries to reverse price deflation. At the same time, the collapse or decline of so many major banks greatly reduced the availability of loans for development and even trade finance. Developing countries were faced with a desperate challenge. Many were determined to industrialize to replace some of the products previously imported, but they would have difficulty paying the cost of imported machinery and financing both the long-term investment and the short-term trade since they had typically relied on financing by foreign banks.

Nazi Germany provided both a model to imitate and a source for needed machinery and other industrial goods. The major policy tools, as in the Nazi case, were foreign exchange controls, supplemented by tariffs. Such controls enabled national economies to plan trade and capital flows according to national priorities. In the case of Nazi Germany, the priority was restoring full employment production in existing industries and accelerating rearmament. In ISI planning, the goal was to develop new industries most suited to countries with scarce capital and relatively low consumption. ISI industries were those that substituted for existing imports, including especially mass consumer products produced by light industry, such as textiles and clothing, food processing, building materials, and simple consumer manufactured products.

The term "light" industry refers to industries that are both small-scale and labor-intensive, whereas "heavy" industries, such as steel, vehicles, machinery, shipbuilding, chemicals, and oil refining, are the large-scale or capital-intensive or both. Heavy industries demand much more capital to initiate, typically provided by long-term credit. They often require more engineering expertise as well. ISI countries would import needed industrial machinery and technical assistance from Germany in exchange for raw material products in short supply there, including wheat, cotton, beef, phosphorous, copper, oil, and rubber. Much of the exchange of products between Germany and these early ISI countries was organized as countertrade, that is, physical barter trade without using scarce foreign exchange or credit (Hirschman 1981). As detailed in the next section, tariffs and exchange controls would favor necessary imports such as machinery and provide strong protection to ISI industries so they could develop without strong foreign competition.

There were significant differences, however, between ISI as supported by Nazi business nationalism and the ISI designed by American business internationalists. Germany's main interest in developing countries was as a source of raw materials. This is in fact the main interest that had drawn European and American investors into the developing world during the preceding century. A new element was that ISI stimulated export demand for German machinery. The overdevelopment of this sector was desirable for the Nazis since machine-building industries would also contribute to the capacity for sustained mechanized warfare. When war eventually shut down much of Germany's overseas trade, any excess machine-building capacity could be switched to making weapons. Meanwhile, until the start of the war, Germany used countertrade not only to supply current needs but also to stockpile scarce strategic materials. Japan tried similar policies, but less successfully. The main limit of German-sponsored ISI was that Germany, with its own stringent capital controls enforcing national priorities for investable funds, could provide little financial support for ISI. By contrast, postwar US-sponsored ISI prioritized mobilizing both domestic and foreign sources of capital, including both public and private financing, thereby more successfully abetting a bullish pace of development.

ISI implementation

ISI was implemented jointly by the US government, including agencies newly created for that purpose; multilateral organizations, such as the World Bank, IMF, United Nations Development Program (UNDP) and various regional organizations; private business internationalists; and the governments and business leaders of ISI countries. As mentioned above, the broad goals and some of the policy details for postwar ISI were drafted first by the private organizations of US business internationalists, involving especially the CFR and its War and Peace Studies Group, the Committee for Economic Development, the National Planning Association, and the National Foreign Trade Council. The overlapping memberships of these groups included most of the large internationally competitive businesses interested in foreign trade and investment. Detailed development plans for each country were drafted by US government agencies, such as the Economic Cooperative Administration, which evolved into the US Agency for International Development (USAID), and multi-lateral organizations such as the World Bank. ISI plans were implemented for most countries in Latin America, South and Southeast Asia, Iran, South Korea, Taiwan, Turkey, and a few countries in Africa, including Algeria, Egypt, Ghana, Kenya, Morocco, South Africa, Tanzania and Tunisia (Maxfield & Nolt 1990: 55–59). ISI presents a paradox of highly protectionist program sponsored by pro-trade internationalist interests, which is why it is usually attributed only to Third World nationalists, ignoring the strong business backing it had, especially in the USA.

ISI had several component objectives. Since capital was scarce in developing countries, it encouraged diverting domestic capital toward targeted industries using various incentives, supplemented by private foreign capital invited to set up new factories and newly created government-run development banks to provide subsidized low-interest loans. ISI did not encourage the development of private banking because for-profit banks would have difficulty competing with government banks that were often paying higher interest to depositors than they were charging on loans, the difference subsidized by government revenue or foreign aid. Foreign exchange controls (insofar not evaded) discouraged wealthy people from sending their capital abroad while the protections and subsidies to industries favored under ISI encouraged them to invest instead in these profitable new industries.

Foreign exchange controls typically involved multiple exchange rates administered through a government-controlled central bank. Which exchange rate applied depended on the purpose of the transaction. ISI exchange control rules assigned the most favorable exchange rate to importers of productive machinery and raw materials required for ISI. Likewise, imported funds used to finance capital investment in ISI or for government purposes would be awarded a favorable rate of exchange. On the other hand, importers of non-essential products, tourists, exporters of capital, and traditional exports like agricultural products and minerals would also by forced to exchange money at an unfavorable rate. Traditional exporters would thus be disadvantaged as compared with free trade, since they would pay high prices for importable goods and receive relatively less local currency in return for their foreign exchange earnings. Exporters were forced to help subsidize the new industries developed under ISI.

Tariff schedules were revised under ISI plans. Previously tariffs in many countries had been designed to maximize revenue, so they were applied to a broad range of products, but not so high as to discourage significantly the volume of imports, and thus the reduce tax revenue. Under ISI, tariffs on goods necessary for the new industries were reduced or eliminated. Tariffs on imports that would compete with new domestic products were raised. In many cases, the combination of tariffs and exchange controls made the cost of imported products so high that imports competing with domestic ISI output virtually ceased. In those instances, tariff revenue actually decreased, so new taxes had to replace the revenue lost to governments by the more extreme tariff schedule. Both the elimination of some tariffs and the increase of others to prohibitive levels tended to reduce governmental tariff income. Primary tariff objectives shifted from gaining government revenue to protecting targeted industries.

Like all economic policies, ISI produced winners and losers. Those who invested in industries protected by ISI policies typically made high and secure profits. These included both domestic manufacturers and foreign multinationals that jumped ISI tariff barriers to set up branch plants within each protected economy. Among American companies, big winners included the large meat-packing and canning firms like Armour and Swift, consumer products companies like Proctor & Gamble, and electrical equipment manufacturers like General Electric and Westinghouse. These last two and many other companies also profited as exporters of productive equipment for the new industries and the infrastructure required by them. The losers included traditional exporters, some of them foreign businesses, and agriculture, which suffered higher prices and taxes without much compensating benefit. Third World politicians and government officials also benefitted from the many opportunities for corruption under ISI. The power to award foreign exchange licenses, subsidized develop-ment bank loans, and other favorable government policies promised to enrich beneficiaries who would therefore eagerly pay a cut of their windfall to officials for the privilege of becoming a protected ISI capitalist. Corruption in many countries was more severe than under similar exchange control regimes in Nazi Germany and the Soviet bloc because police efficiency was lower.

Development emerged as a subfield of economics that justified ISI in its early decades and thus seemed to contradict the teaching of every other field of economics. Whereas most of economics emphasized the superiority of market solutions, development economics advocated major government regulation of the economy. Whereas international trade theory argued that various countries have a comparative advantage in some goods more than others and should produce only those things in which they have a comparative advantage, develop-ment economics emphasized dynamic comparative advantage. Countries could transform their economies from exporting primarily raw materials to eventually producing industrial products competitively. Most industry was considered footloose in the long run, meaning that it could be profitably located in any country, given the right initial incentives to establish itself and then thrive. As the quote opening this chapter suggests, industrialization, rather than being the privilege of a favored few, could become universal.

Exceptions to ISI

ISI was not implemented in every country. Furthermore, even where ISI was implemented, it sometimes departed from the ideal advocated by US business internationalists. Three types of countries did not have much ISI development: (1) very small countries, since their small size gave them a national market too limited to develop a full range of efficient light industries; (2) most oil-producing countries, since the oil industry, dominated by powerful American companies, was the "traditional exporter" that would have been taxed under ISI to support industrialization and in most oil-exporting countries oil interests were powerful enough to prevent this; and (3) countries, mostly in Africa, still effectively dominated by the former colonial power. As Cox (1994) discusses in relation to Central America, some countries in the first category were encouraged to form customs unions to implement ISI within a larger economic area. A few countries where oil companies were strong did nonetheless implement ISI, including Iran and Indonesia. In Africa some of the countries most interested in ISI were also the most anti-colonial and most sympathetic to the socialist bloc, often jeopardizing their prospects for significant aid from developed Western countries. On the other hand, in other countries ISI was resisted by the former colonial power. France, in particular, retained significant neo-colonial influence in many of its former colonies.

For example, in Vietnam France's business interest largely involved export of raw rubber and silk to supply France's processing industries. Although the USA supported France's effort to reassert its control over Indochina until the Geneva Conference ended the first Vietnam War in 1954, the USA and France were at odds on economic policy. US development agencies promulgated ISI plans for Vietnam that were typical of those in other countries. Like most ISI plans, they involved squeezing export interests, such as the French-owned rubber plantations, to subsidize ISI. After Geneva, while the French had cut a deal and made their peace with the Communist forces, the USA increasingly took up the fight to defend an anti-Communist South Vietnamese regime against subversion influenced by the establishment of a Communist state in the north. Subsequently France became one of the foremost critics of the US policy in Vietnam, in part because the regime installed by the US in the south followed ISI priorities rather than those of the French exporters. However, ISI never really took hold in South Vietnam because the extreme economic disruption and distortion caused by the US war there increasingly undermined both industry and agriculture and drove the economy toward one based on services to the

US military and corruption, an economy that became unviable and collapsed as the US forces withdrew (Kolko 1985).

Many oil rich countries were among those that never implemented ISI, but other mineral-rich countries were also among those that never sustained an ISI effort because of the powerful influence of foreign mining interests. A major example of this is the former Belgian Congo, which after independence in 1960 became the Republic of Congo and, for a time, Zaire. It is rich with deposits of copper, diamonds, uranium, and other minerals, but these have always been exploited by foreign interests. At the time of independence, rival business groups struggled for influence over the new government. US and Swedish mining interests lined up against a British-Belgian business consortium to gain control over Congo's resources while both opposed Congo's initial drift toward non-alignment and possible help from the Soviet bloc. Even when one or the other group gained influence in the capital, opposing interests were able to continue opposition by funding mercenaries and secessionist movements, most notably in mineral-rich Katanga province (Gibbs 1991). The polarization of Congo's fragile political order between rival business interests was repeated in many other developing countries that were similarly unable to overcome their dependence on traditional exports, often dominated by foreign interests.

Some countries did welcome ISI, but took it in a direction less favored by the USA. Leading countries of the Third World movement, including India, Egypt, Indonesia (until 1965), and Tanzania, tried to position themselves between the capitalist world and the socialist bloc by accepting aid from both while remaining wary of investment from foreign multinational corporations. India, for example, developed its light industry in classic ISI fashion, but also developed heavy industry with help from the Soviet Union. These mixed cases typically had uneasy relations with the USA. Other countries, such as Brazil, completed the first stage of ISI rather quickly during the 1950s. After that point, US internationalists had originally intended that ISI countries would shift to exporting light industrial products and gradually dismantle ISI controls. Instead, Brazil and some other advanced countries moved toward deepening ISI, in other words, they began to apply ISI protection to new sectors, usually heavy industries like steel and automobiles. The problem is that such industries had huge capital needs that neither foreign nor domestic capitalists would or could provide. Therefore governments stepped to finance state-owned industries, which was unacceptable to US internationalists. It pointed toward permanent Soviet or Nazi style business nationalism, thereby aborting any transition to ELI. This led to intense and often violent polarization between local business nationalists and US business internationalists and their allies in government and international organizations committed to graduation from ISI to ELI.

Transition from ISI to ELI

The original objective of the business internationalists who designed ISI was for it to be a temporary expedient to develop new industries that could eventually become competitive enough to export cheap light industrial products back to the developed countries. The major problem with that plan is that it required sacrificing the interests of business nationalists in the developed countries that could not easily compete with low-wage production from developing countries. For some giant multinationals like GE, this was not a problem because GE could maintain its most capital- and technology-intensive industries in the USA and other developed countries while moving output of light industrial products, such as light bulbs and home appliances, to low-wage countries, thereby rationalizing its global production operations. On the other hand, major labor-intensive industries in developed countries, such as textiles, clothing, and footwear, did not develop multinational companies to manufacture in low-wage countries. They remained protected by tariffs, exchange controls, and quotas, such as the Multi-Fiber Agreement (MFA). Developing countries could not transition from ISI to ELI as originally intended unless developed country markets could be opened more to imports. It was precisely because the textile industry lacked powerful US multinational corporations that it remained one of the last bastions of protectionism.

Developed country markets were opened only gradually. First, exchange controls were removed in most of Europe by 1958 and in Japan by 1964. Tariffs, however, remained an obstacle to imports. These were reduced significantly as part of the Kennedy Round of GATT negotiations completed in 1967. The USA further reduced obstacles to Third World exports in the Generalized System of Preferences (GSP) introduced in 1975. The MFA, a major worldwide quota system affecting clothing and textiles, was only gradually phased out by the end of 2004. Therefore, it was difficult to "graduate" countries from ISI to ELI. Many of the earliest export successes were among the developing countries of East Asia that benefitted from demand for light industrial products generated by the US military operating in the region during the Vietnam War. These included the four so-called "Asian Tigers" because of their fast growth during the 1960s and 1970s: South Korea, Taiwan, Hong Kong, and Singapore. However, the last two were small city-states. Hong Kong never implemented ISI and Singapore dismantled it after breaking away from Malaysia to become an independent nation in 1965. South Korea and Taiwan both had close relations with the US military forces garrisoning their countries, which helped them gain export orders during the war and thus begin to have a chance to transition to ELI. Latin American countries, on the other hand, had fewer opportunities for exporting manufactured products to the developed countries until after these economies were opened more fully. Therefore, many of them followed Brazil's example and tried to deepen ISI to new industries, in the process often clashing with the USA. As more and more developing countries reduced their ISI-era protectionism, they also began to be able to trade more with each other.

Transition from ISI to ELI involved a number of extreme policy changes. First of all, exchange rates were consolidated into a single rate and then exchange controls were eliminated, making currencies freely convertible and capital flows easier. Second, government development banks were either eliminated, privatized, or commercialized. As commercial banking replaced development banking, deposit rates fell relative to loan rates so that deposit banking could become a profitable private business. Third, tariff rates were reduced so that many less competitive businesses were bankrupted by lower prices and increased foreign competition, while at the same time they faced higher cost of capital from rising loan rates. Business nationalists often suffered heavily during the transition. On the other hand, traditionally competitive export sectors, often mining or agriculture, and successfully competitive new export businesses prospered after the transition. Foreign financial institutions flooded into many developing countries when exchange controls were lifted and banking laws liberalized. ELI strongly favored internationalist interests both at home and abroad.

However, the transition from ISI to ELI was politically difficult in most developing countries. This entailed business internationalists unilaterally abrogating their alliance with many of the Third World nationalists whose fortunes had been built during ISI. Since awarding government-controlled perks was such an important power under ISI, many government officials and legislators had become corrupt or were themselves investing in ISI businesses, so they sided with domestic business nationalists against ELI liberalization that would threaten protected industries. In many cases, resistance ELI was only swept away by foreign-supported military coups. Even when the transition was not violent, it was often induced by strong pressure from abroad in the context of foreign exchange and debt crises that were such a common feature of late ISI. Since deepening ISI required more and more capital, but private capital formation was limited by ISI restrictions, many countries financed ISI deepening with heavy foreign borrowing, then suffered foreign exchange crises when foreign loans dried up and anemic export growth was insufficient to finance the foreign currency needs of growing imports and debt-service payments. As major internationalist banks lost confidence in ISI, transition to ELI was often the only alternative to major loan defaults. Since ISI is no longer supported from abroad, nearly every country eventually made the transition to ELI.

The transition to ELI also made economic development theory almost irrelevant as a distinctive field. Economic development theory was invented to justify the ISI exception to free market economics and to trade according to static comparative advantage. Beginning in the late 1960s, ISI policies began to come under widespread criticism within economics through a series of massive detailed studies, often funded or supported by institutions like the World Bank. By the 1970s, ELI was becoming orthodoxy. In recent decades, ISI has been all but forgotten, or, if remembered at all, recast as a failed anti-market policy by misguided Third World nationalists. In fact, ISI was a great success for many of its inventors, promoting the globalization of many industries within giant multinational corporations. Second, it did jump-start the industrialization of many developing countries that had previously been predominantly agricultural. South Korea is one of the most spectacular examples of this, but there are many others, including Brazil. Although many businesses did not survive the transition from ISI to ELI, many others did, and formed the basis for the manufacturing export success of many developing countries today. But ELI requires no exceptional theory of development, since private business exporting competitively to world markets is a generic capitalist game.

Developing countries and the third globalization

Today what used to be called "developing countries" have been rebranded by Wall Street wags as "emerging markets," a term I deplore, but it does vaguely suggest that they are "emerging" from ISI, or, in some cases, socialism, toward an ELI orientation to world "markets," as long as we remember that the so-called "markets" into which they are emerging are rife with cartels and other forms of private power. Nick Robins (2006: 35) claims that at least 60 percent of international trade today occurs within corporations or between subsidiaries of the same corporation. Much of the rest is subject to one or another form of cartel, including the financial consortia that dominate sovereign and other large-scale lending. "Emerging markets" now include even China, emerging from socialism, but much of Chinese export industry manufactures products under contract from foreign corporations and the Chinese IPO business, which recently surpassed that of the USA to become the world's largest, is dominated by a few huge US investment banks earning even fatter fees than they can gain on Wall Street (Zhang 2014). However, constrained and channeled by private power, the industrialization of the developing countries has provided world capitalism with a plethora of low-cost sources of products, especially the labor-intensive products of light industry. These emerging low-cost producers have increased the deflationary competitive pressure in many product lines worldwide.

The success of ELI is thus one of the reasons for the deflationary pressure in the world economy today, which is discussed more in the concluding section of Chapter 14. Most of the light industrial products produced in the world today can be produced efficiently and exported from any of dozens of countries. The vigorous competition among available suppliers keeps world wholesale prices low, although consumer prices might not reflect the full degree of the low cost of production wherever retail companies exercise sufficient market power to keep price markups high. Because so many countries supply the world with roughly the same manufactured products, such things as textiles and clothing, shoes, household appliances, and electronic devices, no one country can have significant cost increases without quickly losing market share to others.

This need to keep export prices low induces many countries to keep their currency relatively undervalued. Such undervalued currencies tend periodically to attract massive inflows of foreign capital eager to purchase underpriced assets. It is very difficult to both keep export prices attractive and keep asset markets from overheating as foreign "hot money" flows in to take advantage of bargain asset prices. Any unusual inflow of foreign capital, because it bids up demand for the local currency, tends to cause it to rise in value, thereby raising export prices and jeopardizing export success, creating a self-limiting bubble when investors realize that falling exports will not sustain rising asset values. Funds then flow out again to collapse the bubble and typically force a currency devaluation. Reinhart and Rogoff (2009), in their massive study of dozens of foreign exchange crises, find that one of the surest indicators of an impending crash and devaluation is the prior massive influx of foreign capital. Boom and bust is stronger than ever in a globalized economy. What goes up must come down.

Among conventional economists, Krugman (2009) studies this tendency toward repeated bubble economies better than most, but his free market ideology blinds him to the central role of private power and strategy in this trend toward growing instability. Like many admirers of Keynes, Krugman seems to believe that better government regulation could mitigate this increasing tendency toward "depression economics." But I think he is misguided to imagine that we can return to the kind of Keynesian regulation that corseted private power during the interlude of the world wars and the Great Depression when globalization and liberalization trends temporarily reversed. Real alternatives to ELI only existed during the period when there was international support for them, either from the USA during the ISI period or from the Nazis during the 1930s or from the socialist bloc until 1991. Today developing countries cannot secure financing for development without playing by the rules of the globalization game. Those rules are not set by governments or by economists, but by those who dominate the global financial business.

13 Cold War polarization and security today

Now the maintenance of this pattern of Soviet power, namely, the pursuit of unlimited authority domestically, accompanied by the semi-myth of implacable foreign hostility, has gone far to shape the actual machinery of Soviet power as we know it today. ... The security of Soviet power came to rest on the iron discipline of the Party, on the severity and ubiquity of the secret police, and the uncompromising economic monopolism of the state. ... Soviet pressure against the free institutions of the western world is something that can be contained by the adroit and vigilant application of counter-force at a series of constantly shifting geographical and political points, corresponding to the shifts and maneuvers of Soviet policy, but which cannot be charmed or talked out of existence.

George Kennan (1946)

Since the end of World War II international relations theory divided sharply into rival liberal and realist schools of thought; at the same time the world was polarized between the Soviet-led socialist camp and the capitalist "free world." Realists like Kennan focused on security issues in a bipolar world fraught with Cold War tensions and the potential of a nuclear holocaust. Liberals focused on the possibilities of increased global governance through institutions like the United Nations and overcoming national rivalries through regional integration, most dramatically within the European Community, as discussed previously. For liberals, the supreme danger of nuclear war made cooperation via arms control and disarmament all the more necessary and desirable for all. Both schools partially understood one aspect of the Cold War international system: corporatism explains both.

Corporatism, recognizing the power of business within the "free world," understands why the Cold War world had to remain polarized until the disintegration of the Soviet Union in 1991. Soviet-style socialism and capitalism are not just two ideologies, or ways of thinking, but two fundamentally different ways of creating power and wealth. Each did pose a real threat and challenge to the other. Business internationalism's inherent competitive threat to the socialist bloc was not just a "semi-myth," as Kennan contended. Ironically, although the Soviets had an elaborate theory of how the capitalist bloc world would succumb to socialism because of internal contradictions between workers and capitalists, the free world did not have a comparable *political realist* theory of the internal contradictions of the socialist bloc. Yet it was ultimately the internal contradictions of the socialist bloc that generated its unexpected demise. Free world idealists might credit a universal human desire for freedom, but this would explain a bottom-up revolution against socialism, not the top-down elite restructuring that actually ended the Soviet system with surprisingly little bloodshed and turmoil. By exploring the business foundations of modern societies, corporatism explains both the integration of the former socialist bloc into a world of business internationalism and yet why this apparent victory of liberal principles produces neither the stable cooperative world of liberal dreams nor the renewed great power wars of realist nightmares.

Liberalism at least has idealist arguments for why the Soviet bloc failed. Realism is bereft of any realist explanation of how such an imposing super-power can just disintegrate without even a war or massive revolution. If a superpower really can be so fragile, then the entire realist perspective treating great powers as unified and durable entities is highly suspect. Indeed it is. Realism has not paid much attention to other instances when great powers suddenly declined for reasons unrelated to defeat in international war. France, during its lengthy civil war between Protestants and Catholics starting in the sixteenth century, is a case in point. If great powers can be vulnerable to sudden disintegration because of system-wide polarizations of power, as during the Classical Greek world of the Peloponnesian War, then IR realism is utterly lacking a *political* realist understanding of polarized power, as found in Thucydides and Aristotle. IR realism is in fact idealistic about the modern state, believing it to be a far more cohesive and unified instrument of international power than it is, even a state as seemingly monolithic as the Soviet one.

The nationalist-internationalist struggle over trade policies was a principal polarization within and among modern states since the decline of mercantilism and the rise of Manchester Liberalism. It remains a divisive issue within many nations to this day, although the global trend since World War II favors business internationalism. The Cold War struggle between ascendant business internationalism in the free world and defensive socialist economic nationalism is in many ways a continuation of the unfinished business of World War II, when business internationalists were able to overcome the Nazi challenge only with Soviet help. The subsequent falling out of these wartime allies was inevitable. No amount of liberal openness or diplomacy could have reassured the Soviets because business internationalism did in fact pose a fundamental threat to their power. Socialist central planning is an extreme form of economic nationalism that cannot survive the divisive threats and attractions from competitive internationalist business.

Contrary to the optimistic liberalism of the immediate postwar era, George Kennan understood the fundamental antagonism of the two systems at the dawn of the Cold War, and thus crafted the strategy of containment celebrated ever since by most realists, and later by many Cold War liberals as well, as the essence of strategic wisdom, although some realists have criticized his strategy of containment for being too passively reactive to Soviet moves rather than surprising the Soviets with American initiatives that they could not easily counter. Regarding the dominance of liberal thinking in Western circles, Kennan may have been tactically right. In the flush of postwar optimism, too many liberals did err on the side of optimism about the prospects for successful cooperation with the Soviet Union within the United Nations framework. But Kennan was wrong in a larger strategic sense, just as Stalin was realistic, not paranoid, to fear the subversive threat of postwar Western initiatives, like United Nations' collective security and the Marshall Plan for the reconstruction of Europe. Regardless of the intentions of its architects, the emerging postwar world order was a real competitive threat to the Soviet system, even if some of its champions could not imagine why.

Kennan was ultimately wrong, however, along with his more proactive realist critics, because the successful strategy for business internationalism to subvert and undermine the Soviet bloc was not containment, but engagement, through economic and political détente. Containment abetted the economic isolation that reinforced and justified Soviet economic and military nationalism. Economic engagement ultimately subverted the Soviet bloc by polarizing its elite between internationalists benefitting from continued engagement and economic nationalists threatened by it. Ironically, the oil and gas price spikes of the 1970s that so deeply concerned Western liberals about the future of the capitalist economies also deepened the rift within the Soviet Union by increasing the power and potential wealth of the Soviet oil and gas sector. Realism could not see inside the superpower shell to perceive this contradiction. Liberalism failed to discern realistically the emerging basis for private power within the Soviet bloc. Only a corporatist approach adequately grasps both the opportunities and threats within the Cold War international system.

Polarizing threats of the Cold War era

During the aftermath of World War II Stalin's "socialism in one country" became a socialist bloc, adding the countries of Eastern Europe, China, North Korea, and eventually Vietnam and Cuba. On the one hand, many in the Western "free world" viewed the socialist bloc as a fundamental threat to their way of life. They were not wrong. On the other hand, the economic (I prefer to say business) nationalism of the socialist bloc could not thrive in contact with the "free world" because the temptations of gaining wealth from commerce with the capitalist countries would quickly subvert and corrupt socialist planning. Extensive border and currency controls enforced by police surveillance and repression were not merely a cruel or arbitrary adjunct to socialist rule in these circumstances. They were a vital necessity. The potential profits from arbitrage between capitalist and socialist prices were so high that the nationalistic isolation of the socialist bloc countries could not be maintained without the greatest police state vigilance. The hysteria against "capitalist roaders" during the Chinese Cultural Revolution was not all hype.

Although the socialist bloc attempted to develop an economy autonomous from the capitalist world, in fact it became increasingly involved in the world economy during the 1970s and 1980s. The huge increases in world oil prices during the 1970s tempted the Soviet Union into becoming a major exporter of oil and natural gas. Its economic plans were soon dependent on importation of advanced technology and agricultural products paid for by energy exports. Meanwhile several Eastern European members of the Soviet Bloc borrowed heavily from Western banks to help prop up their oil-dependent economies. When oil prices plunged during the 1980s, the Soviet Union itself was hard hit. Its output stagnated and it was forced to cut its trading subsidies to some of the weaker bloc members, including some suffering from a debt squeeze as interest rates rose. The costly war in Afghanistan further drained Soviet resources and morale.

I have not yet seen a comprehensive and well-researched economic history of socialist bloc intercourse with the West that includes all the subterranean elements. Yet there is anecdotal evidence from various sources that smuggling goods and exporting liquid capital from the socialist countries was a significant factor in the ultimate demise of the socialist bloc. Even during the height of the Cold War, the Iron Curtain was somewhat porous. Until the Berlin Wall was erected in 1961, people and wealth exited there. Various other borders were not perfectly secure.

Particularly as trade between the socialist bloc and capitalist countries increased during the latter part of the Cold War, the increasing cross border business, as closely monitored as it was, still provided numerous opportunities for corruption and evasion of socialist laws. This is why economic engagement with the socialist bloc proved more subversive than a strict policy of isolation and containment. Although conservative anti-Communists in the West often howled at any increases in trade with the socialist bloc, in fact this was the most potent means of subverting socialism.

The policy of economic engagement with the socialist bloc emerged in Europe during the mid-1960s with the *Ostpolitik* of West German Chancellor Willi Brandt and French President Charles de Gaulle's growing defiance of US efforts to maintain a quarantine on trade with the socialist bloc. Finland had long traded with the Soviet Union. Sweden increased its trade too. European opposition to the US war in Vietnam also encouraged other countries to resist the Cold War imperative to avoid intercourse with the socialist bloc. Not only trade, but private loans to socialist countries began to grow.

The evidence for how much capital leaked out of the socialist bloc through these channels is hard to quantify, but it is noteworthy that with the rapid development of the Eurobond market during the 1960s, large numbers of small denomination anonymous bearer bonds were sold. Apparently most of the early customers were East Europeans and Latin Americans seeking to evade their countries' strict exchange controls to squirrel away wealth in safe and liquid foreign assets (Ferguson 2010: 220). All that exiled wealth could only be enjoyed if the owners either exiled themselves as well or in the event of the fall of the Iron Curtain. Either way it represented the growing investment of relatively elite members of socialist societies in a post-socialist future. Just as the British bond market attracted bond investors from Napoleon's Europe who helped finance Napoleon's defeat, socialist elites were investing more and more in a future in which their smuggled wealth could be openly enjoyed. The development of Hong Kong's capital markets had a similar effect on China.

Just as opportunities for commerce with the capitalist countries tended to undermine the economic controls required to maintain business nationalism in the socialist bloc, the demonstrated success of the socialist bloc countries with planned industrial development threatened capitalist influence in developing countries, as described in Chapter 12. The polarization of the Cold War was not a product merely of ideological differences that could be resolved by changing one's mind. The polarization was fundamentally rooted in the powers and vulnerabilities of contrasting forms of invested wealth. The relative success of either the business nationalist-led (socialist) or the internationalist-led (capitalist) bloc would erode the wealth and opportunities of the other.

Nuclear deterrence

Most liberals and some realists argue that the invention of nuclear weapons has rendered great power war so horribly destructive that war among the nuclear powers is no longer a viable option. Diplomatic solutions therefore must prevail. Other realists, notably Marc Trachtenberg (1991), contend that even during the nuclear era balance of power still matters. Nuclear threats have been used successfully even if nobody has attacked an enemy with nuclear weapons since 1945. Nuclear weapons are not just for deterrence. Nations have had active plans for using them and have used threats of their use for diplomatic leverage. Historical records show that nuclear powers have seriously considered attacking with them on several occasions during the Cold War, even though the con-templated attacks ultimately were averted. Liberals are right to argue that nuclear weapons have greatly raised the stakes of war so that great powers are more likely to avoid it. But realists are also right to point out that war remains not quite as "unthinkable" as we might wish. However, realists also under-estimate the deterrence to war from business interdependence, especially since the decline of a pure containment strategy. Economic engagement gave powerful interests an important stake in peaceful development.

One argument for nuclear weapons that is not so often enunciated is that they seem relatively economical. This is a significant argument for business and other interests opposed to high taxes during peace time that are required to sustain relatively more expensive conventional forces. Both US President Eisenhower and his Soviet contemporary, Premier Khrushchev, made deep cuts in conventional military forces because they believed that nuclear weapons were so decisive that they rendered most conventional forces redundant, if not obsolete. Both justified their cuts economically. Since nuclear weapons are so destructive, large numbers are not required to deter an enemy. However, the policies of both leaders were reversed by their successors. Presidents Kennedy, Johnson, and Reagan initiated large conventional military expansions. Khrushchev was overthrown in 1964 in large part because of his military cutbacks in favor of consumer goods industries and because of Khrushchev backing down during the Berlin and Cuban Missile Crises. The new Soviet leaders appeared to believe what Trachtenberg argues, that the balance of power still matters for great power diplomacy. Eisenhower, with a government strongly representing business internationalists, famously warned at the end of his administration against the power and influence of the "military-industrial complex." This statement has been misinterpreted by those assuming that business as a whole is a unified power elite. It would have been utterly out of character for Eisenhower to be warning against business power in general. But he was aware of polarization within US business and supported business internationalists interested in international cooperation and economy against business nationalists most benefitting from military contracts and consequently using their influence to exaggerate enmities and avoid military cuts.

Most of the nuclear threats during the Cold War were made against powers that did not yet have nuclear weapons, such as the Soviet Union during the 1946 Iran crisis and China during the 1958 Taiwan Straits crisis, or that appeared significantly weaker. Until the 1960s, Soviet nuclear forces able to reach the US itself were few and vulnerable. The Soviets had many nuclear forces that could attack US troops and allies in Europe and Asia, but not the US homeland. On the other hand, if the US attacked first with nuclear weapons, until the 1960s it might have had a chance of destroying all of the Soviet's strategic nuclear forces able to reach the US and some if not most of the Soviet forces targeting Europe. The US nuclear war plan at the time envisioned only one option: a massive all-out attack.

When President Eisenhower first came to power, a serious planning exercise, Solarium, actually studied whether the US should launch an all-out preemptive nuclear attack at the first serious Soviet provocation. The study argued that the US had an overwhelming advantage in nuclear forces at that time (1953), but eventually the Soviets would develop survivable nuclear forces that could launch a devastating second strike on the US home territory even if the US attacked first, so the chance for "victory" in a nuclear war would eventually disappear. If the Soviets were dangerous now, the study contended, they would become even worse if they retained conventional superiority in Europe and Asia but also developed a survivable second-strike nuclear force, thus deterring the US from a preemptive nuclear attack or even the credible threat of one in the event of a lesser conflict. Eisenhower eventually rejected Solarium's recommendation for a preemptive nuclear war because he found that the US at that time had so little intelligence about where all the Soviet nuclear forces were located that the US military leaders could not assure him that a first strike would destroy all the Soviet retaliatory capability (Trachtenberg 1991). Instead, the US began U-2 spy flights and eventually spy satellite overflights to determine with precision where all the Soviet forces were located.

The most dangerous time of the Cold War was probably the period from 1960–62. By then the US had much better intelligence about Soviet forces, knew the Soviets had few intercontinental ballistic missiles (ICBMs) that could reach the US and knew their locations. The Soviets had a few submarines with nuclear missiles deployed near the US coasts, but these were vulnerable because of the short range of the missiles and the need to surface to fire them, which would give US forces some chance of detecting and destroying them before they could launch. The Soviets dared to put mobile nuclear missiles in Cuba in 1962, which gave the Soviets, for the first time, significant survivable nuclear forces that could potentially deter a US preemptive attack. Furthermore, the Soviets had deployed several submarines to Cuban waters, each with at least one nuclear torpedo. The submarine captains had pre-authorization to use them against US forces if attacked. The submarines were all detected, but their nuclear attack capability was apparently not known to the US at the time; neither were their orders. US Navy ships very nearly did attack the submarines. US planes were poised to bomb the missile sites. Except for a last minute diplomatic resolution, the Cuban missile crisis may have led to nuclear war of almost unimaginable destructiveness.

The Cold War balance of nuclear terror began to stabilize in the aftermath of the Cuban missile crisis as both sides came to recognize the utter futility of nuclear war in the context of mutually assured destruction (MAD). The elements of this emerging balance included, first, the strengthening of NATO conventional forces in Western Europe, especially the completion of the rearmament of West Germany, the disengagement of France from colonial wars in Indochina and then Algeria, the disengagement of Britain from colonial wars in several places to focus its army on the defense of Germany, and the strengthening of the US Seventh Army in Germany. Stronger NATO conventional forces in Europe suggested that a potential Soviet conventional attack might be halted without necessarily resorting to nuclear weapons, though in fact Soviet doctrine did not anticipate a major offensive operation in central Europe without support from nuclear arms. Second, perhaps more importantly, first the USA and then the Soviet Union deployed dozens of nuclear-powered submarines able to strike the homeland of the other power with nuclear missiles on short notice. These submarines were stealthy enough that the chance of a few surviving an initial enemy attack was high, thus any enemy first strike could always be followed by a devastating second strike. During the 1960s, in the event of nuclear war, no matter who struck first, MAD became unavoidable.

Internationalist interests within socialism

China joined the Soviet-led socialist bloc during the 1950s, but within a decade opted for an independent path. China was the first major socialist country to begin abandoning central planning and resort to a market economy, beginning in the 1980s. By the 1990s, China had become one of the world's major exporters just as socialism was collapsing elsewhere. China's development path has been somewhat unique. Its fragmented and protected internal market system has produced three major interest blocs: internationalists profiting from rapid export growth and foreign investment to become an integral part of the world economy; nationalists who are competitive within the national economy, but depend on protectionism to survive; and a huge and fast-growing localist sector that produces for local markets in particular counties or provinces, but would not survive in free competition with the leading national producers, let alone against the world market leaders.

China's political economy since market reforms began has been an alliance between internationalists and localists at the expense of nationalists, including China's military-industrial complex. Dramatic political decentralization has given control of local industries to local officials and their cronies, now often private capitalists. In much of China, these local officials use their power to prevent competition even from other Chinese producers from bankrupting inefficient local industries. In a few favored coastal enclaves, local officials attract foreign investment and local businesses produce competitively for the world market, constituting the powerful but narrowly based bloc of internationalists. Some nationalist producers survive, but are increasingly beleaguered. They are squeezed between local protectionism segmenting the national market; increasing foreign competition, especially since China entered the World Trade Organization (WTO) in 2000; and the declining relative importance of national government and military procurement. Since China entered the WTO and is rapidly developing its internal transportation system, however, the localists are under increasing pressure. A possible backlash against current policies might occur if localists and nationalists unite in a xenophobic alliance against the consequences of China's increasing economic openness (Nolt 1999), but I see the chances of this rapidly diminishing with the increasing unification of the internal Chinese market and the continuing success of China as a global export powerhouse.

Truly massive opportunities for Soviet enterprises to earn hard foreign currency emerged during the two "oil shocks" of the 1970s during which crude oil prices first quadrupled and then doubled again. The first oil shock during 1973–74 occurred as oil producing Arab countries embargoed oil to the US and other Western countries for supporting Israel with massive resupply of arms during the 1973 Arab–Israeli War. The second oil shock occurred during 1979–80 with the Iranian Revolution and the subsequent crisis of US–Iranian relations after American hostages were seized at the US Embassy in Tehran in retaliation for the USA admitting the deposed Shah of Iran. Many Iranians feared that he would be re-imposed on Iran as he had been after a CIA-supported coup against the elected Iranian government in 1953. Both oil crises contributed to severe recessions in the Western world and a growing feeling of vulnerability and helplessness among many Americans.

In the short run these crises seemed to bring big benefits to the Soviet Union as well. Arab countries at first moved closer to the Soviet Union as their major arms supplier and supporter against Israel. Yet this trend was soon reversed as the USA brokered the 1978 Camp David Accords, bringing peace between Egypt, the largest Arab country, and Israel. US aid and arms soon flowed into Egypt, displacing Soviet influence there. On the other hand, Iran, a long-term US ally, became more hostile. It has been a major arms customer and trading partner of the Soviet Union and then Russia and China ever since. Even more importantly, the huge increase in oil and gas prices was a great economic boost to the Soviet Union, a major exporter of both products.

The Soviet Union benefitted even more when a consortium of Western European businesses helped finance a massive pipeline project from Soviet gas fields to Western Europe during the 1980s, much to the consternation of President Ronald Reagan and over his strong opposition. At the same time he was boosting US military spending and condemning the Soviet Union as an "evil empire," those weak-kneed Euro-socialists seemed to be appeasing the dreaded Communist superpower. Meanwhile the Soviets were squandering part of their oil and gas windfall in a military buildup of their own, and an expensive and frustratingly ineffective invasion of Afghanistan. It looked like the darkest days of the Cold War were recurring.

Reagan gets too much of the credit for ending the Cold War and the Soviet system for his supposedly tough stance and bravura "tear down that wall," slogan uttered in Berlin. In fact the venal Europeans did much more than the hardline Cold War crusaders to exacerbate contradictions within the Soviet empire. The Eurobond financiers of Soviet capital flight and the European financiers of the gas pipeline provided a carrot far more subversive than Reagan's impotent stick was threatening.

Whereas under socialist economic planning, similarly to ISI planning discussed in the previous chapter, the increasingly massive export earnings of the oil and gas sector were diverted to fund less efficient and competitive enterprises and of course the Soviet Union's own massive military-industrial complex. It obviously seemed an increasingly raw deal to those at the helm of this and other successful Soviet export industries, such as aluminum and other non-ferrous metals. These internationally competitive industries constituted an internationalist bloc with an intense distaste for giving away the hard currency profits of their industries to other, weaker nationalist sectors of Soviet business. These contradictions were increased as some socialist countries began to borrow heavily from Western banks, especially during the 1980s, at the same time that oil and gas prices began falling, making it harder for the socialist bloc to earn through exports the foreign exchange it needed to fund increasingly expensive debt payments. It is no surprise that many of the leaders of the post-Soviet Russian state had and continue to have close ties to the oil and gas sector. The detailed unfolding of Russia's elite realignment may take some time to investigate and document, an effort that is not particularly safe in Russia today, but the basic outline is clear for those with an understanding of business and private power.

Global security today

Since the end of the Cold War, the prospect of war among the great powers has virtually vanished. Realists cannot admit this, because it would render their theory almost irrelevant. They try to conjure a new menace somewhere, for example, claiming a rising threat to the world order from China. Others try to hype the problems of terrorism or an "Axis of Evil" involving small "rogue" nations, but these are ridiculous exaggerations. Terrorism is a police problem. Rogue nations are all too weak to initiate war against great powers with any hope of success. China is now the world's second largest economy, or third if the European Union (EU) is counted as one unit, but China is still little more than half of either the US or EU economies. China is a regional military power roughly comparable to India, but in by no stretch of the imagination a super-power on the scale of the US (Nolt 2006). Furthermore, China is prospering well in the current internationalist world order. It has no incentive to bite the hand that feeds it. China is rising in alignment with the incentives and opportunities of the internationalist world order, not in opposition to it.

Not only is the USA the world's only remaining military superpower and the biggest national economy, it also has formal military alliances with most of the world's other significant powers. Of the top ten national economies in the world today, Japan, Germany, France, Britain, and Italy are all US allies. Only China, Brazil, Russia, and India are not. None of them, however, are allies of each other. The next five largest economies – Canada, Australia, Spain, Mexico, and South Korea – are also US allies, or, in the case of Mexico, closely aligned to the US in the North America Free Trade Association (NATFA). The richest country pegged as a member of the "Axis of Evil," Iran, is not even in the top twenty. US wealth and military power is today hegemonic to an extent never before witnessed in world history.

This does not mean the US is, as a realist might imagine, all-powerful to impose its will on any other country. Military power today has significant capabilities, but also severe limits in terms of the political and certainly the economic problems it can solve. Military power by no means trumps all other forms of power. In fact, liberals are right to argue it is generally of limited utility in international affairs today. As the recent US wars in Iraq and Afghanistan demonstrate, defeating a country's formal military forces may be much easier than pacifying or successfully governing it. Military force can break a country, but it cannot easily put it back together.

Liberals have long argued that war is a more and more irrational pursuit for nations in an interdependent and economically fragile world, given increasingly costly mechanized warfare. And, we should add, the costly and frustrating burden of occupying a broken or failed state. Realists, on the other hand, have reveled in the gross failure of liberals to anticipate the two devastating world wars of the twentieth century, not to mention a number of lesser wars and rumors of war that continue from time to time to roil the international system. Liberals have correctly identified some of the trends tending toward peace while neglecting some other trends, such as imperialism and nationalist-internationalist polarization, which have, during the first half of the past century, provoked sufficient mutual antagonism to incite war.

Yet today the nationalist-internationalist rivalry that so polarized the international system through World War II is largely resolved in favor of inter-nationalist hegemony. This is the business basis of "American" hegemony, which will endure even if the USA declines in relative military capabilities. The long-term weakness of business nationalism, of uncompetitive business, is that as the international environment becomes more globalized and competitive, it tends to disappear, bankrupted, reformed, or acquired by its more competitive internationalist rivals. It is conceivable that a severe crisis in the world economy could recreate a large reservoir of uncompetitive business in some corner of the globe that could erect new barriers to trade to protect itself, but for now that seems quite unlikely (Nolt 1997b).

Recently it has become fashionable to argue that the world is slipping into a new round of conflicts and wars based on deep cultural differences across the globe rather than economic interests or great power politics. One of the most influential proponents of this idea is Samuel Huntington (2011). This sort of explanation is offered as a key reason for the surge of terrorism exemplified by 9/11 terrorist attacks on New York's World Trade Center and the Pentagon. Cultural diversity does exist across the globe and indeed within virtually every juridicial nation. However, internationalist hegemony is countering the tendency toward cultural conflict by promoting global multiculturalism. Internationalist hegemony has also produced a remarkably global business culture. If any culture is ascendant in the world today, it is surely this global business culture. Most major global corporations today, no matter where their headquarters are located, employ people from dozens of countries, transact business with thousands of local partners across the globe, and operate under the laws and customs of dozens of different nations. Terrorism remains a fringe phenomenon outside of this global business system. Like crime in any country, it is a serious social problem, but it does not remotely threaten to overturn the world order.

Cultural boundaries, however drawn, are quite permeable to the operations of internationalist business and have proved little obstacle to it. Within any of the great cultural traditions, however defined, whether Islam or the Judeo-Christian West or Greater China, and so on, internal divisions and distinctions are ram-pant. Nearly any business organization or group of business organizations cooperating together has far more cohesiveness and consistency of purpose than Islam or Greater China or any other such cultural abstraction. In fact, business organizations as collective actors tend to be at least as cohesive and coherent in their activities as nation-states. Yet business as a social and political force fails to attract the kind of sustained study it deserves.

If we are indeed witnessing in our age the end of great power war, that does not mean the end of international conflict. Private interests remain polarized, as they must under a credit-driven economic system such as capitalism. The global economy remains chronically unstable. However, the lines of creditor–debtor and bear–bull conflict do not correspond neatly with national borders. They polarize private interests and their allies in government within every nation. The strategic conflict between bears and bulls is not likely to be the cause of a new round of wars, as consequential as it will be for the trajectory of the global economy and the distribution of wealth. In the final chapter we explore the brave new world of casino capitalism.

14 Global casino

Both Hegel and Marx believed that the evolution of human societies was not open-ended, but would end when mankind achieved a form of society that satisfied its deepest and most fundamental longings. Both thinkers thus posited an "end of history"; for Hegel this was the liberal state, while for Marx it was a communist society. ... It meant ... that there would be no further progress in the development of underlying principles and institutions, because all the really big questions had been settled. ... liberal democracy remains the only coherent political aspiration that spans different regions and cultures around the globe. In addition, liberal principles in economics – the "free market" – have spread, and have succeeded in producing unprecedented levels of material prosperity, both in industrially developed countries and in countries that had been, at the close of World War II, part of the impoverished Third World.

Francis Fukuyama (1992: xii–xiii)

Liberal Francis Fukuyama, contemplating the end of the Soviet bloc, the decline of war, and even of ideological politics, proclaimed the end of history in the Hegelian sense. Many liberals like him note that the human species has been domesticated so thoroughly that violence itself seems to be receding to a few failed states and a lunatic fringe. Now the only wolves that remain seem to be on Wall Street or in superhero fantasy films. I have to admit a certain nostalgia for history; not for its blood, but for its dynamism and hope. The liberal vision today seems mired in mundane consumerism and mere administration. Economists too, celebrated the "end of history" that Ben Bernanke captured in his phrase, "the Great Moderation." It almost convinced me, as contrarian as I am, that a book like this could have little use in a world of technological marvels and bureaucratic management.

Almost, that is, until I was shaken out of my own complacency to revisit the theory of bears, bulls, and the strategic determination of the business cycle that first presented at a conference 20 years ago. The world economic crisis of 2008 directed my attention to the significance of financial derivatives, which until then I, like most educated people, knew nothing about. Studying derivatives turned out to provide the missing key to the central polarization of our era. History, in Fukuyama's Hegelian sense, is not over, but the dynamic of our age is barely perceptible to most people, including him. Unlike the battlefields of past wars and revolutions, the conflicts of today are so remote from the perceptible experience of most people as to be nearly invisible. Neither liberals nor realists have a clue. Yet the financial Olympians of our day impact us no less whether or not we perceive their existence. Fukuyama (1992: 328–29) illustrates his own utter incomprehension of even the most elemental facts of his celebrated "free market" (within appropriately skeptical quote marks even in his own text) by writing:

> There will be plenty of metaphorical wars – corporate lawyers specializing in hostile takeovers who think of themselves as sharks or gunslingers, and bond traders who imagine … that they are "masters of the universe." (They will believe this, however, only in bull markets.)

This last parenthetical sentence illustrates two fundamental errors typical of liberals who love the "free market" but know nothing whatsoever about how it actually operates. Fukuyama seems unaware that bond traders make most of their income from trading fees, and thus the volume of business, not the direction of the market, and that if they expect a bear market not only can they continue to earn trading fees, but can often make money even faster on their own account as shorts. The very idea of a short position seems never to have occurred to him. Yet few of the real "masters of the universe" maintain wealth and power without knowing how to make money in bear markets. His textbook innocence of real business is reflected in his broader Platonic idealism in asserting that liberal economic principles, no matter how misleading or unrealistic, are "producing unprecedented levels of material prosperity." Platonic abstractions such as his produce nothing but obfuscation. It is real business activity, typically conducted in fragrant violation of all the textbook rules of liberalism, rationality and perfect markets, that produces the material prosperity Fukuyama celebrates. Marx's materialist inversion of Hegel's idealism is apt here. It is not the abstract principles of philosophers that produce the world, but the real activity of everyone else. Study *that* and you might learn something.

The previous chapters of this part outlined key developments portending Fukuyama's vision: the end of great power war, the demise of the Soviet bloc, the reduction or elimination of many trade barriers, the unification of much of Europe, and even the decline of a distinctive problem of economic development. All of these represent a triumph for business internationalism: the world's most competitive firms enjoy the globe as their playground. Contrary arguments, such as Samuel Huntington's (2011) concern for a supposed global culture clash, focus on noise at the margins rather than the overwhelming success of business and consumer culture worldwide to ameliorate, manage, and homogenize. Fukuyama does recognize this result better than Huntington, if not its cause. For example, I first taught in China over three decades ago and then again for the past seven years. Chinese young people are today so much closer culturally to those in any other part of the world; I am amazed more by the convergence than by any remaining cultural differences. The instabilities and polarizations of our world today stem less from the residual tribalism of the past than they do from the latest innovations in the citadels of private power.

The contemporary global financial system, with its massive proliferation of financial derivatives, is significantly different from what prevailed for most of the twentieth century. Polarization between bears and bulls has intensified, along with the intensity and frequency of serious financial crises. Those portions of the financial and regulatory system that used to promote some degree of financial stability are nearly all gone. They have been replaced by almost overwhelming interest in economic instability, focused within finance but extending beyond it into commodities trading as well. Short-term interest rates are now the lowest they have ever been in world history, which makes leveraged financing of speculative positions extremely attractive. High-stakes gambling has now taken the place of sober financial strategies in nearly all the world's major financial institutions. The market power of large firms is magnified manyfold by making leveraged bets on prices they manipulate. A stunning example of this is the ongoing scandal that exposed the cartel of large banks that collectively sets the benchmark London Inter-Bank Offer Rate (LIBOR) that is widely used as a reference rate to price variable loan rates worldwide and then whispers upcoming changes to their in-house derivatives traders "speculating" on the very rates the LIBOR cartel has the power to set. Rich financial earnings have spilled into politics, making reform much harder, since the big money is all in financial gaming. Instability is inevitable, chronic – and profitable.

The explosion of derivatives trading has fundamentally changed the global political economy. Traditional banking is declining. It was based on taking deposits as the major liability and holding loans as the major asset. Now major banks make most of their profit from fees for originating loans and creating tradable securities and from trading all forms of securities, especially derivatives. Loans are securitized and sold to investors rather than remaining on the books of banks. Whereas traditional banking had a bias toward stability – though prone to periodic crises – contemporary financial companies thrive from *instability*, which raises the price of and demand for derivatives to hedge risk. Derivatives are also used speculatively to magnify the advantages of market power, since anyone able reliably to move prices can efficiently bet on those same price movements and thus profit from a self-fulfilling prophecy. The only limitation to the ballooning of derivative-based leverage is the never-ending search for "sucker funds," unwary pools of investable funds that can be committed to the wrong side of insider derivatives bets. The 2008 world financial crisis was the first in what are likely to be a series of such crises as wrong-side bets are unloaded on unsuspecting investors. Derivative investors' appetite for crises may tempt them to exaggerate international incidents to provoke the kind of wild price swings that earn the biggest returns for derivative investors on the right side of history. The high-stakes churn of bears and bulls in all of the world's asset and commodity markets must thoroughly polarize and corrupt politics.

Governments are still quantitatively important. Government's share of GDP is not shrinking much. But globalization and the nearly irreversible liberalization of finance have markedly reduced the economic options of governments. Governments are increasingly acted upon rather than being strategic actors in their own right. Few social scientists have yet detected this trend. This is one of the lessons of the 2008 global financial crisis and now the debt crisis in several eurozone countries. Governments are not "withering away" the way Lenin expected under communism or as liberal transnationalists predicted. But government capacity for strategic action is withering. Government influence is still important, but more inertial than strategic, as Hyman Minsky understood. The inertia of governments may still restrain the wildest gyrations of derivative-fueled speculation, but most strategic social initiative is exercised by private business. Not only are the powers of governments withering, but also the decline of military nationalism erodes personal identification with the nation. Realism's conception of unified nation-states, always an idealization, is now almost wholly obsolete. Corporatism is the only perspective of international political economy that can even begin to understand contemporary global dynamics.

The demise of the Soviet bloc completed the internationalist victory that started with World War II. Business internationalism now rules the globe as never before. The military hegemony of the US and its allies is virtually unchallenged. American military hegemony is less significant though than the economic hegemony of business internationalism. Globalization, the opening up of the world economy, has so weakened business nationalism almost everywhere that the centuries-long nationalist–internationalist struggle is fading into obscurity. Business nationalists, who are by definition not competitive at world market prices, cannot survive free trade. As world trade became freer, business nationalism weakened and gradually disappeared as a significant interest bloc. This is why liberals like Fukuyama can imagine "history" at an end, but it is not because of the universal triumph of some abstract principles, but of real powers in the private sector.

Business might have become more unified, except that at the same time trade was disappearing as an issue, business cycle fluctuations consequently intensified as well. "History" has not ended because at least one major and perennial "big question" remains: the cyclical struggle between bears and bulls. The intensity of this polarization increases as derivatives come to dominate financial markets, since every movement of prices now equally creates winners and losers owning the opposite sides of derivative contracts. The nominal face value of all the world's derivative contracts has ballooned from a massive US$600 trillion at the time of the 2008 crisis to about $1.2 quadrillion today, roughly 20 times world GDP! Behind Fukuyama's idealist complacency there remains a titanic business battleground of unresolvable tension.

Polarization via financial derivatives

Whereas so much of the mass media, if they mention derivatives at all, proclaim them to be too complicated for ordinary people to understand, in fact the salient elements of derivatives are simple and stark. Derivatives are financial contracts, like stocks and bonds. They are also potentially valuable assets. However, their value is vastly more volatile than the value of traditional assets, because rather than representing title to something of value, like a share in a company or a loan, they are a wager on the future price of some other specified asset, called the underlying. A type of derivative known as a swap is more complicated and diverse, but for now consider only two kinds: futures and options. All futures and options have two sides: an issuer (seller) and a buyer. Just like most bets, one must win and the other lose. Therefore each one simultaneously creates equal and opposite long and short positions. Both sides cannot win. They are inherently polarizing.

Futures and options have one significant difference. Futures *require* the owner either sell (short) *or* buy (long) a specified quantity of the underlying asset at/by the maturity date. Options *allow* the owner to either sell (put) or buy (call) the underlying (see Figure 4.1). If the price moves opposite the direction bet by a future contract owner, the owner loses and must pay the issuer. If the same happens in the case of an options contract, the owner only loses the price paid for the option, since it is now worthless. Long futures and call options are bullish positions, betting on a price rise. Short futures and put options are bearish positions. Futures and options are typically short-term assets, like long and short positions taken for centuries by means of asset loans. The stated maturity date may be as little as one day in the future or some other period. Most are no more than 90 days, since betting on prices much farther in the future than that is very risky. However, if two parties agree on a longer term, any future date is possible.

Typical futures and options implicitly have a fixed face value, similar to a bond, which represents the value of a specified quantity of the underlying traded at strike price promised in the contract. For example, one could own a short currency future requiring sale of £10,000 at $1.50 each for a total face value of $15,000. However, unlike a bond, the face value tells you little about the actual value of the derivative because that depends more on the relationship between the strike price and the actual market price of the underlying at the time the derivative is exercised, meaning the specified trade is executed. Actually, derivatives are more like pure gambling in the sense that very seldom is the underlying asset actually possessed or traded by either party. They settle the contract based on the price difference alone. In this example, if this contract were executed when the price of a British pound was actually $1.40, it has a total value of at least $1,000, since the owner could have bought £10,000 for $14,000 and immediately sold them at the strike price and earned $1,000 profit. Thus if this case occurs when the contract is exercised, then the owner is paid $1,000 by the issuer. On the other hand, if the exercise price is above the strike price, the owner must pay the issuer the difference. The bigger the difference between the exercise price and the strike price, the larger the total payoff to one side or the other. If the exercise price is exactly the same as the strike price, the face value is zero, so the owner only loses the price paid to buy the contract in the first place, which is usually a very small fraction of the face value, often a few percent. Since the price of derivatives contracts is very low for most assets at strike prices either at-the-money or out-of-the-money, enormous leverage is possible, just like it is much cheaper to bet on a horse race than to own the horse. Furthermore, the price of derivatives increases as volatility of the underlying increases. The more unstable markets are the more valuable derivatives become.

Economists often claim that derivatives increase the stability of financial markets by redistributing risk from those least willing to bear it to those more willing and able. However, as we discovered during 2008, many of those owning these bets do not know what risk they are bearing, since either side of a bet may be packaged into another financial product that obscures the nature and risk of the underlying bets. Thus the original issuer may no longer be the one obligated to cover the contract. During the recent crisis, this was done on a massive scale. Derivatives are not complicated in their essence, but they can be used to create deliberately opaque financial products, such as synthetic bonds. Furthermore, economists' confidence in the stabilizing effect of derivatives is based on their imagined world without private power. When derivatives are combined with private power and strategy, they become powerfully destabilizing. In actual fact, derivatives are often used by powerful market insiders to make self-fulfilling bets on prices they can manipulate. The only limit to this kind of rigged game is finding enough sucker money that can be invested in the wrong side of these insider bets, since few rational well-informed investors would bet against a powerful insider, unless they have a strategic way to defeat the opposing play. Derivatives are simple, but there is no limit to the complexity of the strategies that can be executed using them.

Textbooks argue the safest use of derivatives is to hedge against the risk of losses for assets you own, though this can be highly risky when combined with leverage. For example, if an oil company has a tanker loaded with 100,000 tons of crude oil on a two-month ocean voyage, it might buy a put option on that quantity of oil with a strike price equal to the market price when it purchased the oil. If during the voyage the price of oil goes up, the option is useless, but the oil is more valuable. If the oil price goes down, the oil will be sold for less, but the put option will make up the difference, so the company, in essence, is buying insurance against a price decline. This sort of contract is most like what economists are thinking about when they claim that derivatives redistribute risk. Of course, if oil prices do fall, the issuer of the derivative (or whomever he has sold his side of the contract to) loses money on this contract. If the price does not change, the owner of the option loses only the cost of the option, but losses or even income lower than the cost of borrowing can potentionally bankrupt heavily a leveraged position.

Hedge funds are named for another popular use of derivatives, which is to take a highly leveraged hedged position with perhaps slight asymmetries between the put and call options (or comparable long and short positions). This sort of hedged position is often designed by a financial engineer. If the price of the underlying goes up, the call option pays off. If the price goes down, the put option does. It sounds like a sure bet, but it is not. Since options do cost money, such a position will lose money if the price is fairly stable. They make a profit only if the price movement during the life of the contract is a greater percentage than the cost of the option. Furthermore, many hedged positions are leveraged by using borrowed money to increase the potential profit and thus can go bankrupt if the price movement is too small. Hedged positions profit most from instability.

Speculative positions have become such a driving force in many asset markets today that contending private powers rather than value governs increasingly volatile prices. For example, today most large consumers of petroleum products, such as airlines and shipping companies, avoid purchasing oil products at market prices, since the market price is so drastically subject to the vagaries of speculation. Instead, large purchasers negotiate long-term supply contracts with oil companies to buy at a stable price. This saves the cost of hedging their commodity values using options. It also renders market prices increasingly superfluous to the real economy, except for their effect on redistributing wealth among rival investors – and potentially generating financial crises if too many players are bankrupted by any particular series of price swings. Furthermore, as the LIBOR case illustrates, whereas through most of history cartels were primarily concerned with raising prices, the prevalence of derivatives allows cartels to potentially profit from price swings in either direction, as long as they place their derivatives bets first before moving the cartel price. Economists continue to fixate on market prices as an efficient means of signaling real value and scarcity, while more and more real business abandons free markets to the speculators in return for the stable assurance of contracted or cartel pricing. The market is being displaced less by socialist planning by governments, than by private business agreement. Liberals like Fukuyama have no clue about these real historical trends, since they are largely blind to private power.

Swaps, the third type of derivative, have exploded into a huge market in the hundreds of trillions of dollars of contract face value just in the past two decades. The three main types are interest rate, currency, and credit default swaps. I will talk most about the latter because of their importance during recent crises. All swaps involve two parties brought together by a broker, which is usually an investment bank. The two parties essentially agree to swap two disparate revenue streams or future payoffs and pay a fee to the broker to arrange the deal. Interest rate swaps typically involve trading fixed for floating rate interest payments. Parties entitled to each kind of payment swap with the other for the more desired kind. Currency swaps involve swapping specified income streams in different currencies, for example, a British airline operating in the USA might arrange a currency swap with an American airline operating in Britain, the British company swapping its dollar earnings for the American company's pound earnings. Currency swaps may reduce the risk of earning income in one currency while having to pay most expenses in another. These two kinds of swaps are usually complex deals arranged on an ad hoc basis.

Credit default swaps (CDS) are different. They are more like insurance against bond default. The owner of the CDS on a particular bond is paid the face value of the bond by the issuer of the CDS if the original issuer of the underlying bond defaults. The value of a CDS goes up as the risk of bond default increases, so owning CDS contracts is another way, often inexpensive, to short a bond. CDS contracts on common bonds are such standardized contracts that they may have public prices and may be frequently traded. There can be a perverse interest in a CDS, since a powerful player can buy CDS on a bond and then use market power to force down its price or increase the risk it will default by cutting other sources of credit to the issuer or simply spread bad news about them. Even if the bond does not default, the market price of the CDS is likely to rise to the profit of its owner. It is like buying insurance on your neighbor's house and then profiting by burning it down. This sort of perverse incentive was at the heart of the crisis of 2008 and may also be involved in the current Eurobond crisis.

Like bonds, derivatives may profit their owner even without being exercised, since they have a fluctuating market value based on the estimated likely payoff of the underlying bet. At any time when the price is up, the owner may choose to sell the derivative rather than holding it to maturity. The problem is that there is such an enormous and complex variety of derivatives, the market for any particular one may be quite thin. That is, many are illiquid. Some derivatives contracts are fairly common and standardized enough that they can be traded on public markets at quoted prices. Others are traded privately, often because they are too complex or obscure for a public market to handle.

While the basic properties of individual derivatives are not so difficult to grasp, investors and financial firms that own a complex portfolio of many different derivatives, often bought and sold daily at many different trading desks within a large organization, have a very difficult management problem to keep track of the fluctuating value of all of them in real time, especially those that do not have readily available market prices. These problems are debated within the fields of accounting and finance, especially the subfield of risk management. Statistical models are used to assess risk, but they all suffer from the fatal flaw discussed in Chapter 4. They can only be adequate for routine periods when all the underlying asset prices are behaving in a quasi-random way. The measure of risk typical in mathematical models is based on the historical variance of the price of the asset. But anyone who works in the retail side of the financial business knows that regulations require customers to be told, when shown historical price trends, that history is no guarantee the future performance will be similar. Indeed this is true. When unexpected things happen, for example, when any asset or group of assets is "in play" because investors with market power and strategic intent are deliberately influencing the price, no formal model of either risk or derivative pricing is of much use. When any economy enters a crisis phase, a culminating point, as discussed in Chapter 5, then all routine calculations go haywire. Calculation of risk departs from the realm of financial engineering and enters the realm of strategy.

The world financial crisis of 2008

The worldwide crisis of 2008 was arguably the worst financial crisis in world history. The Great Depression of the 1930s was worse in terms of unemployment, stock market collapse, and sheer human misery, but the various financial crises that occurred during that time did not bankrupt the biggest banks in any major country, except for one in Germany. During 2008, most of the largest banks and some of the largest insurance companies in the US, Britain, and several other countries were effectively bankrupt. Regulators had to decide which would be allowed to fail and which would be bailed out with huge injections of public funds to restore their capital reserves. Government intervention on such a massive scale to save private financial firms is also a first. Without government funds to backstop the financial system, the world would likely have experienced a depression worse than the 1930s. All business depends on credit. During 2008, credit seized up, even for some of the largest companies in the world.

At the heart of the 2008 crisis were CDS on mortgage-backed securities (MBS). The latter are not particularly new. They figured prominently already in the crash of 1893 (Levy 2012: 164–65). MBS are bonds issued by a corporate entity created solely for the purpose of owning a pool of mortgage loans. That entity issues the bonds, pays whatever coupon rate, and redeems the bonds at maturity using the income streams generated by the mortgage debtors' payments. Because so many diverse mortgages are owned by the pool, statistically the typical historical default rate should be known and the default of some of the mortgages figured into the risk and price of the bonds. Because mortgage interest rates are higher than what corporate borrowers typically pay, MBS tended to have a high coupon rate, making them attractive to investors. Combining loans into pools and issuing bonds from these pools is known as securitization or collateralization. The resulting bonds are often called collateral debt obligations (CDO). MBS are a common type of CDO, but many loans today are securitized in this way. This allows banks to profit from the fee income for originating loans, but absolves them of the risk of owning the loans.

MBS and other CDO contracts are made even more attractive by techniques known as structured finance that divide each pool into tranches represented by distinct bonds. The risk of default is thus further lowered for most MBS owners because the riskiest or equity tranche is assigned all the losses in the pool until the loss exceeds its total share of the pool's assets. So, for example, if bonds of the equity tranche were 10 percent of the total pool and mortgage losses in the entire pool were less than 10 percent, the higher tranches would suffer no default losses at all. Thus MBS from the higher prime tranches, the majority of almost every pool, tended to be both high yield and apparently low risk enough to receive the coveted top AAA credit rating from private bond rating agencies. Institutional investors and others required to offer safe returns but also expected to offer high returns snapped up MBS as fast as they could be created. Bullish demand soon outstripped the supply.

Supply was increased in three bullish and highly risky ways. One was that investment bankers demanded from mortgage lenders more and more "product" no matter how risky the underlying loans, since, at worst, only a portion of the loans would default and the higher tranches would still yield high returns and get AAA credit ratings. Therefore mortgage lenders pushed loans on anyone since they earned a fee on each loan and took no risk because any loans they originated would be quickly sold to investment bankers to feed the burgeoning pools to create more MBS. Therefore "liar loans" with unverified documentation proliferated. The default risk expected in the mortgage pools was based on the historic risk of default, but as average loan quality deteriorated, the rate of default would soon climb rapidly.

The second way to create more loans was to use low "teaser" rates of interest for the first few years of a loan that would later increase dramatically. Low income people might be able to afford the interest at first, so more customers could be induced to borrow. Either they did not understand what would happen later or they bullishly expected that when the higher interest rates kicked in they could refinance their home with a new loan based on the expectation that by then its market value would have risen sufficiently that they would have some equity in it and thus be able to afford to refinance long-term at lower rates. Many of these loans began to default around 2007 when house prices peaked so that borrowers soon discovered that with accumulating interest they owed more on their house than its current market value. They were "upside down." They could actually save money by declaring bankruptcy and abandoning the house to the bank. Millions did. These foreclosed homes were then thrown onto the market by banks eager to liquidate them, forcing house prices even lower and causing even more borrowers to become upside down.

The third way was even more ingenuous. It is the ultimate bullish trick since it is unlimited by the quantity of underlying mortgage loans. This was the invention of synthetic bonds. These are bonds that are created using as the underlying asset the issuer's side of CDS contracts on other MBS. This is a bond secured by derivatives based on the value of other bonds. For example, whereas the buyer of a CDS is effectively buying insurance on the underlying bond, the issuer of that CDS insurance receives an income stream, the "insurance" payments from the CDS purchaser, which can fund the income stream required to pay a high coupon rate on the bond. The capital in the pool to redeem the bonds at maturity can be any safe asset, such as Treasury bonds. The higher the risk of the underlying bonds, the higher the CDS payments and therefore the higher the coupon rate could be set on the synthetic bonds. Since the underlying asset in the pool is safe, many of these bonds too earned the highest credit rating by using the techniques of structured finance to create tranches of varying risk.

This invention of synthetic bonds provided a perfectly symmetrical way to inflate a bubble by simultaneously fulfilling the demand of both bears and bulls. The issuer's side of the CDS is the bull bet. It supplies the demand for high-yield bonds that will not default unless the underlying MBS default, thus triggering the CDS contracts contained in the pool to pay the face value of the underlying bonds. It was possible to issue CDS on MBS in huge quantities because wise shorts had an almost unlimited appetite for betting against the bubble that was so obviously, to anyone who understood the game in all its dimensions, bound to fail rather soon. Although I have used CDS as the example of the derivatives funding a synthetic bond, in principle any long-side bet would suffice, such as call options, long futures, or the issuer's side of a put option. Issuers, typically large banks and insurance companies, who themselves believe the short position is the smart one, can simultaneously profit from selling short bets to like-minded bears while off-loading their long position, the issuer's side of the derivatives contract, to a pool that uses it to create synthetic bonds. As the culminating point approaches, the volume of trades climbs as the bank earns fees from both bears and bulls without much risk of its own.

There is strong circumstantial evidence that the investment banks issuing structured financial products knew they were creating a short-lived bubble both because some of their trading desks were actively shorting the MBS they were selling to customers and, less noted but even more telling, in order to keep the game viable the investment banks were willing to hold the worst of what they called "toxic waste," the risky equity tranches of the mortgage pools, virtually unsalable, on their own balance sheets or those of corporate entities they controlled, called special purpose vehicles. Their special purpose was hiding toxic waste. Because this waste would almost certainly result in losses, many investment banks bought very expensive CDS insurance on it. Since the high risk of this "waste product" was obvious to the CDS issuers, the cost of this insurance was very high, so high in fact that it would make no sense to pay it for very long. The only point to buying it at all is because you expect a crisis quite soon. It is like buying expensive fire insurance on your own home but not worrying about the cost because you are secretly planning to burn it down and collect the insurance payment. If that is your plan then it would make no sense to delay long. The investment banks' willingness to buy expensive CDS protection on the worst toxic waste is among the best evidence that they knew the crisis must come soon. They could be confident of this because they themselves had the power to trigger it merely by bearishly tightening credit.

Subsequently one of the most famous of the shorts was hedge fund manager John Paulson. He was absolutely convinced that real estate prices were ascending in an unsustainable bubble. He was delighted to discover that investment banks could offer him a low-cost way to short MBS by buying CDS insurance on them. They even helped Paulson pick some of the most risky bonds to bet against. At first he could not quite figure out why the banks were so eager to sell CDS protection to him. Who was holding the bullish side of the bet? He could not imagine how there could be so many bulls eager to bet that the bubble would continue to grow. In fact the reason was that the investment banks were packaging most of the bullish side of the CDS contracts into their synthetic bonds that were in such high demand from investors, especially institutional investors who wanted to be acclaimed for their high-performance portfolios with apparently low risk. Many bulls seemed to be lulled into a false sense of security by the AAA rating of the bonds they bought. In any case, for most bulls who were fund managers, it was other people's money at risk anyhow. Bankers were simultaneously feeding the bears and the bulls. The appetite of both seemed to increase as the culminating point approached, just as in Keynes' analysis of the 1929 crisis. The proximate trigger for the crisis is debatable and almost trivial. A bubble is bound to burst if it keeps inflating. It often takes only a pin prick to initiate the process. Rapidly rising default rates on the underlying home mortgages during 2007–8 brought the whole pyramid of bullish speculation tumbling down.

Skeptics of my account might wonder if the insider bankers were so smart, how so many banks ended up insolvent. It is important to realize that the interests of senior bankers were not the same as those of owners of bank stock. Financial shares did take a huge tumble during the crisis. Some fell to nothing. Stockholders suffered, but few bankers who were insiders in this game lost much from that. They were paid (or paid themselves) huge bonuses and fees based on the large volume of business they transacted. They were paid for deal flow regardless of whether the assets sold subsequently profited their customers and regardless of the risks to their own bank's capital and earnings. The financial companies that failed did so largely because of losses incurred on "toxic" CDOs they had created but had not yet sold. That is, some were bankrupted by their losses on unsold inventory. On the other hand, some of the more successful banks and bankers were shorting the same assets they were selling to customers, so they profited handsomely when their customers lost. Few banks today are partnerships like the famous investment/merchant banks of the past, wherein partners' own capital was at risk if their banks failed. The stock value of today's corporate banks is not so closely tied to the fortunes of the bankers that run them. During the crisis, many banks became insolvent, but few bankers did.

Short-term credit in crisis

All economic crises originate in the short-term credit system, which is virtually ignored in most textbooks, which substitute instead discussions of money supply. So-called "money supply" is an epiphenomenon of the credit system. I do not say credit market because there are many non-market aspects to the credit system. It is a fount of private power. The meaning of changes in what economists measure as the money supply is unclear without reference to the underlying causes in the credit system. Money supply merely measures the stock of funds in certain sorts of bank accounts. The stock of funds in the measured accounts may grow because real economic transactions are increasing, the typical textbook assumption, or because speculative transactions are increasing, funds are being transferred in from other sorts of accounts not counted as "money," or because people are increasing their reserve funds in anticipation of an economic crisis. In other words, an increasing money supply could be a bullish or bearish sign. Money supply in the USA actually increased during parts of the Great Depression as people increased their cash reserves, signaling a drop in the velocity of money. Even reserve funds can have multiple uses. Textbooks assume their purpose is defensive, to avoid bankruptcy, but they can also be committed aggressively to fund either bull or bear positions, since a crisis is also an opportunity for those with uncommitted reserves, as any real strategist understands.

Short-term credit is a far more important vehicle than monetary policy for exercising private power because it is more precisely discriminatory than money, as mentioned in Chapter 8. That is, changes in the value of the dollar or euro have broad effects, but if private creditors, acting strategically, want to discriminate against specific debtors or classes of debtors, such as the most aggressive bulls, they can do so using credit policies reinforced by positions built using derivatives. Traditionally, short-term credit meant primarily bills, but today other forms are of growing importance, including especially the repo market. Repo market borrowing is the source of much of the trading capital for hedge funds, investment funds, and the trading desks of banks. Repo borrowing is most often overnight borrowing to fund that day's trading positions, mostly established using derivatives. Repo borrowing is typically very inexpensive because loans are secured by assets such as "safe" government bonds or bills. The explosive growth of short-term trading in recent decades has led to an explosive growth in short-term borrowing by banks and other financial companies to fund their trading positions. Traditionally we think of banks as creditors, but nowadays they are also and often more importantly, heavy borrowers. Even a slight increase in their daily cost of borrowing can destroy the profitability of their heavily leveraged trading positions and even jeopardize the solvency of banks and other investors.

Debt bubble

The crisis was only solved by piling on more debt in a world already more indebted than ever before. Public attention has been focused on government debt, including that used in several countries to bail out the huge financial corporations bankrupted during 2008–9. But the crisis did not cure financial companies of their appetite for debt-leveraged derivatives gambling. In fact, it has only increased since then, reaching a level double the already extra-ordinarily high level of 2008. The growth of derivatives trading is the largest cause of the massive bubble in short-term borrowing by financial companies. There is no end in sight.

This massive worldwide debt bubble is still growing. Such massive debts impose a severe constraint on economic growth. The bulls are chained. Any major growth that starts gaining momentum is likely to be choked off quickly because bullish growth is fueled by growing demand for credit that tends to raise interest rates, but the world today is too full of "debt cows," companies and countries growing slowly and saddled with heavy debt, including especially a great many heavily leveraged financial companies. If real interest rates rise above their current world-historic lows levels, many debt cows will not be able to afford the increasing costs to service their debt. Companies will face bankruptcy; countries will face debt default. Many countries in Europe are teetering under their debt load today, as I write.

There are four solutions to heavy debt: bankruptcy (or default for countries), belt-tightening to pay it back, growing out of it, or massive inflation. The first two are bearish. The last two are bullish. Widespread bankruptcy through another severe recession would wipe out much debt, but also many companies and jobs in the process. Belt-tightening is another bearish solution. If widespread it becomes a vicious circle, because the more people, companies, and countries cut their spending to pay back their debt, the more they depress demand. Economists often discount this by suggesting that whoever is receiving the debt repayments may increase their spending, but this is only true if they are not tightening too. Many creditors today are themselves indebted and vulnerable, and thus may prefer to use debt repayments from others to reduce their own indebtedness. Some authors, such as Keen (2011) and Hudson (2012) advocate another bullish solution: a debt jubilee, write down, or default without bankruptcy. While these are possible solutions, they would be difficult to implement without a significant political defeat of private creditors followed by a comprehensive reform of the credit system. If banks and other creditors know such a debt jubilee is even possible, they are likely to lend much less and charge much higher interest rates to compensate for the increased risk of loss of capital. Credit power will not be surrendered easily.

Debt cows are by definition slow growing. They cannot grow fast enough to outgrow their debt. Worldwide restraints on bullish growth reinforce this. In much of the world today, as in Japan since its great bubble burst in 1990, very low interest rates, available especially to creditworthy governments and the most inveterate financial gamblers of the largest financial corporations, are combined with stricter credit rationing for other potential borrowers, including for productive investment. If a truly free market for credit existed, rising asset values would trigger growing demand for credit to buy into this bullish market that could only be curtailed, as in the past, by rising interest rates. But such a heavily indebted world as ours is allergic to higher interest rates, and banks, funding their speculative positions with cheap short-term credit, have little interest in spoiling the party for themselves, even as they ration the credit available for others.

The debt-deflation of the 1930s was finally ended when the US government and private companies financed the World War II and postwar boom. The US at that time had significant reserves of unused private productive capacity and was not nearly as heavily leveraged as today, especially the financial sector. During the 1940s through 1960s, there was still much opportunity for bullish growth. Today there is less. Standard textbook macroeconomics long worried whether government borrowing would "crowd out" private borrowing and thus retard growth. Today it seems a greater problem comes from private speculative borrowing crowding out borrowing for productive investment, making it increasingly difficult to grow out of such debt (Hudson 2012).

Some today, recognizing that the US, Britain, Japan, and even Germany are restrained by high debts, look to China and India as engines of growth. Many talked of the fast-growing "BRICK" countries, Brazil, Russia, India, China, and Korea. Russia has stumbled badly in its relations with Ukraine and in the corruption of its economy. All the BRICK countries are dependent for their growth on exports and thus on the overall buoyancy of the global economy. They cannot continually grow faster than the global markets that buy those exports. Furthermore, as their export growth begins to slow, the other major driver of their economies – investment spending – tends to drop quickly to avoid accumulation of expensive excess industrial capacity or an excess supply of housing and other real estate leading to another collapse in those asset prices. Investment demand is especially volatile since it is investment in future productive capacity that will be redundant if growth slows. As growth slows, it is the fastest growing countries that have the largest share of GDP devoted to investment goods and which therefore have the farthest to fall, as happened to Japan when its bubble burst a quarter century ago after decades of unprecedented growth (Koo 2009). Rather than being engines to sustain growth, at least some of the BRICKs are more likely to fall heavily in a global crisis, accelerating broader economic decline.

If it is not possible to grow out of this debt, the default solution would seem to be massive inflation of currencies to devalue debt denominated in fixed monetary units. This would, of course, benefit long-term debtor interests, including most governments, but it might not be opposed by most major banking interests as vigorously as in the past since the securitization of many loans has left banks more footloose than ever before. Loans at fixed interest devalue with inflation. So do bonds. These traditional assets of major banks are now disappearing from their balance sheets. If banks wished to author a major inflation, they would, of course, first position their assets to profit from it, for example, by taking short positions on long-term bond prices, taking the flexible interest side of interest rate swaps, swapping an inflation-prone currency for a strong one, etc. One should not assume that because big banks were historically bearish they will be so today after so fundamentally restructuring their balance sheets. Using properly designed derivative positions, it is possible to profit from any direction of change, assuming your counterparties avoid bankruptcy and actually pay you, or, as happened during the 2008 crisis, debts of defaulting counterparties are paid by the government. Any movement to higher inflation that was not supported by most of the big banks could be stopped by them by bearishly tightening credit, as in past crashes.

Alternatively, before opting for inflation, big banks might bearishly tighten public credit in major countries with large public debt, which is happening today in several European countries, including Britain. Raising the interest rate cost of large public debts has the advantage that countries cannot go bankrupt, as corporations do, and in the contemporary business environment, major countries are unlikely to default on debt. Raising its cost instead forces public spending cuts and tax increases. However, since government spending in most countries is now a significant portion of national income, cutting it has broad bearish effects on aggregate demand, perhaps leading to a deep recession or depression, thus it would be difficult to limit the effects to government spending alone. On the other hand, a new round of government cuts and asset sales might raise new opportunities to finance IPOs for private corporations taking over former government assets and roles. Such privatization of government functions may disadvantage many, but if banks profit from the new financing opportunities thus created, it might be a tempting strategy for them.

The exact strategy of major interests is less predictable than many believe. Understanding that is the essence of the strategic method. Extraordinary force comes from doing the unexpected successfully. Extraordinary profit often follows. As soon as you think you have your opponents figured out, but they know that you think you know what they will do, further fostering your illusory expectation is their ordinary force; surprising you with a different tack is their extraordinary force. Doing what is unexpected or what people think is out of character for you or against your interest also makes it easier to dissemble and ascribe your exercise of power to someone or something else. Thus you are both more likely to attain your objective and less likely to get the blame from those who would oppose you, because it seems so implausible that you would do such an uncharacteristic thing. Having power means not only having great inertia or mass, it also means having the flexibility of strategic choice. What adversaries must learn are the signs and signals that their rival is building positions indicative of a strategic reversal or realignment. In business such clues are easier to read if you understand the various ways private positions are established and the strategic purposes they portend.

The instability of the third globalization

The era since World War II, the heyday of business internationalism, may be considered the third globalization. It has accelerated in particular during the last quarter century as Europe unified, the Soviet bloc disintegrated, the world became significantly more peaceful, China became an export powerhouse along with scores of other developing countries, world trade barriers fell, the internet made communications easier, and derivative trading exploded to transform global finance. This third globalization bears some similarities to the two that preceded it.

The first globalization is also known as the age of exploration. It is the era of mercantilism in political economy. During that era, the world was explored and world trade developed almost entirely by private capital, including the capital invested in the armies and navies of the great trading corporations like the British and Dutch East India Companies. Mercantilism has been miscast by realism as an era of state dominance. States did not dominate the world's oceans and trade; private corporations did. Even numerous wars among the monarchs of Europe were possible only because of leveraged financing by private capital. The centralization of private capital was the most enduring feature of this era. Whereas the great trading companies that were its hallmark faded away during the next era, some of the great banks and insurance companies endured. Another legacy of the mercantile era was a huge accumulation of public debt. The mercantile era ended with a public debt bubble that caused a revolution in France and made Britain, the most successful mercantile power, the center of global finance.

The second globalization is known as the free trade era because the monopoly barriers to trade and many of the dangers that plagued world trade during the mercantile era were greatly reduced. Financial exchange and export of capital was facilitated by big private banks, such as those of the Rothschild family, and corporate banks, most famously the Bank of England. Because of the relatively free trade and metallic monetary standards largely free from government interference, the second globalization was also known as the era of laissez-faire. It came to a crashing end in World War I and after another huge round of public debt accumulation. However, the business basis of classic liberalism had been eclipsed for decades before the gold standard lapsed in 1914. Laissez-faire liberalism was undermined by the devastating impact on indebted corporations of the deflation of 1860–95 and the consequent enormous concentration of business into huge groups that clamored for tariff protection to secure their monopoly power and aggressive overseas expansion to secure new markets and the credit advanced to develop them. Neither liberalism nor realism grasps the business foundations of imperialism, the end of the liberal era. Whereas the first globalization concentrated power in great mercantile and banking companies, the second globalization witnessed the formation of conglomerates of enormous size, combining dozens of huge industrial and commercial companies under the leadership of finance.

The second globalization was followed by an interlude of a third of a century framed by two world wars and the Great Depression. During this period, governments regulated economies to an unprecedented degree. Except for a brief interlude during the 1920s, private finance declined in influence and business volume while being regulated by governments in many new ways. Trade declined significantly, again, with the brief exception of the 1920s, as barriers to trade increased and governments managed trade, especially during wartime. Today, given the perspective of the centuries, it is possible to see this as an interlude, an interruption. However, for many this war era seemed like a baseline for the future, especially since its effects lingered on for decades after 1945. Regulation of trade and finance persisted, and in the cases of the socialist countries and the developing world, were even enhanced in the postwar decades. Therefore for many of those who grew up during this era, government regulation of economic life seemed the dominant reality and an irreversible trend, but the third globalization did reverse this trend.

The third globalization emerged gradually after the war. It was implicit already in the peace aims of business internationalists. However, it encountered significant resistance from business nationalists, including socialists. It took some time to gain traction. Gradually, however, the war aims of business internationalists were consolidated, certainly far more successfully than after World War I. However, by the time business internationalism succeeded broadly, previous globalizations had faded from living memory, so the third globalization seemed to many people like something completely new and unprecedented. The term "globalization" itself was coined as a way to describe this unique era, but may be applied retroactively to the other two because in fact this era is not so unique. There are some important parallels between the third globalization and the first two.

Like the first globalization, the third has developed an enormous debt bubble, though without war as the proximate cause. Private debt is bigger than public debt today. The biggest component of private debt is the debt of financial interests, largely to finance gambling with derivatives. The mercantilists gambled primarily on war. Contemporary investors gamble on everything on a vast scale. The enormous debt accumulated during centuries of mercantile war became a constraint on war during the liberal second globalization. Much of new debt was channeled to more productive uses such as building railroads and then heavy industries. World War I caused a massive new accumulation of public debt that hobbled the interwar period. Added to these was an explosion of private corporate debt, particularly in the USA, to fund productive investment in new industries like automobiles and radio. The current debt bubble is unique in history. Although public debts are a big part of it, private debt has also exploded, as in the USA during the 1920s. The unique difference, however, is the composition of that private debt. Dividing it into households, financial, and non-financial corporations, during the 1920s, the last was the biggest portion. Debt had financed fast growth through productive investment. The debt of financial companies was the smallest. This is to be expected since traditional banks tend to be net creditors.

Today this has reversed. Especially in the most financially developed countries such as the USA and Britain, financial companies as a whole provide the largest component of private debt. In recent decades their profits have come increasingly from their trading activities, primarily using derivatives, rather than from the traditional deposit banking of economic textbooks. Even worse, they finance their trading activities with highly leveraged short-term borrowing, often overnight loans. That is, they borrow each day what they need to fund that day's trading activities. Since most trading today depends on great volume and enormous leverage to make a profit, anything that lowers the rate of profit on trades or raises the cost of short-term borrowing can turn large profits into large losses overnight. Since these trading activities do not legally require the capital reserves of traditional government-regulated deposit accounts, most banks and other financial companies are leveraged to an extraordinary degree. Their assets may be 40 or 50 times their capital.

High leverage increases profits, but at high risk. Even with assets 25 times capital, it takes a mere 4 percent average losses on assets to become bankrupt. This is why so many financial companies worldwide could fail simultaneously during 2008–9 and require bailouts. The entire financial system is today both exceedingly profitable and precariously fragile.

The strong conservative bearish banks of the past are gone. All are traders now; all are broker-dealers. Banks do take tactically bearish (and bullish) positions in their derivatives trading, but the strategic bears of past globalizations are dead. The enormously bullish bond market since 1981 must be near an end, since high-quality bond prices cannot rise much higher nor yields fall much lower, especially as debt piles up. The transformation of the biggest banks into enormous hedge funds is one reason the current debt bubble can grow so large and the response of big banks, which in the past would have been to raise short-term discount rates, is instead to demand that discount rates remain as low as possible, indeed, the lowest in world history, because it is cheap short-term credit that fuels the derivative trading bubble. Raising the cost of these gambling games would cause many of them to fold, to the great detriment of financial profits. So-called central banks, myopically or ingeniously focused on consumer price stability and ignoring asset price bubbles, are in fact committed to serving the trading interests of the great private banks, which have become the "projectors and stock jobbers" that Adam Smith decried.

The third globalization occurring today has two countervailing tendencies that together paper over the real instability at the heart of our age. On the one hand, like the first globalization of mercantilism, this age is creating a great debt bubble, which should, as it did then, portend inflation. On the other hand, like the second globalization of the later nineteenth century, there are strong deflationary tendencies in the world economy. Freer trade and rapid technological development, then as now, have tended to lower real costs of many products dramatically. There would be bearish deflation now as there was then except for the countervailing effect of an enormously bullish debt bubble, which acts strongly to raise asset prices, including real estate, which enters into the cost of most other things to one degree or another. The net result is roughly stable consumer prices, part of what Ben Bernanke called "the great moderation," but only because ballooning mountain of debt roughly counteracts strong deflationary tendencies. Whenever the debt bubble becomes untenable, which will occur with any rise of interest rates toward historically normal levels, the massive deflationary pressures will become manifest, causing widespread bankruptcies and defaults among so many public and private debtors gorged with debt, as in the series of depressions of the later nineteenth century. This is not a period of great moderation, but an era of unregulated extremes. Attention to private power and strategy is necessary to have any hope of predicting its course.

Selected bibliography

Ackerman, K.D. (1988) *The Gold Ring: Jim Fisk, Jay Gould, and Black Friday, 1869*, New York: Harper Business.

Adler, M. (2010) *Economics for the Rest of Us: Debunking the Science That Makes Life Dismal*, New York: New Press.

Aggarwal, V.K. (1986) *Liberal Protectionism: The International Politics of Organized Textile Trade*, Los Angeles: University of California Press.

Ahamed, L. (2009) *Lords of Finance: The Bankers Who Broke the World*, New York: Penguin.

Allen, F.L. (1989) *The Great Pierpont Morgan*, New York: Dorset.

Alletzhauser, A.J. (1991) *The House of Nomura: The Inside Story of the Legendary Japanese Financial Dynasty*, New York: Harper Perennial.

Amar, A.R. (2005) *America's Constitution: A Biography*, New York: Random House.

Anderson, P.J. (2009) *The Secret Life of Real Estate and Banking*, London: Shepheard-Walwyn.

Angell, N. (2012[1913]) *The Great Illusion: A Study of the Relation of Military Power to National Advantage*, Memphis, TN: Bottom of the Hill Publishing.

Atkinson, A. (1981) *Social Order and the General Theory of Strategy*, London: Routledge.

Bagehot, W. (2013[1878]) *Lombard Street: A Description of the Money Market*, London: Paul.

Barnhart, M.A. (1987) *Japan Prepares for Total War: The Search for Economic Security, 1919–1941*, Ithaca, NY: Cornell University Press.

Barofsky, N. (2012) *Bailout: An Inside Account of How Washington Abandoned Main Street While Rescuing Wall Street*, New York: Free Press.

Baskin, J.B. & Miranti, P.J. (1997) *A History of Corporate Finance*, Cambridge: Cambridge University Press.

Beck, L.W. (ed.) (1963) *Kant: On History*, Indianapolis, IN: Bobbs-Merrill.

Berger, S.D. (ed.) (1981) *Organizing Interests in Western Europe: Pluralism, Corporatism and the Transformation of Politics*, Cambridge: Cambridge University Press.

Birchler, U. & Bütler, M. (2007) *Information Economics*, London: Routledge.

Bird, K. (1992) *The Chairman: John J. McCloy and the Making of the American Establishment*, New York: Simon & Schuster.

Birmingham, S. (1967) *"Our Crowd": The Great Jewish Families of New York*, New York: Harper & Row.

Bodenhorn, H. (2000) *A History of Banking in Antebellum America: Financial Markets and Economic Development in an Era of Nation-Building*, Cambridge: Cambridge University Press.

Boesche, R. (2002) *The First Great Political Realist: Kautilya and His Arthashastra*, Lanham, MD: Lexington.

Bookstaber, R. (2007) *A Demon of Our Own Design: Markets, Hedge Funds, and the Perils of Financial Innovation*, Hoboken, NJ: Wiley.

Bowen, H.V. (2006) *The Business of Empire: The East India Company and Imperial Britain, 1756–1833*, Cambridge: Cambridge University Press.

Boyd, R. (2011) *Fatal Risk: A Cautionary Tale of AIG's Corporate Suicide*, Hoboken, NJ: Wiley.

Brands, H.W. (2010) *American Colossus: The Triumph of Capitalism*, New York: Anchor Books.

Brewer, J. (1988) *The Sinews of Power: War, Money and the English State, 1688–1783*, Cambridge, MA: Harvard University Press.

Brooks, A.A. (2002) *The Woman Who Defied Kings: The Life and Times of Doña Gracia Nasi – A Jewish Leader during the Renaissance*, St. Paul, MN: Paragon House.

Brown, B. (1987) *The Flight of International Capital: A Contemporary History*, London: Routledge.

Bruner, R.F. & Carr, S.D. (2007) *The Panic of 1907: Lessons Learned from the Market's Perfect Storm*, Hoboken, NJ: Wiley.

Buck, P.W. (1974[1942] *The Politics of Mercantilism*, New York: Henry Holt.

Bukharin, N. (1973) *Imperialism and World Economy*, New York: Monthly Review Press.

Burch, P.H. (1980) *Elites in American History*, 3 vols, New York: Holmes & Meyer.

Burke, P. (1994) *Venice and Amsterdam*, Cambridge: Polity Press.

Caro, R.A. (1975) *The Power Broker: Robert Moses and the Fall of New York*, New York: Vintage.

Carr, E.H. (1964) *The Twenty Years' Crisis, 1919–1939: An Introduction to the Study of International Relations*, New York: Harper & Row.

Chancellor, E. (2000) *Devil Take the Hindmost: A History of Financial Speculation*, New York: Plume.

Chandler, A.D. & Salsbury, S. (1971) *Pierre S. du Pont and the Making of the Modern Corporation*, New York: Harper & Row.

Chandler, A.D., Amatori, F., & Hikino, T. (eds) (1999) *Big Business and the Wealth of Nations*, Cambridge: Cambridge University Press.

Chaudhuri, K.N. (1985) *Trade and Civilization in the Indian Ocean: An Economic History from the Rise of Islam to 1750*, Cambridge: Cambridge University Press.

Chernow, R. (1990) *The House of Morgan: An American Banking Dynasty and the Rise of Modern Finance*, New York: Touchstone.

——(1994) *The Warburgs: The Twentieth-Century Odyssey of a Remarkable Jewish Family*, New York: Vintage.

——(1998) *Titan: The Life of John D. Rockefeller, Sr.*, New York: Random House.

Clark, V.S. (1949) *History of Manufactures in the United States*, 3 vols, New York: Peter Smith.

Clausewitz, C. (1976) *On War*, Princeton: Princeton University Press.

Cohan, W.D. (2008) *The Last Tycoons: The Secret History of Lazard Frères & Co.*, London: Penguin.

Coll, S. (2012) *Private Empire: ExxonMobil and American Power*, New York: Penguin.

Collier, P. & Horowitz, D. (1976) *The Rockefellers: An American Dynasty*, New York: Summit.

Connaughton, J. (2013) *The Payoff: Why Wall Street Always Wins*, Westport, CT: Easton Studio.

Cox, R.W. (1994) *Power and Profits: U.S. Policy in Central America*, Lexington: University of Kentucky Press.

——(ed.) (2012) *Corporate Power and Globalization in US Foreign Policy*, London: Routledge.

Crompton, G. (1927) *The Tariff: An Interpretation of a Bewildering Problem*, New York: Macmillan.

Dalzell, R.F. (1987) *Enterprising Elite: The Boston Associates and the World They Made*, Cambridge, MA: Harvard University Press.

Dattel, E.R. (1994) *The Sun That Never Rose: The Inside Story of Japan's Failed Attempt at Global Financial Dominance*, Chicago: Probus.

——(2009) *Cotton and Race in the Making of America: The Human Costs of Economic Power*, Chicago: Ivan R. Dee.

Davis, C.B. & Wilburn, K.E. (eds) (1991) *Railway Imperialism*, Contributions in Comparative Colonial Studies, No. 26, New York: Greenwood Press.

Dayer, R.A. (1988) *Finance and Empire: Sir Charles Addis, 1861–1945*, New York: St. Martin's.

Duffie, D. (2012) *Dark Markets: Asset Pricing and Information Transmission in Over-the-Counter Markets*, Princeton: Princeton University Press.

Dunbar, N. (2001) *Inventing Money: The Story of Long-Term Capital Management and the Legends behind It*, Hoboken, NJ: Wiley.

East, R.A. (1969) *Business Enterprise in the American Revolutionary Era*, New York: AMS.

Einhorn, D. (2011) *Fooling Some of the People All of the Time: A Long Short (and Now Complete) Story*, updated edn, Hoboken, NJ: Wiley.

Ekelund, R.B. & Tollison, R.D. (1997) *Politicized Economies: Monarchy. Monopoly, and Mercantilism*, College Station: Texas A&M University Press.

Emery, H.C. (1969) *Speculation on the Stock and Produce Exchanges of the United States*, New York: Greenwood.

Feis, H. (1930) *Europe, the World's Banker, 1870–1914: An Account of European Foreign Investment and the Connection of World Finance with Diplomacy before the War*, New Haven, CT: Yale University Press.

Ferguson, N. (1998) *The House of Rothschild: Money's Prophets 1798–1848*, New York: Viking.

——(1999) *The House of Rothschild: The World's Banker 1849–1999*, New York: Viking.

——(2002) *Paper and Iron: Hamburg Business and German Politics in the Era of Inflation, 1897–1927*, Cambridge: Cambridge University Press.

——(2008) *The Ascent of Money: A Financial History of the World*, New York: Penguin.

——(2010) *High Financier: The Lives and Time of Siegmund Warburg*, New York: Penguin.

Ferguson, T. (1995) *Golden Rule: The Investment Theory of Party Competition and the Logic of Money-Driven Political Systems*, Chicago: University of Chicago Press.

Figes, O. (1997) *A People's Tragedy: A History of the Russian Revolution*, New York: Viking.

Fisher, I. (1932) *Booms and Depressions: Some First Principles*, New York: Adelphi.

——(1933) The Debt-Deflation Theory of Great Depressions, *Econometrica* 1: 337–55.

Fox, J. (2009) *The Myth of the Rational Market: A History of Risk, Reward, and Delusion on Wall Street*, New York: Harper Business.

Francisco, L.B. & Fast, J.S. (1985) *Conspiracy for Empire: Big Business, Corruption and the Politics of Imperialism in America, 1876–1907*, Quezon City, Philippines: Foundation for Nationalist Studies.

Frank, R.H. & Bernanke, B.S. (2009) *Principles of Macroeconomics*, 4th edn, New York: McGraw-Hill.

Frieden, J.A. (1987) *Banking on the World: The Politics of American International Finance*. New York: Harper & Row.

——(1988) Sectoral Conflict and U.S. Foreign Economic Policy, 1914–40, *International Organization* 42: 59–90.

——(1991) Invested Interests: The Politics of National Economic Policies in a World of Global Finance. *International Organization* 45: 425–51.

Fromkin, D. (1989) *A Peace to End All Peace: The Fall of the Ottoman Empire and the Creation of the Modern Middle East*, New York: Henry Holt.

Fukuyama, F. (1992) *The End of History and the Last Man*, New York: Free Press.

Furber, H. (1976) *Rival Empires of Trade in the Orient, 1600–1800*, Europe and the World in the Age of Expansion, vol. 2, Minneapolis: University of Minnesota Press.

Galbraith, J.K. (1993) *A Short History of Financial Euphoria*, New York: Penguin.

——(2009) *The Great Crash 1929*, Boston: Mariner Books.

Gibbs, D.N. (1991) *The Political Economy of Third World Intervention: Mines, Money, and U.S. Policy in the Congo Crisis*, Chicago: University of Chicago Press.

——(2009) *First Do No Harm: Humanitarian Intervention and the Destruction of Yugoslavia*, Nashville: Vanderbilt University Press.

Gilbert, F. (1980) *The Pope, His Banker, and Venice*, Cambridge, MA: Harvard University Press.

Gillingham, J.R. (1985) *Industry and Politics in the Third Reich: Ruhr Coal, Hitler and Europe*, New York: Columbia University Press.

Glasscock, C.B. (1935) *The War of the Copper Kings: Builders of Butte and Wolves of Wall Street*, Indianapolis, IN: Bobbs-Merrill.

Graebner, D. (2011) *Debt: The First 5,000 Years*, New York: Melville House.

Greenberg, M. (1951) *British Trade and the Opening of China 1800–1842*, Cambridge: Cambridge University Press.

Grossman, R.S. (2010) *Unsettled Account: The Evolution of Banking in the Industrialized World since 1800*, 2 vols, Princeton: Princeton University Press.

Hammond, B. (1991) *Banks and Politics in America from the Revolution to the Civil War*, Princeton: Princeton University Press.

Harrington, V.D. (1964) *The New York Merchant on the Eve of the Revolution*, Gloucester, MA: Peter Smith.

Harvey, D. (2010) *The Enigma of Capital and the Crisis of Capitalism*, Oxford: Oxford University Press.

Held, P. (2006) *The Confusion of Confusions*: Between Speculation and Eschatology, *Concentric: Literacy and Cultural Studies* 32(2): 111–44.

Henry, J.S. (2003) *The Blood Bankers: Tales from the Global Underground Economy*, New York: Four Walls Eight Windows.

Henwood, D. (1997) *Wall Street: How It Works and for Whom*, London: Verso.

Hilferding, R. (2006) *Finance Capital: A Study in the Latest Phase of Capitalist Development*, London: Routledge.

Hirschman, A.O. (1981) *National Power and the Structure of Foreign Trade*, 2d edn, Los Angeles: University of California Press.

Hobson, J.A. (1965) *Imperialism*, Ann Arbor: University of Michigan Press.

Homer, S. and Sylla, R. (2005) *A History of Interest Rates*, 4th edn, Hoboken, NJ: Wiley.

Horowitz, D. (ed.) (1969) *Corporations and the Cold War*, New York: Monthly Review.

Howard, M. (2002) *Clausewitz: A Very Short Introduction*, Oxford: Oxford University Press.

Hudson, M. (2012) *The Bubble and Beyond: Fictitious Capital, Debt Deflation and Global Crisis*, Dresden: Islet.

Hume, D. (1752) Of the Balance of Power, in *Essays, Moral, Political, and Literary*, Available online at www.econlib.org/library/LFBooks/Hume/hmMPL30.html (accessed April 12, 2014).

Hunt, E.S. & Murray, J.M. (1999) *A History of Medieval Business, 1200–1550*, Cambridge: Cambridge University Press.

Huntington, S.P. (2011) *The Clash of Civilizations and the Remaking of World Order*, New York: Simon & Schuster.

Huston, J.L. (1987) *The Panic of 1857 and the Coming of the Civil War*, Baton Rouge: Louisiana State University Press.

James, F.C. (1935) *The Economics of Money, Credit and Banking*, 2d edn, New York: Ronald.

Johnson, L.L. (1953) *Some Aspects of the European Coal and Steel Community*, PhD diss., University of Oregon.

Johnson, S. & Kwak, J. (2010) *13 Bankers: The Wall Street Takeover and the Next Financial Meltdown*, New York: Pantheon.

Josephson, M. (1962) *The Robber Barons: The Great American Capitalists 1861–1901*, San Diego: Harcourt Brace Jovanovich.

——(1972) *The Money Lords: The Great Finance Capitalists 1925–1950*, New York: Weybright and Talley.

Kahneman, D. (2013) *Thinking, Fast and Slow*, New York: Farrar, Straus & Giroux.

Kaiser, D.E. (1980) *Economic Diplomacy and the Origins of the Second World War: Germany, Britain, France, and Eastern Europe 1930–1939*, Princeton: Princeton University Press.

Kaplan, M.A. (1975) *System and Process in International Politics*, Huntington, NY: R.E. Krieger.

Katz, F. (1981) *The Secret War in Mexico: Europe, the United States and the Mexican Revolution*, Chicago: University of Chicago Press.

Keen, S. (2011) *Debunking Economics: The Naked Emperor of the Social Sciences*, 2nd edn, London: Zed.

Kehr, E. (1973) *Battleship Building and Party Politics in Germany, 1894–1901: A Cross-section of the Political, Social and Ideological Preconditions of German Imperialism*, Chicago: University of Chicago Press.

——(1977) *Economic Interest, Militarism, and Foreign Policy: Essays on German History*, Los Angeles: University of California Press.

Kennan, G.F. (1946) *Long Telegram to Secretary of State George Marshall*, available online at www2.gwu.edu/~nsarchiv/coldwar/documents/episode-1/kennan.htm (accessed August 31, 2014).

Keohane, R.O. (1984) *After Hegemony: Cooperation and Discord in the World Political Economy*, Princeton, NJ: Princeton University Press.

Keohane, R.O. & Nye, J.S. (1972) *Transnational Relations and World Politics*, Cambridge, MA: Harvard University Press.

——(1977) *Power and Intedependence*, New York: Pearson (4th edn, 2011).

Keohane, R.O., Nye, J.S., & Hoffman, S. (eds.) (1993) *After the Cold War: International Institutions and State Strategies in Europe, 1989–1991*, Cambridge, MA: Harvard University Press.

Keynes, J.M. (1936) *The General Theory of Employment, Interest and Money*, London: Macmillan.

——(2011)[1930] *A Treatise on Money*, Mansfield Centre, CT: Martino.

Kiechel, W. (2013) *Lords of Strategy: The Secret Intellectual History of the New Corporate World*, Boston, MA: Harvard Business Review Press.

Kindleberger, C.P. (1973) *The Formation of Financial Centers: A Study in Comparative Financial History*, Working Paper (MIT Dept. of Economics) No. 114.

——(2006) *A Financial History of Western Europe*, London: Routledge.

Kindleberger, C.P. & Aliber, R.Z. (2005) *Manias, Panics, and Crashes: A History of Financial Crises*, 5th edn, Hoboken, NJ: Wiley.

——(2011) *Manias, Panics, and Crashes: A History of Financial Crises*, 6th edn, NewYork: Palgrave Macmillan.

Kolb, R.W. (1988) *Understanding Futures Markets*, 2d edn, Glenview, IL: Scott, Foresman.

Kolko, G. (1985) *Anatomy of a War: Vietnam, the United States, and the Modern Historical Experience*, New York: Pantheon.

Koo, R.C. (2009) *The Holy Grail of Macroeconomics: Lessons from Japan's Great Recession*, rev. edn, Singapore: Wiley.

Krooss, H.E. (1983) *Documentary History of Banking and Currency in the United States*, 4 vols, New York: Chelsea House.

Krugman, P.R. (2009) *The Return of Depression Economics and the Crisis of 2008*, New York: Norton.

Leijonhufvud, A. (1968) *On Keynesian Economics and the Economics of Keynes*, New York: Oxford.

Lenin, V.I. (1939) *Imperialism: The Highest Stage of Capitalism*, New York: International Publishers.

——(1964[1916]) Imperialism and the Split in Socialism, in *Collected Works* 23: 105–20, Moscow: Progress Publishers.

Levy, J. (2012) *Freaks of Fortune: The Emerging World of Capitalism and Risk in America*, Cambridge, MA: Harvard University Press.

Lewis, M. (1990) *Liar's Poker: Rising Through the Wreckage on Wall Street*, New York: Penguin.

——(2010) *The Big Short: Inside the Doomsday Machine*, New York: Norton.

Lewis, W.A. (1954) Economic Development with Unlimited Supplies of Labour, *The Manchester School* 22(2): 139–91.

Lipson, C. (2003) *Reliable Partners: How Democracies Have Made a Separate Peace*, Princeton: Princeton University Press.

Lisagor, N. & Lipsius, F. (1988) *A Law Unto Itself: The Untold Story of the Law Firm Sullivan & Cromwell*, New York: William Morrow.

List, F. (1977) *The National System of Political Economy*, Fairfield, NJ: Augustus M. Kelley.

Lubetkin, M.J. (2006) *Jay Cooke's Gamble: The Northern Pacific Railroad, the Sioux, and the Panic of 1873*, Norman, OK: University of Oklahoma Press.

Lurie, J. (1979) *The Chicago Board of Trade 1859–1905: The Dynamics of Self-Regulation*, Urbana: University of Illinois Press.

Machiavelli, N. (1988) *Florentine Histories*, Princeton, NJ: Princeton University Press.

MacKay, C. (2013) *Extraordinary Popular Delusions and the Madness of Crowds*, CreateSpace.

Mackenzie, D.A. (2006) *An Engine, Not a Camera: How Financial Models Shape Markets*, Cambridge, MA: MIT Press.

Madison, J. (1787) *Federalist Papers*, No. 10, available online at http://avalon.law.yale.edu/18th_century/fed10.asp (accessed March 3, 2014).

Mahan, A.T. (2010) *The Influence of the Sea Power Upon History 1660–1783*, Mineola, NY: Dover.

Matsuda, T. (1979) *Woodrow Wilson's Dollar Diplomacy in the Far East: The New China Consortium, 1917–1921*, PhD diss. Madison: University of Wisconsin.

Maxfield, S. (1990) *Governing Capital: International Finance and Mexican Politics*, Ithaca, NY: Cornell University Press.

——(1997) *Gatekeepers of Growth: The International Political Economy of Central Banking in Developing Countries*, Princeton, NJ: Princeton University Press.

Maxfield, S. & Nolt, J.H. (1990) Protectionism and the Internationalization of Capital: U.S. Sponsorship of Import Substitution Industrialization in the Philippines, Turkey and Argentina. *International Studies Quarterly* 34: 49–81.

McCartney, L. (1988) *Friends in High Places: The Bechtel Story: The Most Secret Corporation and How It Engineered the World*, New York: Simon & Schuster.

McLean, B. & Nocera, J. (2010) *All the Devils Are Here: The Hidden History of the Financial Crisis*, New York: Penguin.

Mearsheimer, J.J. (1990) Back to the Future: Instability in Europe after the Gold War, *International Security* 15: 5–56.

——(2003) *The Tragedy of Great Power Politics*, New York: Norton.

Mill, J.S. (1987) *Principles of Political Economy with Some of Their Applications to Social Philosophy*, Fairfield, NJ: Augustus M. Kelley.

Miller, Edward S. (2007) *Bankrupting the Enemy: The U.S. Financial Siege of Japan before Pearl Harbor*, Anapolis, MD: Naval Institute Press.

Mills, C.W. (1956) *The Power Elite*, Oxford: Oxford University Press.

Milward, A. (1977) *War, Economy and Society 1939–1945*, Los Angeles: University of California Press.

Minsky, H.M. (1982) *Can "It" Happen Again: Essays on Instability and Finance*, Armonk, NY: M.E. Sharpe.

——(2008) *John Maynard Keynes*, New York: McGraw Hill.

Mishkin, F.S. (2011) *The Economics of Money, Banking, and Financial Markets*, 9th edn (version sold in China), New York: Pearson.

Moffitt, M. (1983) *The World's Money: International Banking from Bretton Woods to the Brink of Insolvency*, New York: Simon & Schuster.

Montesquieu (1989) *The Spirit of the Laws*, Cambridge: Cambridge University Press.

Morris, C.R. (2008) *The Trillion Dollar Meltdown: East Money, High Rollers, and the Great Credit Crash*, New York: Public Affairs.

Morse, E.L. (1976) *Modernization and the Transformation of International Relations*, New York: Free Press.

Munkirs, J.R. (1985) *The Transformation of American Capitalism from Competitive Market Structures to Centralized Private Sector Planning*, Armonk, NY: Sharpe.

Murphy, A.L. (2009) Trading Options before Black-Scholes: A Study of the Market in Late Seventeenth Century London, *The Economic History Review* 62: 8–30.

Napier, R. (2007) *Anatomy of the Bear: Lessons from Wall Street's Four Great Bottoms*, Petersfield, England: Harriman House.

Napoleoni, L. (2008) *Rogue Economics*, New York: Seven Stories.

Naylor, R.T. (1987) *Hot Money and the Politics of Debt*, New York: Linden.

——(2006) *The History of Canadian Business, 1867–1914*, Montreal: McGill-Queen's University Press.

Neal, L. (1990) *The Rise of Financial Capitalism: Financial Markets in the Age of Reason*, Cambridge: Cambridge University Press.

Nesvetailova, A. (2007) *Fragile Finance: Debt, Speculation and Crisis in the Age of Global Credit*, Houndmills, England: Palgrave Macmillan.

Nolt, J.H. (1994) *Business Conflict and the Origin of the Pacific War*. PhD diss. Chicago: University of Chicago.

——(1997a) Business Conflict and the Demise of Imperialism, in Skidmore, D. (ed.) *Contested Social Orders and International Politics*, Nashville: Vanderbilt.

——(1997b) Conclusion: The Future of Contested Social Orders, in Skidmore, D. (ed.) *Contested Social Orders and International Politics*, Nashville: Vanderbilt.

——(1997c) *Social Order and War: Thucydides, Aristotle and a Critique of Modern Realism*, Unpublished manuscript.

——(1999) China in the WTO: The Debate, *Foreign Policy In Focus* 4 (38).

——(2006) China Is a Status Quo Power Given Its Commercial Interdependence, *Foreign Policy In Focus*, 11 (28 Nov).

Nowell, G.P. (1994) *Mercantile States and the World Oil Cartel, 1900–1939*, Ithaca, NY: Cornell University Press.

Nye, J.V.C. (2007) *War, Wine, and Taxes: The Political Economy of Anglo-French Trade, 1689–1900*, Princeton: Princeton University Press.

Organski, A.F.K. (1958) *World Politics*, New York: Knopf.

Overy, R. (1996) *The Nazi Economic Recovery 1932–1938*, Cambridge: Cambridge University Press.

Parboni, R. (1981) *The Dollar and Its Rivals: Recession, Inflation, and International Finance*, London: Verso.

Parker, G. (1996) *The Military Revolution: Military Innovation and the Rise of the West, 1500–1800*, Cambridge: Cambridge University Press.

Parker, P.M. (ed.) (2009) *Cartel: Webster's Timeline History 1535–2007*, San Diego, CA: ICON Group.

Parks, T. (2005) *Medici Money: Banking, Metaphysics, and Art in Fifteenth-Century Florence*, New York: Norton.

Parmar, I. (1995) *Special Interests, the State and the Anglo-American Alliance, 1939–1945*, London: Frank Cass.

Patterson, S. (2012) *Dark Pools: High-Speed Traders, A.I. Bandits, and the Threat to the Global Financial System*, New York: Crown Business.

Perkins, D., Radelet, S., Snodgrass, D.R., Malcolm, G., & Roemer, M. (2001) *Economics of Development*, 5th edn, New York: Norton.

Polanyi, K. (1957) *The Great Transformation: The Political and Economic Origins of Our Time*, Boston: Beacon.

Pollard, R.A. (1985) *Economic Security and the Origins of the Cold War, 1945–1950*, New York: Columbia University Press.

Porter, G. (2006) *The Rise of Big Business 1860–1920*, 3rd edn, Wheeling, IL: Harlan Davidson.

Pribram, K. (1935) *Cartel Problems: An Analysis of Collective Monopolies in Europe with American Application*, Washington, DC: Brookings.

Prins, Nomi (2014), *All the Presidents' Bankers: The Hidden Alliances that Transformed America*, New York: Perseus.

Rajan, R.G. (2010) *Fault Lines: How Hidden Fractures Still Threaten the World Economy*, Princeton: Princeton University Press.

Raphael, A. (1995) *Ultimate Risk: The Inside Story of the Lloyd's Catastrophe*, New York: Four Walls Eight Windows.

Rasmus, J. (2010) *Epic Recession: Prelude to Global Depression*, London: Pluto.

Reinhart, C.M. & Rogoff, K.S. (2009) *This Time Is Different: Eight Centuries of Financial Folly*, Princeton, NJ: Princeton University Press.

Renehan, E.J. (2005) *Dark Genius of Wall Street: The Misunderstood Life of Jay Gould, King of the Robber Barons*, New York: Basic Books.

Reuters (2000) *The Reuters Financial Glossary*, London: Pearson.

Rickards, J. (2011) *Currency Wars: The Making of the Next Global Crisis*, New York: Penguin.

Robins, N. (2006) *The Corporation that Changed the World: How the East India Company Shaped the Modern Multinational*, London: Pluto Press.

Robinson, J. (1981) *What Are the Questions? And Other Essays: Further Contributions to Modern Economics*, Armonk, NY: M.E. Sharpe.

Rodger, N.A.M. (1999) *The Safeguard of the Sea: A Naval History of Britain, 660–1649*, New York: Norton.

——(2004) *The Command of the Ocean: A Naval History of Britain, 1649–1815*, New York: Norton.

Rotberg, R.I. & Shore, M.F. (1988) *The Founder: Cecil Rhodes and the Pursuit of Power*, Oxford: Oxford University Press.

Rothbard, M.N. (2002) *A History of Money and Banking in the United States: The Colonial Era to World War II*, Auburn, AL: Ludwig von Mises Institute.

Sampson, A. (1983) *The Money Lenders: The People and Politics of the World Banking Crisis*, Harmondsworth, England: Penguin.

Sayers, R.S. (1976) *The Bank of England 1891–1944*, Cambridge: Cambridge University Press.

Schattschneider, E.E. (1935) *Politics, Pressures and the Tariff: A Study of Private Enterprise in Pressure Politics, as Shown in the 1929–1930 Revision of the Tariff*, New York: Prentice-Hall.

Schroeder, A. (2008) *The Snowball: Warren Buffet and the Business of Life*, New York: Bantam.

Schwed, F. (2006) *Where Are All the Customers' Yachts? or A Good Hard Look at Wall Street*, Hoboken, NJ: Wiley.

Shackle, G.L.S. (1967) *The Years of High Theory: Invention and Tradition in Economic Thought 1926–1939*, Cambridge: Cambridge University Press.

Shelp, R. & Ehrbar, A. (2006) *Fallen Giant: The Amazing Story of Hank Greenberg and the History of AIG*, Hoboken, NJ: Wiley.

Shermer, M. (2009) *The Mind of the Market: How Biology and Psychology Shape Our Economic Lives*, New York: Holt.

Shiller, R.J. (2005) *Irrational Exuberance*, 2nd edn, New York: Broadway Books.

Skidmore, D. (1997) *Contested Social Orders and International Politics*, Nashville: Vanderbilt University Press.

Skinner, Q. (1981) *Machiavelli: A Very Short Introduction*, Oxford: Oxford University Press.

Smith, A. (1976) *An Inquiry into the Nature and Causes of the Wealth of Nations*, Chicago: University of Chicago Press.

Smith, Y. (2010) *Econned: How Unenlightened Self Interest Undermined Democracy and Corrupted Capitalism*, New York: Palgrave Macmillan.

Smithers, A. (2009) *Wall Street Revalued: Imperfect Markets and Inept Central Bankers*, Hoboken, NJ: Wiley.

Smitten, R. (2001) *Jesse Livermore: World's Greatest Stock Trader*, New York: Wiley.

Sobel, R. (1984) *The Age of Giant Corporations: A Microeconomic History of American Business 1914–1984*, 2nd edn, Westport, CT: Greenwood.

——(1988) *Panic on Wall Street: A Classic History of America's Financial Disasters – with a New Explanation of the Crash of 1987*, New York: Truman Talley.

——(1991) *The Life and Times of Dillon Read*, New York: Dutton.

Sorkin, A.R. (2009) *Too Big to Fail: The Inside Story of How Wall Street and Washington Fought to Save the Financial System from Crisis – and Themselves*, New York: Viking.

Spufford, P. (2002) *Power and Profit: The Merchant in Medieval Europe*, New York: Thames & Hudson.

Sraffa, P. (1926) The Law of Returns under Competitive Conditions, *Economic Journal*, 40: 538–50.

——(1930) The Trees of the Forest – A Criticism, *Economic Journal* 44: 89–92.

——(1960) *The Production of Commodities by Means of Commodities; Prelude to a Critique of Political Economy*, Cambridge: Cambridge University Press.

Stern, C.W. and Deimler, M.S. (eds) (2006) *The Boston Consulting Group On Strategy*, 2nd edn, Hoboken, NJ: Wiley.

Stern, F. (1979) *Gold and Iron: Bismarck, Bleichröder, and the Building of the German Reich*, New York: Vintage.

Stiglitz, J.E. (2010) *Freefall: America, Free Markets, and the Sinking of the World Economy*, New York: Norton.

Stone, O. (1987) [Film] *Wall Street*, USA: Fox.

Strachan, H. (2004) *Financing the First World War*, Oxford: Oxford University Press.

Strange, S. (1997) *Casino Capitalism*, Manchester: Manchester University Press.

Strouse, J. (1999) *Morgan: American Financier*, New York: Random House.

Sun-Tzu [Sun Zi] (1993) *The Art of War*, New York: William Morrow.

Taleb, N.N. (2010) *The Black Swan: The Impact of the Highly Improbable*, London: Penguin.

Teichova, A. & Cottrell, P.L. (eds) (1983) *International Business and Central Europe 1918–1939*, Leicester, England: Leicester University Press.

Teichova, A., Lévy-Leboyer, M., & Nussbaum, H. (eds) (1986) *Multinational Enterprise in Historical Perspective*, Cambridge: Cambridge University Press.

Tett, G. (2009) *Fool's Gold: How the Bold Dream of a Small Tribe at J.P. Morgan Was Corrupted by Wall Street and Unleashed a Catastrophe*, New York: Free Press.

Thucydides (2008) *The Landmark Thucydides: A Comprehensive Guild to the Peloponnesian War*, edited by V.D. Hanson & R.B. Strassler, New York: Free Press.

Tilly, C. (1975) Reflections on the History of European State-making, in C. Tilly & G. Ardant (eds), *The Formation of States in Western Europe*, Vol. 8, pp. 3–83. Princeton: Princeton University Press.

Tocqueville, A. de (1840) *Democracy in America*, London: Saunders and Otley.

Trachtenberg, M. (1991) *History and Strategy*, Princeton, NJ: Princeton University Press.

Turner, H.A. (1985) *German Big Business and the Rise of Hitler*, Oxford: Oxford University Press.

US Federal Trade Commission (1948) *Report of the Federal Trade Commission on the Merger Movement: A Summary Report*, Washingon: GPO.

Varoufakis, Y. (2011) *The Global Minotaur: America, the True Origins of the Financial Crisis and the Future of the World Economy*, London: Zed.

Ventelou, B. (2004) *Millennial Keynes: An Introduction to the Origin, Development, and Later Currents of Keynesian Thought*, Armonk, NY: M.E. Sharpe.

Vogel, D. (1989) *Fluctuating Fortunes: The Political Power of Business in America*, New York: Basic Books.

Walter, I. (1990) *The Secret Money Market: Inside the Dark World of Tax Evasion, Financial Fraud, Insider Trading, Money Laundering, and Capital Flight*, New York: Harper Business.

Waltz, K.N. (1979) *Theory of International Politics*, Reading, MA: Addison-Wesley.

Wang, K. (1998) *The Classic of the Dao: A New Investigation*, Beijing: Foreign Languages Press.

Welles, C. (1975) *The Last Days of the Club*, New York: Dutton.

Wennerlind, C. (2011) *Casualties of Credit*, Cambridge, MA: Harvard University Press.

Wheatcroft, G. (1985) *The Randlords: South Africa's Robber Barons and the Mines That Forged a Nation*, New York: Simon & Schuster.

Wicker, E. (2000) *Banking Panics of the Gilded Age*, Cambridge: Cambridge University Press.

Wilson, D. (1993) *The Astors 1763–1992: Landscape with Millionaires*, London: Weidenfeld & Nicolson.

Winters, J.A. (1996) *Power in Motion: Capital Mobility and the Indonesian State*, Ithaca, NY: Cornell University Press.

Wolff, O. (1962) *Ouvrard: Speculator of Genius 1770–1846*, New York: David McKay.

Wright, R.E. (2008) *One Nation Under Debt: Hamilton, Jefferson, and the History of What We Owe*, New York: McGraw Hill.

Yergin, D. (1991) *The Prize: The Epic Quest for Oil, Money, and Power*, New York: Simon & Schuster.

Zhang, T. (2014) *The Analysis of Chinese IPO*, Unpublished.

Ziegler, P. (1988) *The Sixth Great Power: A History of One of the Greatest of All Banking Families, The House of Barings, 1762–1929*, New York: Knopf.

Zuckerman, G. (2009) *The Greatest Trade Ever: The Behind-the-Scenes Story of How John Paulson Defied Wall Street and Made Financial History*, New York: Broadway Books.

Index

Made in the USA
Lexington, KY
08 August 2019